GIANT IN THE LAND:
THE LIFE OF WILLIAM B. JOHNSON

William B. Johnson, from the portrait hanging at the First
Baptist Church of Augusta, Georgia. Courtesy First Baptist
Church, Augusta.

Giant in the Land:

THE LIFE OF
WILLIAM B. JOHNSON

First President of the
Southern Baptist Convention
1845-1851

BY HORTENSE C. WOODSON

Charleston Association Series

Particular Baptist Press
Springfield, Missouri

Originally printed by Broadman Press
Nashville, Tennessee
1950

This 2005 expanded edition with additional
illustrations and index
is published by

Particular Baptist Press
2766 W. FR 178
Springfield, Missouri   65810

Cataloging Data:

• Woodson, Hortense Caroline 1896-1990

• Johnson, William Bullein 1780-1862

• Baptists—United States—History
• Regular Baptists—Georgia
• Regular Baptists—South Carolina
• General Missionary (Triennial) Convention—History
• Southern Baptist Convention—History
• Southern Baptists—Biographies

ISBN 1-888514-24-8   Acid free paper

Printed and bound in the United States of America

To my mother, Mrs. Agatha Abney Woodson, whose ardent love for Old Edgefield—hallowed ground of Southern Baptists—has not waned with the lengthened years, and whose unfailing interest in this undertaking has been a constant inspiration and benediction, this volume is affectionately dedicated.

Acknowledgments

The publishers express their appreciation to Mr. Bill Sumners of
the Southern Baptist Historical Library and Archives,
Nashville, Tennessee,
the First Baptist Church, Columbia, South Carolina,
the First Baptist Church of Augusta, Georgia,
and Mr. Gene Smith of Edgefield, South Carolina
for graciously providing us with the additional materials we
requested for inclusion in this volume.
This publication has been made possible by the generous
contributions of the following:

Trinity Baptist Church, Wamego, Kansas
Tony Mattia, pastor

Capitol Heights Baptist Church, Washington D. C.
Mark Dever, pastor

Emmanuel Baptist Church, Enid, Oklahoma
Wade Burleson, pastor

and by a Southern Baptist brother in
northwestern Oklahoma, who desires that "all
praise be given to God for His matchless grace!"

Contents

[v]

Preface

By Bill Sumners, Director
Southern Baptist Historical Library and Archives
Nashville, Tennessee

My grandfather Sumners was a butcher, farmer, road builder, merchant, and a Baptist. He had an abiding love for the Bible and I still have vivid memories of him reading his tattered Bible on the front porch. My father grew up in a harshly segregated South but taught his sons to judge people not by skin color or where they lived or the kind of clothes they wore, but by the content of their character. He drove a tank through France and Germany during World War II and witnessed the horror of war. He hoped his sons would never have to experience this nightmare. He has been a life-long Baptist. So much of who we are as people depends on others – those who first came to this place and made sacrifices so that we could have a better life. It was these pioneers who built the towns and communities that we live in and the schools and churches we attend.

In 1950, Broadman Press first published Hortense Woodson's biography of William Bullein Johnson, *Giant in the Land*. It is fitting and right that this biography is published once again. Although this work is almost 55 years old, it still provides valuable insight into the life of one of the most important Baptists in American history.

Johnson himself was reflective of the denomination he helped establish. His status in society was not notable or affluent, but that was true of most Baptists in the South in the early and mid-nineteenth century. Johnson like most Baptists of his time was mostly self-educated, but he appreciated the value of education and worked most of his life to establish schools. He was committed to sharing the gospel and to Baptist church polity. While a *Southern Baptist* denominational loyalty was nonexistent in the early nineteenth century, one's identity as a *Baptist* was a meaningful and intentional distinction.

Hortense Woodson, using Johnson's own memoirs to tell much of the story, details the accomplishments of this South

Carolina Baptist. While he may remain unknown to most Baptists, Johnson's contributions to his fellowship were highly significant. Woodson in her address to the South Carolina Baptist Historical Society in 1950 spoke of Johnson's legacy to Baptist work in America by saying:

> Monuments of stone might well be placed not only in Edgefield, but all over South Carolina, over most of the Southern Baptist territory, and up and down the Atlantic seaboard, commemorating the fact that here Dr. William Bullein Johnson preached, prayed, taught, or presided, and they would form stepping stones in the history of Baptists in America.

Those of us would wear the name Baptist need to be reminded that our thoughts and beliefs are shaped by those who have gone before us. The life story of William Bullein Johnson is worth honoring and remembering as it helps us to understand who we are as Baptists.

Publisher's Introduction

The following biography by Miss H. C. Woodson remains the only full-length treatment on the life of William B. Johnson. This is surprising in itself when one considers that Johnson has been described as "the principal architect" of the Southern Baptist Convention.[1] The leading role he had in the formation of what has become the largest Baptist constituency in the world is therefore of great spiritual as well as historical significance. But like so many other "giants" of the past, today the name of W. B. Johnson is largely unknown—even among Southern Baptists.

As the only individual to have been president of both the General Missionary (or Triennial) Convention, 1841-1844, and the Southern Baptist Convention, 1845-1851, Johnson participated not only in the formation of these two conventions in 1814[2] and 1845 respectively, but in the intervening years he assisted in organizing the first state convention among Baptists in the South.

> He was a leader in the formation of the South Carolina Baptist State Convention in 1821, assisted in drafting its constitution and by-laws, wrote the very able "Address" to the denomination, and traveled over the state explaining and defending this innovation. He was vice-president from 1821 to 1825 and president from 1825 till 1852, when he declined reelection on account of ill health.[3]

---

[1] H. Leon McBeth, *The Baptist Heritage* (Nashville: Broadman Press, 1987), 389.

[2] It was Luther Rice who credited W. B. Johnson with suggesting that Philadelphia be the place of meeting for the delegates who assembled to constitute what became the General Missionary Convention in May of 1814.

[3] William J. McGlothin, "William Bullein Johnson," *Dictionary of American Biography* (New York: Charles Scribner's Sons, 1933), Vol. X, 130.

Johnson's energies extended also to his various other capacities as itinerant evangelist, church organizer, pastor and associational moderator in both South Carolina and Georgia. He took an active interest in ministerial training for men and in higher education for women. One of his greatest accomplishments was in laying the groundwork for Baptist theological seminaries in the South.

> When Furman Academy and Theological Institution, now Furman University, was projected, he was leader in the movement. He secured its charter, introduced it to the public, selected its first principal, and during the first uncertain twenty-five years of its history was its chief guide. He was long a trustee of the institution and most of its public documents of a non-legal character were written by him.[4]

At different periods in his life, Johnson was principal of the Greenville Female Academy and the Edgefield Female Academy. He was instrumental in the founding of Johnson Female Seminary (which was named after him) located in Anderson, South Carolina.

In August of 1831, during his pastorate in Edgefield, Johnson experienced a genuine spiritual revival among his people. "I have been present at many such meetings," he wrote, "but none, that I have ever attended, were equal to this....At private houses in the intervals of public worship, prayer, praise, and exhortations were constantly going on. And so deeply was the population of our town impressed with the presence of the descending God, that with a few, very few exceptions, they believed that what they beheld was the work of the Lord." Miss Woodson's stirring account of those days is found Chapter XI of this book.

When William B. Johnson passed away quietly at the home of his son-in-law at Greenville, South Carolina on October 2, 1862, our country was in the midst of a terrible Civil War. Less than a month before, on September 17th, the bloodiest one-day battle ever fought on American soil had taken place at Antietam Creek in

---

[4] *Ibid.* Before his conversion Johnson had planned to enter the legal profession, hence his proficiency in drawing up documents.

western Maryland.[5] Equally tragic to those Americans at the time who held dear the kingdom of our Lord Jesus Christ was the unhappy division that existed among Christians in general, and Baptists in particular. At the beginning of the war there were just over a million Baptists in this country,[6] many of whom soon found themselves shooting at one another on the battlefield.

Yet, as was true of the Presbyterians, Methodists, and others, this "painful division" among Baptists, as Johnson referred to it,[7] occurred years before the Civil War. There is no doubt that the underlying cause for the separation was the contention over slavery.[8] Efforts to keep the General Missionary Convention neutral on the issue proved to be in vain, and in May of 1845 the Southern Baptist Convention was organized at Augusta, Georgia.[9]

---

[5] Killed on that day were 2,108 Union soldiers and 2,700 Confederate soldiers.

[6] *The American Baptist Almanac, 1863* (Philadelphia: American Baptist Publication Society), p. 48, gives the total Baptist population in the U. S. at 1,037,576: 452,711 in the Union states and western territories, and 584,865 in the 11 seceding states. Southern figures however are those of 1860, as no reports were received during the war. According to the 1860 Federal Census, the population of the 11 Confederate states totaled 9,105,000 persons, 3,654,000 of whom were slaves.

[7] See Appendix C, 205. Johnson states the Southern case for the division in his address to the delegates.

[8] That there were abolitionists also among Baptists in the South can be illustrated by the statements of J. B. Gambrell (1841-1921), who would later serve four terms as president of the S. B. C. He wrote that there "were thousands of men in the South who were abolitionists. They would have changed the situation if it could have been done, or if they could have seen any way of doing it without imperiling the social order of the South. I am speaking from what I know by contact with the common people. I myself, was an Abolitionist by instinct, not by birth. It came to me as an original intuition, that everybody ought to have an even chance in this world and I wanted everybody to have an even chance." E. C. Routh, *The Life Story of Dr. J. B. Gambrell* (Oklahoma City: E. C. Routh, 1929), 5.

[9] The actual call for the meeting at Augusta was made by the Board of the Virginia Foreign Mission Society in Richmond, and published in the March 13, 1845 issue of the *Religious Herald*—a two-month notice!

Even at its inception the Southern Baptist Convention was a large body, comprising 4,126 churches with 351, 951 members.[10] And while he firmly believed that the separate organization of the S. B. C. "became necessary," Johnson reminded the assembled delegates at Augusta that "Northern and Southern Baptists are still brethren. They differ in no article of the faith. They are guided by the same principles of gospel order."[11]

Many Southern Baptists today may find it difficult to understand how their forefathers in the faith could not only tolerate the institution of slavery, but actually participate in and even defend it. Yet how many Christians in our own day tolerate, participate in and even defend the present evils in American society? Whose compromise to the prevailing culture can we say is the greater?[12]

As an heir to the early Particular Baptists in South Carolina, W. B. Johnson's contribution to Baptist life in America was not as a theologian, for there were better among his own contemporaries, but rather as a man who was remarkably gifted with organizational and administrative skills—traits which led him into prominent positions where he proved to be a trusted and able executive. And because of his unique and abiding influence which survives today in the institutions that he helped to create, we should all take the time to read Miss Woodson's biography and become acquainted with the life of William B. Johnson.

Terry Wolever

---

[10] Lewis Wingo, "Little Known Facts about the Southern Baptist Convention," *Quarterly Review* (April-June 1984), 40-41, as cited in H. Leon McBeth, *The Baptist Heritage*, 391.

[11] See Appendix C, 205.

[12] A well-stated and commendable "Resolution on Racial Reconcilation," passed by the messengers to the sesquicentennial meeting of the Southern Baptist Convention in Atlanta, Georgia on June 20-22, 1995, not only "unwaveringly" denounced "racism, in all its forms, as deplorable sin," but went on to affirm that "we lament and repudiate historic acts of evil such as slavery" and "we apologize to all African-Americans for condoning and/or perpetuating individual and systemic racism in our lifetime." Would only Christians *en masse* emulate these resolutions concerning other great sins in our own time!

Foreword

During the turbulent years when the breach between the North and the South was growing wider, there lived in the village of Edgefield, South Carolina, a tall, slender man, of remarkable poise and dignity. As pastor of the village Baptist Church, he stood behind the white paling of the rounded pulpit and preached to sinners the error of their ways. There was a gleam in the deep-set eyes and a grimness to his chin; the graying locks combed back from his high, intellectual forehead reminded one of a prophet. The congregation of white and Negro groups listened intently as the minister announced his text: "Fear not, little flock; for it is your Father's good pleasure to give you the kingdom"; or perhaps, "Boast not thyself of to morrow; for thou knowest not what a day may bring forth."

During the week he was about his tasks as rector of the Edge-field Female Academy. Occasional notices in the *Edgefield Advertiser* were signed, "W. B. Johnson, Rector."

Minutes of the church meetings usually began, "Preaching by Brother Johnson." But sometimes the information was given, "Brother Johnson was absent on a visit to the North." At times he was in attendance upon the sessions of the General Convention of Baptists in the United States, which he had helped to organize in 1814 and which he served as president for three years.

"It was my privilege—my honor," said Dr. Johnson, addressing a meeting of the South Carolina State Baptist Convention on May

3, 1845, "to be associated with that noble band of men who organized the General Missionary Convention of our denomination in 1814. . . . Under the fostering care of God, the success of the enterprise then undertaken has been wonderfully glorious, and I had almost indulged the hope that *esto perpetua* might be safely written upon its destiny. But now when our union should be closer, our counsels more matured, and our labors more effective, there comes an awful irruption upon us, cleaving the body in twain."

On May 8, 1845, three hundred or more messengers from the District of Columbia and from the states of Virginia, North Carolina, South Carolina, Kentucky, Florida, Alabama, Mississippi, and Georgia met in Augusta, Georgia, and formed the Southern Baptist Convention. Dr. Johnson, it was said, left Edgefield for the gathering with the proposed constitution in his pocket. When the organization was effected, he was named first president.

Dr. Johnson had been present at the organization of the South Carolina State Baptist Convention in 1821, and succeeded the sainted Richard Furman as president of that convention and as leader of the denomination in South Carolina in 1825. For twenty-eight years Dr. Johnson was president of the state convention, which was organized to foster missions and ministerial education. He was tireless also in his labors for Furman University, and meetings of the Furman board of trustees, of which he was chairman for many years, commanded his scrupulous attention. "Hardly any other man could have filled his place in the days of disaster to the school," wrote Dr. H. T. Cook.

Dr. Johnson was a golden link between Richard Furman, Luther Rice, and other worthies of the early nineteenth century, connecting them with the forward-marching denominational leaders of the latter part of the nineteenth and early twentieth century.

"In after years he will wear a triple tiara as honorable and exalted as that worn by the ecclesiastical potentate," wrote Dr. William W. Barnes, of the Southwestern Baptist Theological Seminary, in recounting the story of an address delivered by Dr. Johnson in a Roman Catholic cathedral on one occasion.

And without subtracting from the worth of the great men who were Dr. Johnson's contemporaries, Dr. Cook wrote of him: "Indeed he stood like a long-leaf pine amid scrubby oaks." (Address written for the Edgefield Baptist Association Centennial, 1907.)

Dr. Johnson's "Reminiscences" "of the brethren in the ministry and of others with whom I have been associated in my ministerial course, with sketch of my own life," are now in the safekeeping of the University Caroliniana Library, University of South Carolina. With permission of the library and the appreciated co-operation of the secretary of the Caroliniana Society, Dr. R. L. Meriwether, I use Dr. Johnson's "Reminiscences" as the basis of this biography, together with the files of the *Edgefield Advertiser* and other valued source material.

I herewith acknowledge with appreciation the help of the following: Mrs. Kate Townes Corbett, of Tampa, Florida, granddaughter of Dr. Johnson, for family data and financial aid, bestowed graciously in memory of her sister, the late Miss Claudia Townes, who had spent years in compiling material relating to their distinguished grandfather; Mr. W. W. Mims, editor of the *Edgefield Advertiser* for unfailing help; Mrs. Eloise Bealle Carpenter, of Birmingham, Alabama, for use of her copy of *The Gospel Developed* by Dr. Johnson, and other helpful family data; the Tompkins Memorial Library at Edgefield, and its librarian, Mrs. W. E. B. Tompkins, for use of the files of the *Edgefield Advertiser* and other volumes; Mrs. Julian Landrum Mims for minutes of the Edgefield Baptist Association and other material; Mrs. Mamie Norris Tillman for use of her library and for assistance in countless other ways; my sister, Miss Elizabeth Woodson, for co-operation at home; Mr. and Mrs. David S. Martin, of LaGrange, Georgia, for generously supplying material; Rev. John S. Wimbish, of Edgefield, for his valued help; Dr. William W. Barnes for typed material; Miss Ruby Callison, of Baptist Headquarters, Columbia, South Carolina, for typing an address on Dr. Johnson from the state Baptist minutes; Mr. A. S. Salley, secretary of the South Carolina Historical Commission, for supplying Johnson and Bullein family records; Dr. Louie D. Newton, Atlanta, Georgia, for helpful sketches; Dr. A. Warren Huyck, Augusta, Georgia, for typewritten copy of minutes of the organizational meeting of the Southern Baptist Convention; Mr. Harry L. Watson, Greenwood, South Carolina, and Mrs. George E. Davis, Orangeburg, South Carolina, for critical reading of the manuscript; authors and publishers for permission to quote from published works; Dr. John L. Hill, book editor, and Mr. Porter Routh, statistical secretary, Baptist Sunday School Board, for helpful suggestions; and others whose help cannot be estimated.

HORTENSE WOODSON

Edgefield, South Carolina

Chapter *I*

Early Life and Family Background

Painstakingly the Rev. William Bullein Johnson, D.D., dipped
his quill in the ink and wrote in careful style:

"On this day—the 13th of June, 1860—I am 78 years of age,
and at the request of my brethren in the ministry and others whom
I highly respect, I undertake the record of ministerial and other
brethren with whom I have been associated in the work of the
Lord; to which I add some sketches of my own life. I engage in
this, I trust, in the fear of God and in the hope of promoting His
cause. I commit it in prayer to His providential disposal.

"I was born on the 13th day of June, 1782. My parents were
Joseph Johnson and Mary Bullein. They had three children, of
whom I am the only survivor. (The others died in infancy.) My
father, being of a roving disposition, was often absent from home
and I was therefore less under his instruction and example than
my mother's.

"She was an intelligent and pious woman and bestowed great
pains on my intellectual and moral culture. She taught me to read
in my fourth year, so I read acceptably before its close in Hervey's
'Meditations' and began the Latin Grammar two weeks before I
entered my 6th year.

"She sought to imbue my mind, at an early age, with profound
reverence for the Holy Scriptures as the Word of God, and for
this purpose often spoke to me of the Savior, of Noah, Abraham,
Joseph, Paul and other worthys [worthies] recorded in the Bible.
She taught me also the great principles of the doctrine of Christ
which were so impressed upon my mind that they were of great
service to me when I began to preach.

"My education was defective in consequence of want of means

to have a collegiate course, and I entered upon the study of law without previous training for such a course. Soon afterwards God in His providence called my honored Mother to her eternal rest. The loss of such a counselor and friend was a severe calamity. But God in mercy provided for my abode in a pious and intelligent Baptist family who were our particular friends."

Dr. Johnson was born at John's Island, near Charleston, South Carolina, of a family whose names were associated with the history of South Carolina Baptists from earliest years. A score of years before William Screven came to the colony, when Baptists were formally organized about 1696, members of the Bullein (Bulline, Bullen, Bulling) family had sought this place of refuge from the persecutions inflicted upon Dissenters in the Old World.

The Bulline family were of the Particular Baptist faith, of strongly Calvinistic beliefs, holding to the doctrine of personal election and close communion of the elect only; as opposed to the General Baptist faith which rejected personal and unconditional election, admitting the possibility of universal repentance and baptism in Christ and relapsing from grace.

In a lawsuit involving the Particular and General Baptists over possession of property in 1745, Thomas Bulline testified that his father, one of the original trustees, was a Calvinistic Baptist; and when the court decision gave an equal share in the property to the Particular and General Baptists, Nathaniel Bulline was one of the ultra-Particular group said to have observed June 24, 1745 as a day of fasting and prayer when a covenant was signed reaffirming their Calvinistic principles. Nathaniel Bulline was one of the group to whom Martha Fowler conveyed in 1755 a new lot "to and for, the only proper use Benefit & behoof of all and Every People, Known by the Name of Anti-paedobaptists Owning and Acknowledging the Doctrines of Personal Election & Final Perseverance, & disowning and denying Arian Arminian and Socinian Principles."

A century after the Charleston Baptist Church was founded, the register of Incorporated Church, Charleston, 1793–1800, lists among its members: Joseph Johnson, father of William Bullein

Johnson; Richard Furman, Charles Screven, and Joseph Bullein Cook, whose lives were to be interwoven with the life of young Johnson, then studying law at Georgetown.

Joseph Bullein Cook was the son of Rev. Joseph Cook, who married first, Elizabeth Bullein, and second, her sister. The Bulleins were remarkable for special courtesy and piety, Dr. James C. Furman told a descendant of Dr. Johnson. There were many of the name, and all connected, in the early days, but the male line is now extinct in South Carolina.

Joseph Johnson married Mary Bullein, whose mother was also named Mary, possibly the wife of Nathaniel Bullein. A memorial pin owned by Mrs. Kate Townes Corbett, granddaughter of Dr. Johnson, has inscribed upon it the names: "Mrs. Mary Bullein, died 15 Sept., 1780, age 49; Nathaniel Johnson, died 21 Sept., 1780, aged 13 days; Mary B. Johnson, died 25 Feb., 1788, aged 10 days." Mrs. Mary Bullein was the mother of Mrs. Joseph Johnson, and the two infants were children of Mr. and Mrs. Joseph Johnson.

Joseph Johnson was said to be of English descent. A descendant, writing of William Bullein Johnson, states: "I have heard my father say in speaking of his paternal ancestors that they came out as officers in the British colonial government."

Many young men of the wealthier class went to England for their higher education. Joseph Johnson is said to have attended Oxford University and to have brought back many books from England, largely religious and educational. Dr. Johnson once told a daughter that he just missed being born at sea. Whether or not his parents had come from England at that time or from another part of this continent is not known. The Revolutionary War was then in its final stages, with South Carolina as the last base of the British. Because of the unsettled conditions, the family probably found a temporary abiding place at John's Island, and later went to Georgetown, some distance up the coast, where William Bullein Johnson spent his boyhood.

Coastal Carolina, with its extensive plantations tended by Negro slaves, its moss-hung trees in virgin forests, and its spacious homes where hospitality abounded, was a center of culture and leisurely living. In 1791, when William Bullein Johnson was a lad of nine years, living in Georgetown, George Washington was entertained there.

The gracious and beautiful Mary Bullein Johnson was one of those who planned the reception for the beloved first President, and she presented her young son to him. Dr. Johnson told of attending the reception with his mother and of shaking hands with the President.

Rev. John Waldo was a noted teacher in Georgetown during the early years of William Bullein Johnson, and he is said to have attended the Boys' Academy under the Rev. Mr. Waldo.

Dr. Johnson esteemed Mr. Waldo's learning and ability highly, and in later years in his own schools he used Latin and English grammars written by Mr. Waldo. William Bullein Johnson is said to have become proficient in French and to have had broad acquaintance with English, French, and classical literature.

The Brown University Historical Catalogue lists William Bullein Johnson as having received the A.M. degree in 1814, and the Honorary D.D. degree in 1833.

During his formative years in Georgetown, Dr. Johnson came under the influence of two great Baptist ministers, Rev. William Staughton and Rev. Edmund Botsford.

Regarding his early association with them, Dr. Johnson wrote:

"When I was about ten years old I enjoyed the privilege of Dr. Staughton's ministry with the advantage of an intimate intercourse with him for one so young. . . . And during my law studies I had the privilege of Mr. Botsford's ministry, with the advantage of an intimate intercourse with him also. Dr. Staughton was an Englishman of remarkable amiableness & popularity, & of great & varied literary opulence, which he was always ready to impart to others. . . . I asked him to explain to me a passage of Scripture, & with a benignant smile he said, 'My boy, I will bring you some writings, that you may see what wise & good men have said upon it,' and repairing to his study he brought out Gill & others, & read their views & gave his own. He was so plain & affectionate & eloquent, that I could remember more of his sermons than those of any other preacher. . . ."

While religious services were held at Georgetown no doubt for many years, there was no formal organization there for Baptists until 1794, when Johnson was a young boy living there. Rev. Oliver Hart and Dr. Richard Furman had come from Charleston at different times to preach there, and in June, 1794, the church was constituted with thirty-six members. The Rev. Mr. Staughton had assisted in constituting the church and served as supply pastor for a year. He was succeeded by Waldo, who supplied until the arrival of Botsford in 1797.

Dr. Furman, first president of the General Convention of Baptists in the United States, with whom Dr. Johnson was associated in his early ministry, made a deep impression on the young boy who heard him preach in Georgetown.

"My acquaintance with this man of God began when I was a boy," he wrote, "& I well remember the deep & solemn impression which his grave & ministerial appearance made upon my mind, young as I then was; an impression which was deepened by a more familiar knowledge of his character."

Both Dr. Furman and Oliver Hart wore robes, suggesting the dignity and form of the Church of England.

William B. Johnson was one of twenty men who presented the petition of incorporation of the "Antipedo Baptist Church of Georgetown" in 1801. He had not made a public profession of faith at that time. He had been instructed in the letter of the law and knew by rote the doctrines for which his forefathers had been persecuted, but his spirit had not been quickened by the Holy Spirit. The light that was to shine with effulgence about him later through a personal experience of salvation had not yet kindled its flame within his soul. The faith of his fathers—even the faith of Particular Baptists—was his by inheritance and teaching; and it was to become his by regeneration.

Dr. Johnson made his home with a Keith family in Georgetown after the death of his mother in 1799.

"At the close of my law studies," his narrative continues, "I removed to Beaufort District & became a member of my Father's family which consisted of himself & his wife, a lady whom he had married a suitable time after the decease of my Mother. In December, 1803, I followed his example and married Henrietta Hornby, a niece of my stepmother. In my Father's second marriage he

[5]

obtained a pious, excellent lady who was a very affectionate wife to him and a kind Mother to me."

His stepmother was "of the Presbyterian order, but happily became a Baptist. . . . My wife was a descendant of the Hornby and Kelsall families and by birth an Episcopalian." She, too, became a Baptist.

Henrietta Hornby and William Bullein Johnson were married December 10, 1803, according to the family Bible record.

"She was an excellent wife and mother," Dr. Johnson records. "To her I am greatly indebted for her judicious support in my ministerial course. She facilitated me in my departure for appointments and gave a cordial and welcome greeting on my return. She sedulously performed the duties of a Mother, supervising with great care the early training of our children in the nurture and admonition of the Lord."

The second wife of Dr. Johnson's father, Joseph Johnson, was Elizabeth Bellinger Kelsall. Her sister, Henrietta Kelsall, had married Philip Hornby, and it was their daughter, Henrietta Hornby, whom William Bullein Johnson married. The maternal grandparents of Henrietta Hornby Johnson were John Kelsall and Mary Bellinger. Landgrave Edmund Bellinger was an ancestor, as was Richard Baker, one of the early judges of the Court of Common Pleas in South Carolina.

Chapter II

Conversion and Early Ministry

The Spirit of God was moving upon the face of the United States of America when the nineteenth century dawned, lighting the fires of evangelism, rekindling the flame of Christian education, speaking again his timeless decree, "Let there be light!"

In 1794 the Charleston Association recommended a general concert of prayer by all denominations for a revival of religion, to be held on the first Tuesday in January, April, July, and October. These prayer services continued for several years.

The camp meetings which began in Kentucky in 1797 were "like a few drops before a mighty rain, when compared with the wonders of Almighty grace which took place in the year 1800," declared Rev. James McGready, of the Presbyterian Church. When the first of the "general meetings" in which Presbyterians, Methodists, and Baptists participated in South Carolina occurred in 1802, Rev. James Jenkins, a Methodist, wrote Bishop Asbury: "Hell is trembling, and Satan's kingdom falling. Through Georgia, South and North Carolina, the sacred flame and holy fire of God, amidst all the opposition, are extending far and wide. I may say with safety, that hundreds of sinners have been awakened and converted this year in the above-named states."

The revival spirit was felt in the Baptist churches of South Carolina, and in the peak year of 1803 the membership in the Charleston Association had risen to 2,316 in the 28 churches forming the association, with 418 baptisms that year, compared with a membership of 1,982 in 1799, when 41 were baptized.

Young men, born when the nation was in swaddling clothes, felt a quickening of spirit as one century closed and another spanned before them. Luther Rice, at his home in Northborough, Massa-

[7]

chusetts, yielded to the impelling force of the Spirit in 1802. Two years later, in South Carolina, William Bullein Johnson, brilliant young lawyer of Beaufort, heard the insistent Voice as he tossed upon his couch—his spirit in unison with the restless waves of the Atlantic; and knew no rest until the reproachful Countenance before him changed to a look of forgiveness, and he felt within himself a quiet serenity like the calm after storm. The Master of wind and wave had spoken again: "Peace, be still!"

A decade later, Rice and Johnson were to become moving spirits along with Richard Furman and other great leaders in the effort to "elicit, combine and direct" the energies of Baptists all over the nation for the propagation of the gospel.

"We passed the summer of 1804 in the Town of Beaufort whose inhabitants were then blessed of the Lord with a deeply interesting revival," wrote Dr. Johnson. "Of the numbers who were immersed & united with the Baptist Church there were several families of Episcopalians of the first standing in the state. And there were about six ministers who came out of that revival, whose labors have been instrumental of great good to the churches."

Dr. Henry Holcombe, pastor at Euhaw Church 1791–1798, had moved from the Euhaw neighborhood to Beaufort in 1795 because of sickness in his family.

"The beautiful town of Beaufort had long been the residence of an enlightened, wealthy, & refined community," according to Dr. Johnson. "But at the time of Dr. Holcombe's becoming one of its inhabitants, there existed among the people generally, with a few honorable exceptions, a strange destitution of spiritual religion. The new birth was held in contempt, & a violent prejudice prevailed against the Baptists. Here the Doctor raised the standard of the cross, & though attempts were made by the ungodly to turn his ministerial exercises into ridicule, he maintained his ground unmoved."

Dr. Holcombe served Beaufort as an "arm" of the Euhaw Church, about twenty-five miles distant, until his removal to Savannah, Georgia in July, 1799. A revival which began under Holcombe at Beaufort continued throughout the Euhaw congregation under his successor, Rev. Joseph B. Cook. With a greatly increased membership, it was decided to divide the church, and the

Beaufort Baptist Church was constituted January 27, 1804. The pastor of the newly constituted church was the Rev. Mr. Cook, who had been dismissed or transferred from the Euhaw Church.

Another dismissed from Euhaw to join the Beaufort Church was Joseph Johnson, father of William Bullein Johnson.

The revival in Beaufort continued with force and power during 1804 under the pastor, the Rev. Mr. Cook.

"It was at the close of that revival that, I trust, I was brought to a saving knowledge of the truth as it is in Jesus," Dr. Johnson relates. "This was effected by the instrumentality of a pious female —Miss Lydia Turner of London, who, like her sister Lydia of Thyatira, was a seller of purple. On her way she stopped at Savannah, where she and her household, consisting of two female assistants and herself, were immersed & united with the Baptist Church at Savannah under the Pastorate of Rev. Dr. Holcombe. Miss Turner possessed a strong, capacious mind & ardent piety, but an affectionate & grateful heart. It was the privilege of my Father & myself to shew her some little kindness; & in return she labored for my conversion in earnest conversation & fervent prayer. And I trust that she did not labor in vain. This excellent sister labored not for me alone; but for others also in whose conversion she was very useful, for God honored & blessed her in his glorious work, in directing them to the Lamb of God who taketh away the sin of the world. Her piety was of an elevated character, & her arguments & views produced a greater spiritual effect upon my mind than any that had been urged upon my consideration before. One evening after reading the Scriptures & prayer, I retired to bed, & on closing my eyes there appeared before me a Form like that of the Lord Jesus, with a countenance expressive of distress, indicating that, although *He* had died for *my* sins, *I* had not received *Him* as *my Savior*. This filled my heart with distress & sorrow. After some time I became more calm & fell asleep. In the morning when I awoke my attention was drawn upward to the right, where I beheld the same form I had seen the night before. But O how changed! Instead of distress in His countenance, joy beamed forth upon the attendants around Him, of whom I seemed to be one. He looked upon me with a benignant smile, & a moral change most happy came over my spirit. I felt as tho' the gates of Heaven were opened before me; and in this happy frame I continued for some weeks.

"Although an entire revolution of a spiritual nature was internally effected, my convictions for sin were not of the distressing, alarming character that marks the exercises of some of God's dear children in their conversion to Him. Mine were of a gentler kind, tho' I trust not the less genuine. They were such as are indicated in the following Scripture—'I drew them with cords of a man, with bands of love'—Hos. 11:4. I had a vivid sense of my ingratitude to God for all His abounding kindness to me, & felt that nothing short of mercy could save me, & that the sacrifice of Christ was the only foundation of a sinner's hope: Far deeper have been my convictions for sin; of its heinousness, its polluting character & damning nature, since, than during, the exercises of my transition from a state of sin to a state of holiness & grace.

"My relations & friends were struck with the change of my countenance & manner. They observed that the usual gaiety & wildness of my face & deportment had given place to a seriousness & sobriety indicative of an internal change. And when they learned the cause, joy and gladness filled their hearts. As 'out of the fulness of the heart the mouth speaketh', I began to talk to my unconverted young friends about their salvation, but as Adam was too strong for young Melancthon, so I found him too strong for young Johnson. One only listened with a happy result. And it was my privilege to go down into the water with her & with her to be buried with Christ in immersion. O! what a day was that baptismal day! An autumnal sun (in October 1804) arose that day in cloudless majesty, & at the appointed time, crowds were seen wending their way to the beautiful river, whose inflowing waters from the Ocean seemed to welcome the candidates with the numerous audience. Arrived at the Bank, I gave out, by permission of the Minister, the hymn which begins, 'Jesus! And shall it ever be', &c. The singing of this hymn by the vast assembly seemed to unite & sweet was the sound of praise that ascended to the Heavens. Then followed an appropriate address from my good brother Cook, a relative after the flesh, & pastor of the church. He then offered a solemn prayer to the throne of grace, & at its close proceeded with the candidates to the flowing stream & immersed them into the name of the Triune

God. Returning from the water the audience sang with great energy & harmony up to the house to which I had repaired for a change of habiliments, & by the time I was ready to join them, it seemed as if the music of heaven had come down to earth. As I left the water, a young friend grasped me by the hand, exclaiming, 'O that I was worthy to be as you now are.' This young friend soon had the desire of his heart granted to him, & it was not long before he became a minister of Jesus."

* * * * *

"In January 1805, I was called by the Church to the public exercise of my gifts, & straightway I preached Christ to the people.

"My first public effort was made in the pulpit of the Euhaw Baptist Church Edifice of St. Luke's Parish, Beaufort District. The minister of the church was Rev. Aaron Tison—an excellent man & an effective preacher, tho' destitute of human learning. He was soon after my preaching in his pulpit removed from his earthly labors. As my efforts had been acceptable, it was considered providential, & the attention of the church was directed to me as his successor. Preparatory to any action, however, I was requested to become a member of the church. Having complied with the request, I received, & accepted, a call to the office of Pastor; and on the first Lord's Day in January 1806, I was set apart to the Pastorate —Rev. Dr. Henry Holcombe & Rev. Jos. B. Cook assisting on the occasion."

During his connection with the Euhaw Church and its branches, "the Great Head of the Church was pleased to bless his people with a valuable accession of precious souls," says Dr. Johnson. This he attributes in large measure to a meeting of the Charleston Association, which was held at Euhaw Church in November, 1804. That was probably the first of the large denominational meetings attended by William Bullein Johnson, as he had been baptized only the month before.

He relates that news of the revival at Beaufort that summer had spread to the upper sections of the state, and many from various parts of South Carolina and Georgia attended that meeting of the

Charleston Baptist Association at Euhaw, expecting great manifestations of grace among the new converts from Beaufort.

". . . At that meeting a number of the members of the Beaufort Baptist Church were in attendance with the life & enthusiasm of their late great revival. Many of them had been recently immersed, & were in the fervor of their first love. It was at this time that the first opportunity was afforded to the Baptists of the upper country & of Beaufort to unite in the Annual Associational Meetings. Those of the upper country had heard of the revival, & expected much spirituality & love among the brethren & especially among the new converts; but when they saw them coming in their fine carriages, & clothed in their fashionable habiliments, their hearts sunk within them. Ah! said they, we left a cold religious region, & expected to be warmed by the fires of glowing love, which had animated the more southern disciples, who had been basking in the rays of the Son of righteousness. But vain are our expectations. Instead of being warmed & animated in our religious course, we are in danger of losing what little religion we brought with us. But when they became acquainted with the brethren from the Beaufort revival, & held spiritual intercourse with them, they said —Ah! we were mistaken. *They* have indeed the religion of Jesus & it is good for *us to be here.* There is no danger of losing any religion here that is worth having. Happy was the season of enjoyment to the brethren & sisters assembled at Euhaw. . . . Strong spiritual attachments were formed, that led to the interchanges of Ministerial visits between the upper & the lower country brethren, that were profitable to the churches, & promoted the interests of the Savior's kingdom."

One can imagine the keen excitement of young Johnson as he reached Euhaw for that meeting and watched other delegates arriving from all over South Carolina; his close attention as letters from the churches were read, queries discussed and statistics recorded by Clerk John M. Roberts; and his feeling of awe when the moderator, Dr. Richard Furman, arose to preach from the text: "Teaching them to observe all things whatsoever I have commanded you: and, lo, I am with you alway, even unto the end of the world."

"It was shortly after this meeting," Dr. Johnson writes, "that

I commenced my ministerial labors with the Euhaw Church & her branches; & it was not surprizing that they were attended with manifestations of the divine favor."

The Euhaw Church, at that time on a branch of Euhaw Creek, and adjoining the high road leading from Georgia to Charleston, about sixty miles down the coast from Charleston, was constituted as a distinct organization on May 5, 1746.

When Dr. Johnson became pastor, the membership had been reduced by the dismissal of members who constituted the Beaufort Church, and there were probably less than 100 members; but, as he says, the membership was soon afterward increased.

"My position was nearly central to the District, which opened to me a wide field of usefulness, that I was permitted to occupy with manifestations of the Divine Blessing, but not without persecution from the wicked," he wrote. "The church was one of the oldest in the State, with a branch, or arm, as sometimes called, about 21 miles distant. To this arm I preached statedly once a month on Saturday & Lord's Day, & on my way I preached on Friday at a Deacon's house." That was the May River branch.

He commenced another arm about twenty miles distant in an opposite direction, "which was much prospered of the Lord tho' the settlement was notorious for dissipation. At the tavern a gambling club statedly assembled two nights in the week, & spent the time till morning in their sports. Dancing, horse racing, & foul language were common amusements. Under the first sermon one young man was awakened, & obtaining mercy, was baptized & united with the church, as soon as opportunity offered, and he subsequently became a Deacon. I preached in private homes once a month, until a church edifice was erected, & in the third year a church of twenty-six members was constituted in Prince William Parish, Beaufort District, called the Lower Saltketchers, among whose members were some that had been ring-leaders in the dissipation of the settlement."

One instance of the persecution to which Dr. Johnson referred as attending his early ministry occurred shortly after his acceptance of the call to the Euhaw Church. Of that he writes:

"About the time of my acceptance to the call of the Euhaw church, there removed into the neighborhood a gentleman with

whom in our youthful days I had been very intimate. He had un-
happily become very dissipated, & conceived great opposition to
me on account of my religious change. As his dissipation increased,
his opposition kept pace with it, until at length he determined on
doing me some bodily harm, & for this purpose he enlisted some
congenial spirits in his service, & sallied forth at the appointed
time. On their way, they stopped for supper at a friend's house,
& the lady soon learning their design, delayed the preparations to
a very late hour,—the husband meanwhile supplying the party
liberally with liquor, so that when they left the house, they were
unable to find their way to mine. In their wanderings they met with
a negro of whom they asked the way, but he knowing their intention, gave them a wrong direction. Being unable to ascertain their
position until daylight, they gave up the pursuit; & thus in God's
good providence, I escaped unharmed. Of this meditated injury I
knew nothing, until some years after, when I had removed to Savannah. Meanwhile my enemy had obtained mercy of God, &
immediately he visited me to announce the good news, & make
confession of his former hostility to me, & his unsuccessful effort
to do me bodily harm. Our interview was joyful, & to our merciful
God we offered up the praise of grateful hearts."

Many other events transpired during the first years of Dr. Johnson's ministry to show forth the power of God.

"In the neighborhood of the arm of the church 21 miles distant,
to which I preached on Saturday and Sunday, there lived a
respectable & intelligent gentleman, who statedly attended with his
family on the public institutions of the Gospel. On a sacramental
occasion I passed his house on the way to the meeting on Saturday;
& seeing no preparations for his going out, I rode up to the door &
enquired the cause. He said that as the weather was gloomy, he had
intended not to go; but as I had called he would accompany me, &
forthwith ordered his carriage. On the way he exacted from his
wife, who desired to be immersed & united with the church, a
promise that she would not make an application on that day.
During the sermon he felt for the first time the conviction that he
was a sinner, & as soon as the service closed, he released his wife
from her promise. Accordingly as soon as the opportunity was
presented she embraced it, & was upon the evidence of her faith

in Christ cordially received. During the night, however, her husband's mind was much distressed about it, & as he told me afterwards, he would have given anything to release his wife from submitting to the Ordinance. On the next day, she was immersed, & partook of the Lord's supper with the Church.

"The convictions of her husband deepened until he became really sick, & sent for physicians. He grew worse & sent for me. On my arrival I found that the cause of his sickness had not been understood, & that of course the proper remedies had not been applied. A temporary mental derangement produced by his agony of mind on account of his sins, & requiring spiritual remedies, was treated as a common case of insanity. His head was shaved & blistered. Soon after my arrival, he asked for prayer, & as we rose from the service, 'O!' said he, 'if I could only hear such prayers every day, I should get well.'

"The physicians came in soon after & attended to their patient; & then we were invited to supper. At the close of the repast, the physicians began, in an indirect manner, to inform me that ministerial visits to their patients were regarded as an interference with their practice. In reply I said, 'Gentlemen, I fear that you misapprehend the design of my visits to your patient. You may think I come to harrow up his feelings & to terrify him with horrors of the damned, that he may be converted. Not so. I come not to interfere with your mode of practice for the recovery of your patient, but to pray for God's blessing upon your efforts, that you may be the means of restoring him to health. My office then is auxiliary to yours, not antagonistic.' Being infidels, no impression was made on their minds, & they took their leave, saying that either the patient's ministerial or medical friends must leave him. I remained, & they departed, not to return.

"On the next morning I proposed the removal of the patient to my habitation—fifteen miles distant—to which he readily consented, but his wife felt some reluctance, & I advised her to retire to her closet, & ask the Lord's direction. She did so, & returned satisfied that it was their duty to go. A message was immediately sent to a neighbor to ask the loan of his close carriage for the use of his master. 'What does he want it for?' asked the neighbor. 'To go to Mr. Johnson's,' was the reply. 'Your master,' rejoined the neighbor, 'will die if he attempts to go that distance'; and added, 'there are cases on the books which shew that Mr. Johnson may be hung for his death.' The neighbor nevertheless sent his carriage & as neither the gentleman nor myself feared the hazard, we all set out as soon as the necessary preparations could be made. The patient gathered strength as we made progress, & by the divine blessing arrived at my habitation before the setting of the sun, & in an improved state of health.

"I sent the next day for a physician, who favored the visits of a judicious minister of Christ to his patients; & by the blessing of the Good Physician of the body & the soul, I had the great satisfaction of seeing my guest become restored to health in both. I had also the additional enjoyment of seeing him stand forth in the presence of the largest audience I had ever seen in the Meeting House; and relate in a clear, consistent spiritual manner, the exercises of his mind in his conversion from sin to holiness, 'from darkness to light, & from the power of Satan unto God'; & then descend into the water, in obedience to the command of his Lord & Master, Jesus Christ, to be buried with Him in baptism. After this solemn act of obedience he was received into the membership of the church, & enjoyed its privileges for many years."

Dr. Johnson served the Euhaw Church and its branches for four years, counting the year 1805 before his ordination.

"In the review of my ministry of four years in connexion with the Euhaw church," he said, "I feel deeply sensible of, & thankful for, the manifestations of grace & mercy abundantly bestowed upon His people & myself during our connexion, which closed in December 1808. Entire harmony in our proceedings rendered our intercourse delightful, & our duties easy. And with one heart & voice we ascribe the glory of all to the Father, & the Son, & the Spirit—one God over all for ever & ever."

When the bicentennial of old Euhaw Baptist Church was celebrated in 1945, particular reference was made to William Bullein Johnson as one of its famous pastors, who left Euhaw and became first pastor of the First Baptist Church, of Columbia, South Carolina.

Chapter III

Removal to Columbia

"In the last year of my pastorate at Euhaw," writes Dr. Johnson, "I felt a strong desire to enjoy opportunities more favorable to improvement, than those at Euhaw; & for its accomplishment, having secured a successor for the Euhaw Church, I resigned my Pastorate & removed to Columbia—the seat of the South Carolina College—in January 1809. As the Chaplaincy was vacant, & the President too feeble in health to perform the duties of both offices, the Trustees were pleased to invite me to occupy the pulpit. I accepted the invitation, & preached on Lord's Days to the end of the session in June, when it was thought best, as the weather became very warm, to remove to the Court House of the town, which was more central to the audience."

When William Bullein Johnson, with his wife and three children, Mary, Joseph, and William, reached Columbia, they probably viewed on an eminence through the lofty forest oaks the original frame State House, built a score of years before; and as they went perhaps on a tour of inspection, their vehicle plowing its way through the frozen mud of the streets, they doubtless scrutinized the one crude house of worship built by the Methodists in 1803 and noted the one hundred or more dwellings. Passing along the tree-lined main business thoroughfare, they would have observed the two-story brick court building where Presbyterians and Episcopalians held their services, and the cotton gin that rubbed elbows with merchant shop and market place. A few more blocks and they would have reached the high brick wall surrounding South Carolina College.

Columbia had been chosen as the site for the capital of South Carolina by the legislature in 1786, when plantations of Thomas and James Taylor were laid off uniformly into streets and the erection of public buildings and dwellings began.

South Carolina College, established by legislative enactment in 1801, had opened its doors January 10, 1805, with President Jonathan Maxcy and one other professor composing the faculty for the original eight students and others who enrolled the first year. Four years later, when the new chaplain, Rev. W. B. Johnson, arrived, the one original Drayton Hall had been supplemented by other buildings, an $8,000 dwelling for the president had been constructed, and a wall enclosed the property. By 1810 there were upward of one hundred students, and forty were on the waiting list. The faculty had increased proportionately.

Along with his duties as chaplain, the zeal of the missionary impelled Johnson to establish the Baptist faith in Columbia.

"I found not many Baptists in Columbia," he relates, "but as it was a growing place, we succeeded in constituting a Baptist Church of thirteen members—nine whites & four colored, on the first Lord's Day in October, 1809, the year of my removal to Columbia. . . . Of this number I had the pleasure of baptizing five persons, the first of whom was Mrs. Ann Taylor, the honored wife of the venerable Thomas Taylor, one of the Revolutionary heroes of South Carolina. This lady was the first person baptized in Columbia. . . ."

Colonel and Mrs. Taylor had been part and parcel of Columbia since its incipiency, and the appellation, "Mother of Columbia," might well be applied to Mrs. Taylor—a woman who had watched over the birth of that city and who set a worthy example in following her own religious convictions, leading in the establishment of a church whose influence has reached many thousands in the course of its long and honored history.

Describing the first baptism and the organization, Dr. Johnson wrote:

"At the appointed time on a beautiful Lord's Day morning of October, a multitude assembled on the bank of the Congaree to witness the Baptismal scene. Profound silence reigned in the whole assembly during the solemn services of the occasion. From the Baptismal water we repaired to the C. House, & after the sermon by Dr. Roberts—[John M.] the constitution of the church was adopted, Rev. Maxcy in the chair as presiding officer. Having succeeded in the constitution of a *church* we were alike successful in the erection of a *Church Edifice* we had the pleasure of seeing dedicated to the service of the Lord on the second day of March 1811."

Dr. Johnson may be considered the founder and first pastor of the First Baptist Church of Columbia. Under his preaching the church was established, and as minister in charge he performed the first rite of baptism.

From the thirteen constituent members the number had grown in 1948 to 2,672.

"The church is unique in the history of Southern Baptists in that among its former pastors was Dr. J. P. Boyce, founder and first president of the Seminary at Louisville, Ky., which was at first located at Greenville, S. C. Another of its former pastors was the first president of the Southern Baptist Convention, Dr. Wm. B. Johnson," reads a pamphlet sketch of the church issued April 15, 1945.

Although Dr. Johnson went to Columbia in order to broaden his education and serve as chaplain of South Carolina College, he soon became absorbed in preaching and did much itinerant evangelizing, traveling both on his own initiative and as an appointee of organized bodies.

His removal to Columbia gave him the opportunity of forming an extensive acquaintance with the brethren and ministry of the denomination in the middle and upper sections, Dr. Johnson records, "among whom I found a body of valuable members of the churches; & of laborious, indefatigable & successful ministers in the Gospel Vineyard. There was, it must be admitted, not a large amount of literary improvement in the churches or the ministry, & some of the latter were, it is true, very ungrammatical in their language, & coarse in their figures; but they were suited to a large proportion of their hearers, & greatly blessed in doing them good."

Such preachers, however, he added, formed the smaller number of the whole body of the ministry.

"The larger number were more improved, though without scholastic learning. Generally obliged to labor through the week, they read their Bibles & other useful books as they rode to their appointments, & by torch light as they sat by their firesides at night. A brother minister of this class told me that he often performed the work of six days in four to save two for preaching & studied by firelight to the injury of his eyes, & it is now with great pleasure that I hear him preach, & know that he is very useful in his Master's cause. The ministers of whom I have been treating dwelt above Columbia."

Dr. Johnson, exponent of ministerial education, contrasted the unlearned ministers of the state above Columbia with those of the middle and lower sections, who were more improved in general than those above.

"This is attributable," he wrote, "to the Divine blessing on the Education Fund established in 1791 by the Charleston Baptist Association & committed to the management of the General Committee of the Churches. This institution had for its object the gratuitous education of pious young men for the ministry. And from its commencement a goodly number of such characters availed themselves of its advantages, & became useful ministers in the middle & lower country among the churches which then formed the Charleston Baptist Association, extending from the Seaboard to the vicinity of Columbia."

Of the beneficiaries of the Education Fund, Dr. Johnson writes particularly of Rev. John Mitchell Roberts, Rev. J. B. Cook, Rev. William T. Brantly, and Rev. Jesse Mercer: Roberts, who established a classical school at the High Hills of Santee and received free of charge other beneficiaries of the Education Fund by way of expressing his own gratitude; Cook, who influenced in great measure his young kinsman, Johnson; Brantly, minister and educator in Camden, Augusta, Beaufort, Philadelphia, and Charleston —founder of the Baptist church in Augusta in which the Southern Baptist Convention was organized during the pastorate of Brantly's son at the same church; and Mercer, for whom Mercer University in Georgia is named. Dr. Johnson wrote of Mercer that he was "the most interesting man, as a preacher, that I ever heard."

The Charleston Association had carried on work in missions and education almost from the beginning of its organization in 1751.

"The Education Fund of the Charleston Association," Dr. Johnson stated, "continues its gratuitous aid to students for the ministry. Of those who have finished their course & entered into rest, I would with great readiness have made honorable mention, but they went forth to their labors in different parts of the state, & into different states, North, South & West, of whom I often heard very favorably, but without sufficient material for my purpose in mentioning them in these reminiscences."

The Association commenced a mission to the Catawba Indians in the state in 1802, wrote Dr. Johnson. "They found in Rev. John Rooker a suitable person for the undertaking, & appointed him to visit the tribe, preach to them once a month for a year, & ascertain the mind of the Chief in relation to preaching & the establishment of a school for their children. The report of Bro. Rooker was favorable, & the Association carried their purpose into effect. This excellent & faithful Brother was appointed the preacher to the nation, & a school was opened under a competent Teacher. Specimens of the penmanship of the scholars were exhibited to the General Committee & Association from time to time, evincing very satisfactory improvement. In 1810 I visited the Station, by appointment of the Association, to act with the Missionary in relation to the establishment, & on looking through it I was much gratified with the orderly state of its affairs. An appointment had been made for me to preach, & on my arrival at the place I found a very large audience of Indians & whites in attendance. The attention & gravity of these children of the forest were of a marked character, far superior to what is sometimes seen in the congregations of the whites in towns & cities of the States. Even the behaviour in religious services that their children exhibit is a pattern for imitation to the more improved children of more polished societies in other places. By means of the Missionary & the School Master, sustained by the Charleston Baptist Association in the tribe of the Catawba Indians, their nation's manners & morals were much improved, & there is reason to believe that the souls of not a few were saved through the riches of grace."

If the erudite Staughton and the unpretentious Botsford were Johnson's mentors in his formative years, the accomplished Jonathan Maxcy was the preceptor of his maturity. In the quiet of the evening, broken perhaps by the occasional sounds of hilarity among the students at the college, the twenty-seven-year-old chaplain often sat in the study of the president's home on the campus and imbibed from the older man truths from Holy Writ. He heard from the lips of Dr. Maxcy an exposition of the parable of Lazarus and Dives which he never forgot.

". . . his eloquence was so overpowering that I seemed to be for the time in the presence of an Angel sent from Heaven to instruct me in the import of that portion of the scripture; and the impression of the truths taught in that parable, as explained by the Doctor, have never been effaced from my memory; nor have they failed to retain the approval of my judgment, as the true exposition of the passage."

Dr. Maxcy had the faculty, according to Johnson, of "throwing with irresistible force into the mind of the hearer, the principle taught, or the duty enforced." A student, he recounts, attended a recitation in Logic, on the subject of the resurrection of Christ, in Watts'. On leaving the recitation room, he said to a fellow student, "I went into the recitation room an infidel, but I left it a believer."

Dr. Johnson relates that he had the pleasure, on a visit to Savannah, of hearing Professor Ogilvie, the popular orator of the day, then traveling as a public speaker. Dr. Johnson requested him to visit Columbia and gave him a letter of introduction to Dr. Maxcy.

"He presented the letter and the Doctor invited him to be his guest. The subject of their conversation one evening was the authority & authenticity of the Holy Scriptures. The Dr., a believer—the Orator, an unbeliever. At the close of an animated conversation on these points, they began to feel the necessity of retirement for repose from their labors. When, to their astonishment, on looking at their watches for the hour, they beheld the light of a new day coming in at the windows. It is said that 'the Eloquent Orator' declared that he never after would venture upon a denial of the authority or authenticity of the Holy Scriptures."

The admiration felt by Dr. Johnson for Dr. Maxcy did not abate with time, and even after a passage of ten years, in reviewing a patriotic address made by the older man, Johnson expressed his high approval:

"I felt that if the Dr. had, at this point, called upon me to do an impossibility, I should have made the attempt. If with such mental power displayed on this occasion, Dr. Maxcy had possessed strong health, & the compass of voice necessary to the full utterance of his exalted conceptions & sublime views, he would have occupied the first position in the rank of Orators & of the Learned. But his constitution was so feeble, that after a pulpit effort, he was obliged to lie still for some time to recover his strength. . . ."

Jonathan Maxcy (1768-1820). James L. Petigru of South Carolina said of Maxcy, "Never will the charm of his eloquence be erased from the memory on which its impression has once been made." - William Cathcart, ed., *The Baptist Encyclopedia* (1881), 762.

Chapter IV

Ministry in Savannah

"In the spring of the year 1811," Dr. Johnson writes, "I received a unanimous invitation from the Baptist church of Savannah in Georgia to become their pastor; & after some thought & much consultation & prayer, I accepted it for the following reasons—I had, in some good degree, accomplished the object of my removal to Columbia. I had also the pleasure of seeing a church formed there; but though she was increasing in numbers, the members were not in pecuniary means adequate to the support of my growing family, whilst the salary offered by the Church in Savannah was. Other considerations of weight induced me to think that, in Savannah my usefulness would be enlarged. I therefore removed in December 1811 to the spiritual charge over which my venerable friend & brother, Dr. Holcombe, had so long, with parental care under God's blessing, presided. In the interval of Dr. Holcombe's departure from Savannah & my arrival in that city, which was about a year, the church enjoyed the very acceptable labors of Bro. Thomas J. Williams, a Licensed Preacher. . . ."

In a volume entitled, *Series of Letters,* by Henry Holcombe, D.D., published in 1812, the author commends to the church at Savannah his successor, William Bullein Johnson, as pastor of that church, and states that Johnson had "pursued his literary studies for several years . . . under the direction of the Rev. Dr. Jonathan Maxcy, President of South Carolina College at Columbia."

"This distinguished servant of the church is in the prime of life," Dr. Holcombe commented, "has an amiable rising family, and success has uniformly crowned his labors."

In addition to his pastoral work in Savannah, he also taught an academy for girls.

By his removal to Savannah, Dr. Johnson again became a member of the Savannah River Baptist Association, of which the Euhaw Church was a part. Shortly after he went to Savannah, the May River branch of Euhaw Baptist Church was constituted as a church, and Dr. Johnson received and accepted an invitation to attend the services. That branch was located a half day's ride from Savannah, in St. Luke's Parish, South Carolina.

"The season was not only agreeable, but of deep interest to my mind," wrote Dr. Johnson, "as I found that, under the blessing of God upon the labors of my successor, the arm of the Church had grown to sufficient maturity for assuming the position of an independent body. And peculiarly spiritual enjoyment accompanied the exercises from the meeting of old friends to take part in, or witness to, the constitution of another church of the Lord Jesus, who should take rank with Sister Churches in the great work of Salvation."

Dr. Johnson's ministry in Savannah extended from 1811 until 1815, and during that period many important events were to take place. The War of 1812 was upon the nation; and during the same period the forces of righteousness were being mobilized against the forces of unrighteousness in the spiritual realm with William B. Johnson as a moving spirit in the co-ordination of Baptist forces for a program of world conquest for Christ.

In the meantime he was concerned with the spiritual state of men and women about him, and he was to have the high privilege of assisting in the ordination to the gospel ministry of one who had been antagonistic to religion only a few years earlier. While Dr. Johnson was pastor at Euhaw, he relates: "I removed with several persons of my church and congregation to a more healthy region, & to them & the neighbors I preached stately on the Wednesday evening of each week. A sister of one of the ladies of our settlement spent a summer with her, & in the latter part of the season, her husband came over from Georgia to pass a little time with his friends & return home with his family. Being informed of my weekly discourses, & that I held the doctrine of election, he conceived a violent opposition to me, & endeavored to enlist a party to assist him in doing me some personal injury, but he could find no congenial spirits to unite with him in his design against me; & thus through the providential care of my heavenly Father I was again preserved from the evil meditated against me."

Continuing, Dr. Johnson writes: "This gentleman became very dissipated, & had nearly made ship-wreck of his fortune, as he had of his morals & his character. But when I saw him a few years after, he had become a new man, & we embraced each other with tears as children of the same Father, & brothers of the same family. It was during the absence of his family on a visit to Savannah, that the Spirit of the Lord came upon him with deep conviction for his sins, awakening him to a sense of his awful condition. Alone. He read his Bible & called on God for mercy. No human agency was near to direct, and teach him. But the Lord was there, the Great Teacher; & the Spirit & word were there, & the work of regeneration & faith was well done. And when he went for his family & told his dear wife of his happy change, her heart overflowed with joy & thankfulness to Almighty God for his great mercy to her dear husband. For she, too, notwithstanding his opposition to the truth, had obtained mercy of God during her visit to Carolina already referred to.

"There was about three miles distant from this gentleman's habitation a meeting house in building during his unconverted state, by which he was riding with a friend, to whom he said, 'That Meeting House is being built for me to preach in. But if ever I'm a preacher, the Lord alone shall be my Teacher.' These words were prophetic & received a literal fulfilment. For he became a Christian, was baptized, entered the ministry, and preached in that Meeting House, whilst his useful life was prolonged on earth. And the Lord alone *was* his Teacher, for he received his theology from the Lord's word & spirit, & from no human teacher.

"It was my privilege, in company with the Rev. Charles O. Screven, to assist in the ordination of this servant of the Lord. The day was fine, & the assembly was very large. The services began at 11 o'clock, & at their close at the meeting house the vast audience repaired to a clear & beautiful stream of water at the distance of two miles, to behold the ordinance of Immersion, administered to seventy-six persons upon the profession of their faith in the Lord Jesus. On their arrival at the beautiful spot, an address on the Ordinance was delivered, a hymn sung & a prayer offered to the Great God, when the newly ordained Pastor descended into the water, accompanied with ten of the candidates, whom he immersed into the name of the Father, & of the Son, & of the Holy Spirit. This was followed by the singing of one verse of a hymn, during which the solemn procession of ten more approached, whom the Pastor received & immersed, when another verse was sung; and in the same manner did the affecting scene proceed to its close. Then—

> "Loud as from numbers without number, sweet
> As from blest voices, uttering joy, heaven rung
> With jubilee, & loud hosannas fill'd
> The vast conclave."

"From this heavenly scene, the multitude returned to the Meeting House, & the church commemorated, in the supper of their Lord, His sufferings & His love.

"The space of time occupied in the services of this holy day closed at 4 o'clock. Protracted as they were, they form an epoch in the history of the church, introductory of a series of services on succeeding Lord's days, on which have been richly bestowed upon the church by her Great Head, the blessings of grace & salvation through the remarkable administration of her honored Pastor. About 2 or 3 years after, I visited the Pastor & his church, & learned with surprise & pleasure that the members had multiplied to five hundred & fifty, twelve of whom were whites & the rest blacks. This great increase was attributed to the blessing of God upon the scriptural arrangements & untiring diligence of the Pastor. This judicious servant of the Lord had divided territorially the colored members of the church into fourteen Districts, & appointed as many Elders as visitors & teachers. The tour of service began with Elder A who went to District No. 1 on a given evening of the first week according to appointment previously made. On the same evening of the second week Elder A went to District No. 2 & Elder B attended on that evening at District No. 1; & thus in regular order the Districts were supplied with the Elders following each other in regular succession. Their duty consisted in praying, singing, & teaching with exhortation & a particular enquiry into the moral condition of the members in each District. On each Lord's Day, after the morning services were ended, these Elders made their reports to the Pastor, who remained to receive & act upon them. By this means, the Elders & members were brought together every Lord's Day, when the necessary discipline was instituted, & both Elders & members received appropriate instruction. And such was the religious & moral effect upon the church & community, that an intelligent & wealthy Presbyterian, who had fifty negroes in the church, told me that he did not feel at liberty to chastise any of them for an offence, before he reported the delinquents to the Pastor, & if he could not reform them, then he would undertake the reform himself. I was also told that the delinquency of servants—members of the church—was often brought to the knowledge of their masters for the first time, through the dealings of the church. Such was the man whom the Lord took from the lowest dissipation, & honored with such distinguished usefulness, in gathering His Elect into His Great Fold."

It happened that Dr. Johnson was in Boston and present at services at the Baptist Church when Dr. Lucius Bolles and his wife became affiliated with that church. The procedure of receiving members he found to be so in keeping with his own ideas that he studied the subject more closely, and finally felt moved to take the matter up with his church in Savannah.

In being received into the Boston Church, Dr. and Mrs. Bolles were transferring from another church, but each gave public testimony as to salvation through regeneration.

"The proceeding was in accordance with my own views, & I enjoyed a spiritual feast in hearing such a spiritual recital from these pious followers of the Lamb. Beginning with their conviction for sin & their deliverance from its condemnation by faith in Christ, they proceeded to speak of peace with God through our Lord Jesus. Then of their trials & sorrows, their triumphs & joys through their victorious Leader, who had led them along the narrow way to that period. The church was strengthened & refreshed, & the happy applicants were cordially welcomed into membership."

Dr. Johnson then proceeded to explain his views. Removal of

members from one community to another rendered a change in church membership necessary, but the Bible gives no rules as to how such changes may be effected. Therefore, principles of church organization must be referred to. The first principle is that each church is an independent body and must determine for itself the fitness of a person for membership, regardless of that person's previous membership in other churches. The second principle is that each church is solemnly charged to preserve a pure, spiritual membership, and therefore cannot commit the duty of judging the qualifications of her members to other hands. That principle is observed in the first application for membership, but is generally neglected in the reception of members from other churches.

The procedure usually is to receive a member upon presentation of a letter of dismission from another church of the same faith and order "without the recital of any spiritual exercises."

"We have no scriptural authority for letters of Dismission, & surely such letters can not have equal value with the recital of the applicant in person before the Church."

Baptism, he pointed out, is not the door of admission into a church "but the consent of the members upon a satisfactory evidence of the applicant's faith & repentance toward God, not before, but after he has put on Christ by Baptism. Hence whenever a membership is formed by a baptized believer, however often, in consequence of removal or otherwise, the same order must be observed, except in some very extraordinary case; & this must be by the consent of the church upon a satisfactory evidence of his faith in Christ. A letter of dismission gives no such evidence, for the bearer may be a hypocrite, or self-deceived. This is evident, as it only testifies that he has been an orderly member of the body from which he is dismissed. . . .

"Although we have no scriptural authority for letters of dismission, we have for letters of commendation. When a member of a church was determined to remove beyond its precincts, he should therefore, before his departure, state the fact to the Body, & request a letter of commendation from them, that wherever he goes, he may carry with him the testimonial of his Christian character, that upon settling himself, he may unite with a church of his religious views; or endeavor to originate one if there should not be

[29]

one in his neighborhood. In uniting with another church, the mode of proceeding adopted by the church in Boston in the admission of Dr. Bolles & his wife should be observed. In forming a new church those who are to become members, should meet together, & organize by choosing a chairman & secretary for the sake of order. Their letters of commendation should then be read & their exercises of renewing & sanctifying grace related. Fellowship being obtained, there should be an understanding of the principles of order, on which a church of Christ should be scripturally formed, & then by a solemn resolution they should enter into the church relation, to be governed in faith & practice according to the teachings of the Scriptures, as the only standard of authority for Christians & Christian churches. Those only who are to be members, can constitute a church; for ministers have no authority to constitute a church of Christ."

To the evangelist belongs the work of baptizing believers into the kingdom of God, even as John the Baptist preached and baptized before the churches were organized after Pentecost. The great work of converting sinners had been going on for several years before Christ died, arose, and ascended into heaven, and came again in the power of the Holy Spirit.

Dr. Johnson outlined precise instructions as to those who desired baptism and membership in a church. A private interview between the minister and applicant, he thought, would afford more freedom of thought and expression on the part of the applicant and would give the minister a better opportunity to teach and explain the doctrines of salvation before a public profession should be made.

As he studied the subject more carefully, he came to the conclusion that it was his duty to teach the members of his church the important truths of church polity. So he proposed to them to devote the afternoons of succeeding Lord's Days to a prayerful and scriptural discussion of the subject.

"To this they readily consented," he wrote, "& I have the high satisfaction to say that the whole was conducted in a brotherly & Christian spirit. A small minority entertained my views, & as I considered them important, & even indispensable to the completeness of the order of a Church of Christ, I resigned my Pastorate,

& withdrew the membership of my wife & myself in the midst of tears, flowing from the whole church. This spiritual Body of Christ's Disciples exercised the freedom of conscience; & therefore cherished no thought of excommunicating those who, from honest & conscientious difference of opinion on religious sentiments, withdrew their membership; & therefore no censure was passed against my wife & myself. So far from it, I had the satisfaction of receiving from the church soon after my reaching home, a committee to request that I would, as often as I could conveniently, preach for them.

"I had made no efforts to form a party, who would stand by me, if the church would not accept my views. Nor had I laid any plans for my future arrangements in such a result. I determined to do my duty & leave the event to God. To my surprize, on Monday a brother of the church came to me to ask advice for himself & others, who had embraced similar views to those which I had taught the church. To which I said, You must ask counsel of God, & act as your conscience shall direct you. At the church meeting of the same week, twelve members of the church asked for a letter of dismission, which was given without censure & without hesitancy; & on the succeeding Lord's Day measures were taken by fifteen members of the Body of Christ to form a church for His glory. This was done in humble & earnest prayer to the Great Head of the Church, for His blessing. The Bible! The Bible! which is the religion of Christians, was our Constitution. This little band encreased by the accession of estimable females, & worthy males, some of whom exercised acceptable gifts."

Chapter V

"Eliciting, Combining, Directing"

Like the old, yet ever new, story of the Christ is the wonder of the story of foreign missions and its beginnings in America. The restless energies of the Baptists—born of the persecutions in the Old World as well as the New; satisfied for a time with the founding of meetinghouses here and there under the rugged preaching of early evangels; reanimated under the earnest leadership of more polished and learned ministers; finding an outlet in educational endeavors, in missionary efforts at home and in contributions to the English missionary movement—at length were to be "elicited, combined and directed, in one sacred effort for sending the word of life to idolatrous lands."

The Baptists of America were ready and waiting.

While the world waited in darkness once before, a Babe was born in a cattle stall and made his bed in a manger of hay. And while the world waited once again, a group of young men gathered around a haystack—emblem of the garnered grain—and prayed. Then and there was born the foreign missionary movement in America.

The Christ child was born to the Hebrew race, yet was a Light to lighten the Gentiles. The young men who dedicated themselves to the work of foreign missions differed in their creed from the Baptists, yet when the light of divine truth shone upon two of them in particular, the events were like to those that befell the Son of God: they came unto their own and their own received them not. Thus it behooved them to turn to the Baptists.

"In 1813," wrote Dr. Johnson, "Rev. Luther Rice visited our Association [the Savannah River] with letters of introduction from the Baptist brethren of Boston proposing the organization of a Baptist Missionary Convention in the United States. The occasion of this visit & proposal was as follows: The Rev. Messrs. Luther Rice & Adoniram Judson had been sent by the Congregationalists of the North as Missionaries to India. As they sailed for the port at which Baptist Missionaries resided, they determined, tho' on different vessels, to examine anew, during their voyage, the subject of Gospel Baptism, that they might be fully prepared for any discussion on the subject with their Baptist brethren in India. The result of this examination was the conviction that the immersion of a believer in Christ is Gospel Baptism. And on their arrival at the distant port, they, with Mrs. Judson, were immersed in the name of the Father, & the Son, & the Holy Spirit. It was then agreed that Bro. Judson & lady should remain in India, preparing for Missionary work, & that Bro. Rice should return to the United States, & if their patrons would not sustain them, that Bro. Rice should confer with the Baptist brethren on the subject of engaging in the great work of Foreign Missions. As was naturally to be expected, the brethren Rice & Judson were not sustained by their patrons, and the opportunity thus providentially presented of entering upon this noble enterprise was readily embraced by our brethren at the North, who without delay remitted a thousand dollars to Bro. Judson & his lady. They also requested Bro. Rice to travel through as many states as would be practicable to engage the Baptists to form Societies, whose delegates would meet at Philadelphia in May 1814, to organize a Baptist Foreign Missionary Society for the United States. Upon this interesting statement from Bro. Rice, he was cordially invited to a seat in the Association; & the proposal to form Societies with the view to organize a Missionary Convention for foreign lands in 1814, was as cordially approved, whereupon a society was formed & organized without delay, to make the necessary preparations for meeting in May 1814 in the city of Philadelphia.

"From our Association Bro. Rice went forth on his agency with the prayers of the brethren, that God would bless him & make him a blessing. And verily God *did* bless him & make *him* a *blessing;* for his labors were indefatigable, & so successful, that, at the time & place appointed for the meeting of the convention, a large delegation was in attendance, forming the elite of the Denomination in the United States of America. Of this body Rev. Dr. Richard Furman of Charleston, S. Carolina, was chosen President; & Rev. Dr. Thomas Baldwin, of Boston, Massachusetts, Secretary. As no provision had been made for a Convention Sermon, the President was, by an unanimous vote, requested to perform the service at night, & in complying with the request, the venerable man of God delivered a very appropriate & acceptable discourse. The organization of this Convention formed an epoch in the history of the Baptists of the United States, that was followed by a most blessed era of successful benevolent effort in various departments of the Kingdom of Christ, that spread the unspeakable blessings of literature & salvation throughout millions of our race in these & foreign lands."

Dr. Johnson's brief account of the formation of the General Convention thus gives emphasis to the important place Luther Rice rightly holds in Baptist thinking. But Rice himself attributed to Johnson the suggestion that the meeting be held in Philadelphia. In the *Christian Index* of January 27, 1835, there is a letter written by Luther Rice telling the story of the beginnings of the General Convention, in which he says:

"After completing the range of development and formation of mission societies here recited, I had conversation with Brother Johnson on the subject of having a meeting of delegates from all the societies of this kind, for the purpose of forming some general combination or concert of action among them. He consented and engaged, that, in case it should be agreed to by the others concerned, he would go personally as a delegate from the Savannah society as far as Philadelphia to attend such a meeting. Immediately, of course, I wrote to all the other societies, stating that fact, and urging the importance of the meeting in Philadelphia as proposed by Brother Johnson."

A letter from Dr. Staughton to Dr. Rice, dated December 17, 1813, possibly in reply to the one written by Rice apprising Staughton of Johnson's proposal, includes the following: ". . . With respect to the place of meeting of the general committee, I think our society ought to be passive. I was conversing last evening with Doctor Rogers on the subject, who is of opinion with myself, that the societies which exist at the greatest distance from some central point should decide for themselves. I am persuaded that our society will acquiesce with cheerfulness in such a decision. Were we to consult personal convenience and gratification, we should at once recommend Philadelphia."

In the name of the Savannah Society for Foreign Missions, Dr. Johnson issued an address to the people of Georgia and adjacent parts of South Carolina, which Dr. Daniel Sharp called "the most able appeal in behalf of Baptist missions which was written by anyone in that period." It was signed by William B. Johnson, president, and William T. Brantly, corresponding secretary, of the society.

In the address are the following significant words:

"Since the secession of our dear brethren, Rice, Judson and lady, . . . several missionary societies have been formed by the Baptists of America. These societies have for their object the establishment and support of foreign missions; and it is contemplated that delegates from them all will convene in some central situation of the United States for the purpose of organizing an efficient and practicable plan, on which the energies of the whole Baptist denomination, throughout America, may be elicited, combined and directed, in one sacred effort for sending the word of life to idolatrous lands . . ."

That is perhaps the first time the words, "elicit, combine, direct," were used in connection with Baptist organizations, and they appear recurrently in other compositions which Dr. Johnson had a hand in writing. He was a member of the committee to draft the constitution of the General Convention, the South Carolina State Baptist Convention, organized in 1821, and the Southern Baptist Convention, and his phraseology is evident in each.

The preamble to the constitution of the General Convention reads:

"We the delegates from Missionary Societies, and other religious bodies of the Baptist denomination, in various parts of the United States, met in Convention, for the purpose of carrying into effect the benevolent Intentions of our Constituents, for organizing a plan for eliciting, combining and directing the Energies of the whole Denomination in one sacred effort, for sending the glad tidings of Salvation to the Heathen and to nations destitute of pure

[35]

Gospel light, do agree to the following Rules of fundamental Principles. . . ."

Provision was made for meetings triennially with not more than two representatives from each missionary society or other religious bodies, each organization to contribute at least one hundred dollars per annum; the election of a board of commissioners, twenty-one in number, called the "Baptist Board of Foreign Missions for the United States," with authority to employ missionaries and conduct the executive part of the missionary concern; the Board to transact business of the Convention between sessions.

There were present at the first meeting thirty-three representatives from twenty societies in eleven states and the District of Columbia. Luther Rice was "appointed, under the patronage of this board, as their Missionary, to continue his itinerate services, in these United States, for a reasonable time; with a view to excite the public mind more generally, to engage in Missionary exertions; and to assist in organizing Societies, or Institutions, for carrying the Missionary design into execution."

The minutes record the decision that Adoniram Judson, "now in India, be considered as a Missionary, under the care and direction of this Board; of which he shall be informed without delay: That provision be made for the support of him and his family accordingly; and that one thousand dollars be transmitted to him by the first safe opportunity: That the Secretary of the Particular Baptist Society, for Missions in England, be informed of this transaction; and that this Board has assumed the pledge given by the Boston Mission Society, to pay any bills which may be drawn on them, in consequence of advances made in favor of Mr. and Mrs. Judson."

Dr. Johnson was a guest of Dr. Henry Holcombe, who was then pastor of the First Baptist Church of Philadelphia.

"I had the honor of being his guest for about a week or ten days," Dr. Johnson wrote. "And in the intervals of business & the public services of the Sanctuary, our intercourse was not only very agreeable to me, but I trust profitable also."

Dr. Johnson had driven through the country in his "chair" to attend the meeting, and A. L. Vail, in *The Morning Hour of American Missions,* says of him: "His quality is well indicated by the position he had attained and the service he had performed locally, and by the zeal which had brought him farther than any other had come to this meeting."

"The labors and successes of our beloved missionaries enlisted the warmest sympathies of his heart," wrote Dr. Richard Furman III. "With an intensity of interest, peculiar to the instincts of a benevolent and pious nature, he contemplated the advancement of the Redeemer's kingdom, and watched the indications of Providence pointing towards the fulfillment of God's decree that the heathen shall be given to his Son for an inheritance, and the uttermost parts of the earth for a possession. For the accomplishment of this glorious work he prayed, he preached and with great liberality, according to his means, he gave."

With the board's appointment of "Mr. Hough, who was twenty-eight years of age, a native of Winsor, Vt., and a member of the Baptist church at Pawtucket, R. I.," as assistant to Judson at its second meeting, and the provision for domestic missions made by the Convention in 1817, an impetus was given to the mission task that must have been pleasing to Dr. Johnson. James E. Welch and John M. Peck were accepted as missionaries "to a Western mission, having reference ultimately to the Western Indians." The corresponding secretary was instructed to write to the Rev. Isaac McCoy, "informing him of the designation of the two brethren to the missionary service in St. Louis and the surrounding country . . . that his application has been received by the Board with emotions of pleasure and satisfaction; and that they request him to inform them whether there is not in that quarter . . . some other station in which a missionary is equally needed, and in which he would be willing to labor."

A communication was also to go to Rev. John Young, of Kentucky, in reply to his letters, "informing him, that on applying to the committee for the Western section of our country . . . they will make such a representation of the case to the Board as their piety and prudence may dictate. . . ."

Dr. Johnson recommended by letter the appointment of Rev. James A. Ranaldson as a missionary in New Orleans and vicinity, and a resolution was passed appointing him; "and that he be requested to visit such of the Indian tribes in that quarter as he has

[37]

referred to in his letter, and others if he can; and inquire into the practicability of establishing schools among them; and that 500 dollars be forwarded to his assistance."

Rice reported in 1817 that he had collected $10,000 in ten months. The receipts of the board for that year were about double the expenditures.

A forward movement that was to claim much of the time and means of the denomination was education. As set forth in another chapter, the Charleston Association had been interested in the education of young men for the ministry a quarter of a century before the organization of the General Convention. Dr. Johnson's interest in the subject of an educated ministry was intensified upon the co-ordination of Baptist forces, and on August 9, 1814, he had written from Savannah to Luther Rice at Boston:

"There is another subject which has occupied much of my thoughts, since my return, to the furtherance of which I am willing to bend my exertions. It is the establishment of a central theological seminary. I think more is to be done in this business northwardly than southwardly; and though I have no pretensions to great talents, learning, influence, or property, yet I am willing to employ what I have received from the Lord, in these respects, for the promotion of His glory in this, or any other way."

Dr. Johnson's views as to an educated ministry are found also in a volume by himself in which he speaks of qualifications for evangelists: "The first and chief of these [qualifications] is, the possession of the saving grace of God in the soul, and manifested in the life by exercises of deep and ardent piety. . . . A second qualification consists in ability to teach. . . . To the capacity for teaching must be added its diligent exercise in seeking an acquaintance with the subjects to be taught. Hence, the necessity of a third qualification, Study. . . . It is the duty of the churches of Christ, to see that the evangelists whom they receive possess these qualifications; and in cases where they have not the means of improvement, the churches should afford them the necessary supply. Hence the importance of establishing and sustaining institutions of learning, at which our young men, who have the ministry in view, may acquire the necessary improvement for the great work."

At the second meeting of the Triennial Convention in Philadelphia in 1817, Johnson heard Dr. Furman as he "placed before the body, in a speech of considerable length and great interest, the very serious and religious importance of a well-informed ministry." Dr. Johnson is reported to have said that Dr. Furman "used his utmost efforts to impress upon each member, and through them upon the churches, the sacred importance of an able ministry and the obligation to make provisions for securing it."

An article added to the constitution of the Convention in 1817 reads:

"That when competent and distinct funds shall have been received for the purpose, the board, from these, without resorting at all to mission funds, shall proceed to institute a classical and theological seminary, for the purpose of aiding pious young men, who, in the judgment of the churches of which they are members, and of the board, possess gifts and graces suited to the gospel ministry."

In conformity with the above article, a school was opened in Philadelphia under the care of Dr. Staughton and Rev. Ira Chase. A few years later the educational program was enlarged with the founding of Columbian College.

In 1814 there was no theological seminary nor state college for Baptists. Such Baptist ministers as were educated obtained their training in institutions other than denominational or in homes under direction of older ministers who possessed libraries and some learning, or by the laborious process of self-culture. Rice saw that ignorance was the most dangerous foe the mission program would have to face, and he urged the founding of a national educational institution corresponding to the newly organized national society. He was ably seconded by other leaders, notably Furman and Johnson.

Chapter VI

A Fruitful Interlude

"During my residence in Savannah," wrote Dr. Johnson, "my eyes became weak, & finding no relief from the remedies prescribed, I consulted a Physician of skill & experience in Columbia, who thought that, if I would remove with my family to that place, he could relieve me. I removed, therefore, & put myself under his care. The church, of which I have already given an account, received me very cordially, notwithstanding my change of views on the subject of Church Polity, & invited me to occupy her pulpit in connexion with her Minister. This invitation I accepted, as my newly acquired views imposed no difficulty in the way of preaching to *any* people.

"As my friend, tho' a skillful Physician, did not succeed, he advised me to visit the White Sulphur Spring in Virginia & drink its waters. I did so & found them effectual. My constitution was renovated & for the preservation of my health, & that of my wife, the Physician advised me, when a suitable opportunity presented itself, to remove to Greenville or Pendleton. As Savannah was not healthy in the summer & autumn, I took this as an intimation that I should not return to that city. And as I was comfortably situated in Columbia in a house & lot of my own, I resolved to profit by the intimation, & continue where I was, until Divine Providence should indicate some other place of greater health & usefulness. I was led to this conclusion in connexion with the above by the following facts—1. I was removed, in the ordering of Divine Providence, without seeking it, from the church in Savannah with whose members I had recently united in their organization; to Columbia at a considerable distance, in which I had united some years before, in organizing a church also. 2. My views of church order, which had originated the formation of the church in Savannah had undergone a change. By my removal, an interdict was imposed upon my enjoying the privilege of *that* church; & an opportunity was afforded me of enjoying the privileges of the church in Columbia, as she was willing to receive me without requiring an abandonment of any of my peculiar views; & I was willing to retain those views as matters of private judgment, never to be advanced to the disturbance of the harmony of the Denomination. With this understanding I was received into the membership of the Columbia Baptist Church. And as the Church was a member of the Charleston Baptist Association, I became again one of the Constituency of that body. . . .

"In the interval between my departure from Savannah & my removal to Columbia, I took a sea voyage by my Physician's advice, on the principle that secret bile was locked up in my system, & that the voyage would enable me to throw it up, & thus restore the health of my eyes. As it was winter, & I had received affectionate invitations to visit New Orleans & preach to the people, I took passage for that city, & on my arrival met with a cordial reception by the few Baptists there. Mr. Paulding, a rich man, had built a long room in the city, in which preaching & other religious exercises were observed on Lord's Days. In this room it was my privilege to preach Jesus & Him crucified for many weeks to a goodly number of immortal beings."

An incident occurred during Dr. Johnson's stay in New Orleans that has been commented upon by several historians. By special permission of Father Anthony, Dr. Johnson preached a sermon in the Roman Catholic Cathedral for the benefit of an orphans' home.

This was a strange occurrence, commented Dr. J. T. Christian, "when it is recalled that Antonio was the acknowledged head of the Spanish Inquisition in this city." Concerning that event Dr. Johnson relates:

"A few days after my arrival, a Committee of ladies waited upon me with a request that I would preach a Charity sermon in behalf of the Female Asylum, for which benevolent purpose an Israelite had given a house & lot worth $10,000. And these ladies, the representatives of their Sisters of Charity, who have charge of the Institution, desirous of improving the premises to render them more available for their noble design, came to ask the aid of the ministry of the Word. For this purpose, they obtained the privilege of Mr. Paulding's Long Room, & the Church Edifice of the Episcopalians, that I might preach & take up collections in both. It gave [me] much pleasure to comply with their request; I have only to regret that larger sums were not contributed for so important a cause. I felt a strong desire to preach, & have a collection taken up for the Asylum, in the Roman Catholic Cathedral, & having made the acquaintance of a lawyer of the city, I suggested to him my desire, & asked if he thought it practicable. He said he thought it might be accomplished, & being willing to make the application, we paid the Head of the Catholics, Father Anthony, a visit. And on opening to him our business, he gave us the privilege of the Cathedral for the purpose asked. 'But,' he said, 'I must see his sermon before he preaches it.' The sermon was sent, & returned with approval. As the audience would be French, the sermon was translated into the same language, & on the appointed Lord's Day, after the Catholic services were ended, the Father waived his handkerchief towards the pulpit, &, ascending it, I addressed a very attentive audience, after which a collection was taken up in aid of the Asylum. Some of the Priests remained in the audience, &, as I was afterwards informed, expressed a favorable opinion of the sermon, tho I had preached it before in English."

Of his other work in New Orleans, Dr. Johnson writes:

"An appointment was made for me to preach on the deck of a ship in the harbor, & besides the crew, we had a goodly number from the city. The sailors paid great attention, as was manifest from the falling tears, which flowed, we trust, from the effect of God's word upon their hearts.

"The citizens of Savannah had recently formed a Tract Society & had received from London a large supply of Tracts in English, French, & Spanish. Of these I took with me a large supply in all these languages, as I expected to find many in New Orleans who spoke all these tongues, and not a few who could read them also. In the work of distribution, I found use for these little messengers of salvation. I visited the poor families, & where I found them unable to read, I read the Tracts to them & talked to them about their souls' concerns. Where they could read I left Tracts, that they might themselves read. I visited the sailors, also distributed among them the precious little messengers of mercy. My vocation, as Colporteur, attracted the attention of the children in the streets, who would run after me, saying, 'Give me some of your *petits livres*,' meaning 'little books.'

"I had the pleasure of finding a Baptist Minister, a Missionary to the city, but his health was too feeble to allow him to preach during my visit. A few days before my departure from New Orleans, I had the pleasure of assisting in the formation of a Missionary Society, auxiliary to the Baptist General Missionary Convention. We collected three hundred dollars, paid one hundred to the Missionary, & remitted two hundred to the Treasurer of the General Missionary Board.

"Having spent several weeks in the service of the Lord not in vain I humbly trust, I took leave of my affectionate brethren & committing myself to the care of my heavenly Father on the Ocean, set sail for Carolina, whose shores I reached in safety, but with no benefit to my eyes."

Dr. Johnson left his wife and children in Beaufort with his stepmother while he was on the trip to New Orleans in 1817. They had mourned the passing of an eight-year-old son the year before, and now the children were, Mary, age 13; Joseph, 11; Claudia, 6; Elizabeth, 4; Charles, 2; and a baby son, William Bullein Johnson, born in July of that year. But the serenity of the family was to be interrupted soon again when they were called upon to give up their eldest son. Dr. Johnson makes no reference to it in his "Reminiscences," but this notation appears, in his writing, in the family Bible:

"Died on Thursday night, the 25th Sept. 1817, Joseph Kelsall Johnson, eldest son of William Bullein and Henrietta Johnson, aged 10 years, 11 months and 27 days. This dear child was a child of much promise, and greatly beloved of his parents. 'The Lord gave and the Lord hath taken away; blessed be the name of the Lord.' Job, 1 ch. 21 v."

Writing of their visit to Beaufort, Dr. Johnson says:

"In the same interval that I went to New Orleans, I visited Beaufort with my family to see my honored Stepmother, & when

I set out upon my voyage, left them with her, whose kindness was equal to that of an affectionate parent. As the vessel, in which I had taken my passage, was delayed in her preparations, I had the pleasure of spending some time with my Mother & the brethren before I set sail. Besides the Beaufort Church, there was a church of the same order with that in Savannah, with which I had recently united in its formation, & with this church in Beaufort I associated in church privileges, as I had not then united with the church in Columbia. This church had for their pastor, Rev. James Graham, a worthy man, & some excellent members were numbered in their communion. Clarinda, of whom I have already given an account [a colored woman] was a member of this church, & rendered great service to the white & colored brethren. This church has since become one body with the Beaufort Baptist church, without being required to abandon any of their former views."

Chapter VII

South Carolina State Baptist Convention

The first State Baptist Convention in the United States was formed in South Carolina in 1821.

"At the annual meeting of this [Charleston] Association in November, 1819, an interesting communication was read by Rev. R. Furman, Moderator, whose object was to unite the Denomination of the State in a State Convention," Dr. Johnson writes. "The objects of the Convention were the promotion of evangelical & useful knowledge by means of religious education; the support of Missionary service among the destitute; & the cultivation of measures promotive of the true interest of the churches in general, & of their love, union, & harmony in particular. The objects of the plan were approved by the Association, & means were taken without delay to bring both before the Baptists of the state. A judicious address was prepared by the Moderator to the Denomination in the State, & it was committed to my hands as Agent to use in visiting the churches & Associations for the purpose of engaging them in support of the noble scheme of forming a Baptist State Convention to carry out the objects proposed. A day was also appointed in December 1820 on which the Delegates should meet. But it was not until the second year, December 1821, that Delegates assembled in Columbia from the Charleston, Edgefield, & Savannah River Associations. There were four other Associations in the State, but their opposition to learning in the ministry lest its usefulness would be injured, hindered their uniting in the coalition. But these fears have nearly all gone, and it is our privilege to number, at this time of the Convention [1860] sixteen Associations, six Missionaries, & one church."

The year 1821 was a pivotal period for the Baptists of South

Carolina. Evangelistic impulses of the past seven years had been keenly felt. Missionary zeal and its important accompaniment, religious education, had taken on new meaning.

The life of the great Richard Furman was drawing to a close, and William Bullein Johnson, in his prime, was his logical successor. Basil Manly was completing his course at South Carolina College and about to begin his ministerial career; Richard Fuller was entering Harvard at the age of 18; and James C. Furman, son of Dr. Richard Furman, was just starting out in life.

The saintly Furman and the zealous Johnson, closely identified with the missionary enterprise of the Triennial Convention, realized the importance of a closer co-ordination of District Associations. But they were faced with the problem of converting anti-missionary and anti-educational groups within their own ranks.

At a meeting of the Charleston Association at the High Hills of Santee in 1818, Dr. Furman had inspired the query: "Would not the formation of a General Association composed of delegates from the several Baptist Associations in South Carolina be desirable and advantageous to the interests of the Baptist denomination?" In addition he introduced the subject in a more enlarged form in a letter from his church, the Charleston Baptist Church, to the association, and included a plan for promoting educational and missionary interests. This was accompanied by a serious address to the other associations. The proposition was endorsed and a committee composed of Richard Furman, John M. Roberts, and J. B. Cook, was named to make a revision and send the address to other bodies and arrange for the proposed meeting.

A thousand copies of Dr. Furman's address were printed and sent out over the state through the agency of Dr. Johnson, William Dossey, and Richard M. Todd.

Nine men met in Columbia on December 4, 1821, and formed the South Carolina State Baptist Convention. They were: Richard Furman, William Dossey, Joseph B. Cook, William B. Johnson, Richard M. Todd, and Lott Campbell, representing the Charleston Association; Rev. John Landrum and Col. Abner Blocker, the Edgefield Association; and Thomas Gillison, the Savannah River Association.

[46]

The meeting was called to order by Dr. Richard Furman, with Abner Blocker, of Edgefield, acting as secretary. Testimonials of the delegates were read and prayer was offered by Dr. Furman. The delegates, "agreeably to appointment," formed themselves into a "regular Body under the character of a Baptist State Convention in South Carolina," with the election of Dr. Richard Furman as president and Col. Abner Blocker as secretary. Visiting brethren, Pauling, Manly, Mayson, Chrestman, were invited to a seat in council.

A resolution was adopted: "This body do consider their union as founded upon the principles of gospel truth, Christian affection and liberality, having for their direct object the promotion of the cause and the interest of the Redeemer."

Associations not represented at this initial meeting were the Broad River, the Saluda, the Bethel, and the Moriah.

A committee to prepare the constitution included Dr. Furman, John Landrum, and W. B. Johnson; and named as a committee to prepare an address to the several associations in the state were R. Furman, J. B. Cook, and L. Campbell. Colonel Davis, deacon of the Rocky Creek Church in Fairfield District, was invited to a seat in the body. The committee on constitution asked for time to prepare the same, and on December 6 they submitted the constitution to the body and it was cordially received. It was agreed that copies of the minutes be sent to neighboring associations and that the address as above referred to be printed in the minutes after being revised by Dr. Furman.

The next annual meeting of the convention was held at Fellowship Meeting House in Edgefield District, near old Cambridge on Saturday before the "first Sabbath in December next"—1822. Dr. Richard Furman was appointed to preach on Monday morning at the second annual meeting, with Rev. Mr. Dossey, alternate. The meeting was featured by the interchange of letters with like organizations, one being received from the General Association of Baptists in Georgia which had been organized shortly after the South Carolina Convention. Saturday and Sunday of the meeting were employed in acts of public worship, closing with the celebration of the Lord's Supper. On Monday morning Dr. Furman preached according to appointment, from the text, "Because of the House of the Lord our God, I will seek thy good" (Psalm 122:9).

Dr. Johnson preached the introductory sermon and prepared the address of the convention to the churches that year—"a document of great ability and penetrated by a thoroughly missionary and evangelical spirit," according to Dr. John E. White.

A resolution was passed approving the formation of "Sabbath Schools," with suggestions as to the method of conducting them.

The third meeting of the convention was held at Edgefield Village Church in 1823. That church had been constituted in April of the same year, with Rev. Basil Manly as pastor, and began at once to take its place as a vital unit in the denomination's program of missions and education. Manly was elected secretary of the convention in 1823.

The Saluda River Association, of which Dr. Johnson was then a member, was represented at the 1823 convention. Dr. Johnson was living in Greenville at that time and thus had the opportunity of enlisting the interest of that association in the State organization.

"I was sent as a delegate to the Annual Meeting of the Association, where I had the pleasure of meeting several agents of the newly formed Baptist Convention," wrote Johnson. "These assisted in the Association's becoming a member of the Convention. But unfortunately at the next Annual Meeting [1824] many of the churches sent an expression of their unwillingness to continue in the Convention, & the Association discontinued their union with that Body. During the meeting, however, a Society was formed, auxiliary to the Convention, Delegates were appointed, & a respectable sum of money was collected & sent to the Convention."

Besides rescinding the resolution adopted the year before by which the Saluda Association became a member of the State Convention, the circular letter read by Dr. Johnson based on the co-operation of the association with the convention was revoked. Johnson was then moderator of the Saluda Association, and, according to T. H. Garrett, "This was indeed a gloomy time to Johnson and many others, who were full of the missionary spirit and zeal."

Upon the rejection of the circular, Dr. Johnson hastily wrote a short paper on "The Alarming Condition of the Churches," of which the following is an extract:

"The present is a season of alarming visitation from the hand of our God. Our churches generally complain of great coldness and declension. Serious troubles exist between some of them, and even between some of their ministers and venerable fathers in the gospel. Very few have been the additions to them, and our number, as a body, has suffered a decrease, as well this year as the last. In the providential arrangement of the Divine hand, indications of His displeasure are strongly marked. The heaven above is as iron, and the earth beneath our feet is as brass. The bottles of heaven are stopped, and the earth withholds her usual supply of kindly fruits for the support of men. Brethren, this dearth of rain upon the earth, and of Divine influence upon the churches, call for solemn prayer and serious self-examination. Is it not evident that the Lord hath a controversy with us? . . . What is the state of our hearts with respect to the exercise of vital religion? Are we careful to maintain secret and close communion with our God? Are we cultivating enlarged views of the Divine glory, character and designs? Are we doing for God what is in the power of our hands as instruments to do for his adorable name?"

The State Convention met that year, 1824, at Coosawhatchie Church, and Dr. Furman presided over the body for his last time. The convention met in Camden in 1825 and elected William Bullein Johnson as president, to succeed the lamented Furman.

On December 3, 1825, the convention presented to the State Legislature a petition of incorporation signed by: William B. Johnson, president; Benjamin S. Screven, vice-president; Basil Manly, secretary; Abner Blocker, treasurer; John Landrum, James Crowther, John Good, Charles T. Mallary, Jesse Hartwell, John T. Coleman, Nicholas W. Hodges, M. Mims, T. Pothill, T. B. Baker, Timothy Dargan, Nathan Johnson, James Graham, William Frippe, Samuel Gibson.

Chapter VIII

Accepts Call to Greenville

The suitable opportunity for Dr. Johnson to remove to the Piedmont, in accordance with the suggestion of his physician, came in 1822 when the trustees of the Greenville Academies invited him to take charge of the female school. Of this he writes:

"In the year 1822 I received an invitation from the Trustees of the Greenville Academies of this State to visit them; & in compliance with their request, informed them that I would do so by Divine permission, & appointed a day on which I would preach to the people. According to appointment I went up, saw the Trustees, & preached to the people. On the next day I had an interview with the Trustees, accepted the office of principal of the Academy, & opened the Institution on the first Monday in the year 1823. I also commenced a stated course of preaching on Lord's Days in the Court House, as there was no House of public Worship in the village. I also opened a Sunday School, which encreased considerably, requiring several teachers. . . . I joined the Baptist Church at Brushy Creek, seven miles out of the Village. . . ."

By November, 1822, he had removed his wife and family of five children to Greenville. The state road, from the seaboard to the mountains, coming through the capital city, Columbia, was probably their route of travel until they reached the vicinity of Greenville.

Children of the family then were: Mary, aged 18; Claudia, 11; Elizabeth, 9; Charles, 7; and William Bullein, 5. Shortly after their residence began in Greenville, on January 12, 1823, another son, Francis Cleveland, was born; and before the end of the decade their family was to be rounded out by the addition of two other children, Henrietta Ann, born in 1824, and Thomas Hornby, in

1827. Down into the valley of the shadow the mother went in 1829, when, as the father wrote in the family Bible:

"On Tuesday, 28th April, 1829, was born to William B. and Henrietta Johnson—a son, but deprived of life, being, as is usually called still born. Its dear mother was in a perilous state in bringing it into existence, but God had mercy on her and on her family that in taking the child he spared the parent."

Several other children of the family had died in infancy, and some of them bore the same names as children born later.

"My removal to Greenville," relates Dr. Johnson, "brought me into acquaintance with two communities of much improvement. The beauty of Greenville & the salubrity of its atmosphere had attracted the favorable attention of inhabitants of the lower country of both South Carolina & Georgia. Numbers were, by these attractions, annually drawn in the summer & autumn to admire its splendid scenery of mountain view, & to enjoy its pure air. A few families of wealth & refinement made it their abode for several months of the year, at whose suggestion the citizens determined to erect two Academies of brick for male & female students. In aid of this noble design, a gentleman gave a lot of 30 acres of land in the North part of the town, on which the edifices were built. In the first year of my residence at Greenville, I had the pleasure of assisting in the formation of a Bible Society; & my elder daughter succeeded in forming a Female Library Society. At Pendleton, about 30 miles distant, the society was larger & more improved, in consequence of a larger number of inhabitants from the low country who were possessed of wealth & learning, & made it their permanent place of residence. A Bible Society, Library, & Schools for both sexes had also been for some time in operation.

"I had the high satisfaction of finding that the churches of the Association consisted of good & substantial members; and that they [so] increased in numbers, that in the eight years of my connexion with the Academy, she sent forth a sufficient number of churches to form two Associations. The ministry of the churches was destitute of scholastic education; but they were sincere, laborious, & earnest in their labors, & their work was blessed by the Great Master."

A few years after he went to Greenville, Dr. Johnson set in motion plans for the First Baptist Church in Greenville, but his recital of the details is in keeping with his reluctance to speak of his own accomplishments:

"In the year 1825, I opened a successful subscription for the erection of a Meeting House for the Baptists, which was built of brick, on a beautiful site which was given by Mr. Vardry McBee, the liberal donor of the land for the Academies. I had the privilege also of baptizing the first white person in the town of Greenville—the wife of a respectable mechanic."

The Greenville Baptist Church was formally constituted November 2, 1831, after Dr. Johnson had removed from that place. During its century and more of life it has exerted a tremendous influence upon the religious and educational life of Greenville. A new building was constructed in 1857, and the original building became the first home of the Southern Baptist Theological Seminary in 1859.

Many church organizations have grown out of the First Baptist Church of Greenville, and by it a large number of Baptist ministers have been ordained.

Along with his school work, Dr. Johnson, as noted, took an active interest in other phases of community and denominational life. Going to the Saluda Association meeting as a delegate from Brushy Creek Church in 1823, he at once became a leader and was moderator during his connection with that association.

Associational meetings in those early years drew large crowds from miles about. Sunday was the great day for preaching, with the entire day given to exhortation and prayer. The attendance was so large that two congregations were formed that alternated in listening to the speaking which began early in the morning and lasted until late in the afternoon. An account of one meeting stated that eleven hundred people slept in tents on the church grounds the Saturday night of the meeting.

While in Greenville, Dr. Johnson was active also in the wider realms of denominational life. The outreach of the General Convention, both in its missionary and educational endeavors, was of vital concern to him. Three times during his stay in Greenville he had gone northward—to Washington in 1823, to New York in

1826, and to Philadelphia in 1829—to meet with the brethren from the different States; and as a member of the Board of Commissioners he met regularly with that group which managed the affairs of the convention between sessions.

The dreams of the venerable Richard Furman, Luther Rice, and William B. Johnson became a reality when the Columbian College opened its doors in January, 1822. Referring to the organization and history of this institution, Dr. Johnson relates in his "Reminiscences":

". . . The plan of the venerable President was the establishment of a Central Theological Seminary of high order, & Institutions in each state in which students should prepare for the Central Seminary, or take a limited course.

"Brother Rice was of the opinion, that the establishment of a well endowed College near the city of Washington under able Professors would materially aid the interests of the Denomination, & might become in one sense, a National Institution, tho' not endowed by the Nation's munificence & authority. He, therefore, collected funds for the College, as well as for the Missionary Enterprize. Buildings were erected on an eligible lot about 12 miles from Washington; Professors appointed, students gathered, & the Columbian College commenced operations under favorable circumstances. In its first year, the College graduated several students, who became useful & distinguished ministers. But in succeeding years, it became embarrassed in pecuniary affairs, & its prosperity declined. It was rising again, however, when the unrighteous & cruel war, now raging in the Southern Confederacy, has again suspended its operations [1862].

"The prosperity of the Columbian College was very dear to our departed Brother's heart. In the dying hour he did not forget it. When asked by the kind friend in whose home he died, to whom he should send his property after his death, he replied— 'The College —Send all to the College.'"

Luther Rice died in old Edgefield District, now Saluda County, South Carolina, at the home of Ryden Grigsby Mays, and is buried at Pine Pleasant Baptist Church cemetery. The South Carolina Baptist State Convention erected a marker over his grave.

Once again during Dr. Johnson's residence in Greenville, death laid its hand upon his family, taking his eldest child, Mary. In sorrow the father penned the words: "Died on Thursday night about 9 o'clock, 11th August, 1825, Mary Bullein Johnson, eldest child of W. B. and H. Johnson, aged 20 years, 10 months and 5 days. She was a dear child and universally beloved."

Meanwhile, Dr. Johnson, as president of the South Carolina State Baptist Convention, was actively engaged in plans for the establishment of a theological school in South Carolina, and at the meeting of the State Convention in Greenville in 1826, final arrangements were made for the school.

The first meetinghouse of the Greenville Baptist Church (now First Baptist) and the first building used by the Southern Baptist Theological Seminary when it was first established at Greenville in 1859. This structure had been built under William B. Johnson's leadership in 1826. The congregation itself was not organized until five years later, in 1831.

Chapter IX

Furman Academy and Theological Institution

Furman University at Greenville, South Carolina, and the Southern Baptist Theological Seminary at Louisville, Kentucky, may trace their ancestry to Furman Academy and Theological Institution, which opened its doors in Edgefield, South Carolina, January 15, 1827.

According to Dr. Johnson: "In the year 1826, at the Annual Meeting of the Baptist State Convention in Greenville the final arrangements were made for establishing an Institution of Learning at Edgefield Court House in the State, by the name of The Furman Academy & Theological Institution. Of this Institution Rev. Joseph Andrews Warne was elected Principal, & in January 1827 it commenced operations with a respectable number of students, five of whom had the ministry in view. Edgefield C.H. was selected the location of the Institution because the citizens made a liberal offer of a building, erected for Academical purposes; & because of its adjacency to the State of Georgia with the desire & in the hope, that she would unite with South Carolina upon the same Institution for both States. Georgia however preferred to establish an Institution for herself, & South Carolina removed hers in the third year of its existence into a central part of the State."

Furman is the oldest of the Baptist institutions in the South, conceived by the founding fathers when the State Convention was organized in 1821; the seed dormant for a while—until the death of Richard Furman in 1825 gave it new being; its actual life span beginning when the trustees of the Edgefield Village Academy deeded the school property to the South Carolina Baptist State Convention.

The Baptists of Georgia were also without proper facilities for

[55]

educating young ministers, and some of that state's Baptist leaders were favorable to the idea of one school for both states. Jesse Mercer and W. T. Brantly, then living in Georgia, had both received aid from the Charleston Association Education Fund and were friendly with the South Carolina Baptists. They attended the meeting of the State Convention held in Edgefield in November, 1823, as representatives of the newly organized general association of Baptists in Georgia and were cordially received. They came for the purpose of discussing the establishment of a joint institution for both states.

Conclusions reached were that the two conventions should unite in one educational institution, to be located in South Carolina within thirty miles of Augusta, and to "embrace ultimately, a general course of literature, scientific and classical; as well as a suitable course of theological instruction." A committee consisting of Thomas Gillison, Esq., Rev. John Landrum, Col. Abner Blocker, Rev. W. B. Johnson, and Rev. B. Manly was appointed to confer with the Georgia brethren in the selection of a site and the arrangement of courses of study; and collecting agents were appointed.

Dr. Johnson, at that meeting of the State Baptist Convention, stood for the first time presumably in the village church in Edgefield which he was to serve later as pastor for twenty-two years; and perhaps he went with Dr. Furman, Rev. Basil Manly, and other members of the committee to the Village Academy to consider that as a possible site for the school that was contemplated. It was only a matter of continuing along the same street, crossing Three Quarters or Academy Branch, and entering the grove where stood the school that had been incorporated a year earlier. And perhaps they were joined there by trustees of the Academy, Eldred Simkins, Sr., John S. Jeter, Matthew Mims, Benjamin Fraser, and Whitfield Brooks.

At the convention in 1824 the committee appointed to collect funds reported that "owing to the disasters suffered throughout the State this year, and particularly to the planting interest, the majority of them had attempted nothing; yet, in general, such efforts as had been made had been crowned with success."

The state had been visited with a severe drought during the summer and from heavy rains and destructive floods during the fall and winter, from pestilence in Charleston and a destructive hurricane over a large part of the state. The sum of $25.00 was the first money reported as having been collected for the new institution. Finding that the Georgia committee had not been active, it was agreed to appoint another committee in South Carolina to select a site anywhere in the state and make estimates as to cost of buildings and other expenses.

When the State Convention met in Camden in 1825, with Dr. Johnson as president, the first business taken up was the proposed new educational institution. The resolution to petition the legislature to grant a charter of incorporation was adopted in order to enable the convention to acquire and hold property for use of the proposed school. The Board of Agents, as the general board of the convention was designated, was instructed to employ a suitable man as agent "who shall devote himself exclusively to the interests of the convention, and who shall travel through the different parts of this state for the purpose of collecting subscriptions and donations, wherever he can, in aid of the contemplated institution, and other important designs of this body," as recorded in the minutes. Dr. Johnson, with John Landrum, Basil Manly, and Abner Blocker, formed a committee named as messengers to the Georgia body to seek their continued co-operation.

The committee appointed to select a site decided unanimously to locate the school at Edgefield, after considering other places, particularly Greenville and Pendleton. Dr. Johnson, then living in the Piedmont section, naturally preferred either Greenville or Pendleton, but a majority of the committee favored Edgefield, and he made the selection unanimous because of his desire to co-operate with the Georgia brethren.

A committee consisting of Basil Manly, pastor at Edgefield; Abner Blocker, Matthew Mims, John Landrum, Benjamin S. Screven, Timothy Dargan, and Samuel Gibson was appointed to "visit the spot and make such arrangements with the trustees of the Edgefield Village Academy and citizens of that place in the selection of a site, as may to them seem best for the institution, and safe, both for the convention and the trustees" (of the Village Academy). It was thought wise to seek a union or some accommodation with that institution to avoid duplication or conflict. The Board of Agents was instructed to take immediate measures to erect suitable buildings and to work out plans for the operation of the school.

The Act of Incorporation, approved December 20, 1825, set forth as objects and purposes of the State Baptist Convention: "to erect and establish an academical and theological seminary for the education of youth, generally, and of indigent pious young men, particularly, who may be designed for the gospel ministry, and for all other purposes necessary for carrying the foregoing objects into effect."

Upon adjournment of the convention, December 6, 1825, the board met and appointed a special committee consisting of Basil Manly, John Landrum, Abner Blocker, and Matthew Mims to complete all details at Edgefield, and appointed Samuel Gibson to travel over the state to collect funds.

The Board met at Edgefield, March 16 and 17, 1826, to transact the important business of transferring the property of the Edgefield Male Academy to the State Convention. Six members present were: W. B. Johnson, Basil Manly, John Landrum, Charles D. Mallary, Abner Blocker, and Matthew Mims. They accepted the property of the Academy and also from Eldred Simkins, Sr., thirty acres of surrounding land, on condition that a "respectable institution" should be established and maintained. Failure to do so entailed a penalty of $2,000 to be paid the trustees of the academy and $800 to Mr. Simkins. The entire property of the academy was pledged to the fulfilment of these conditions. The deeds were signed, March 17, 1826. This was the first property held by the convention.

The board bought as a home for the principal the house and lot of Basil Manly, who was just leaving to become pastor of the church at Charleston, succeeding Dr. Furman. The price paid was $1,400, a thousand of which was to be paid to Mr. Manly and $400 to the institution for the beginning of a library.

They fixed the salary of the future principal as "the entire profits of the school, five hundred dollars in addition to it, and the use of a house and lot free of expense."

Dr. Johnson was authorized to advertise for a principal who

should be "a Baptist minister, and able to instruct in all the branches of literary education, necessary for admission into the higher classes of the most respectable colleges in the United States, and to give such assistance in their divinity studies, to young men designed for the gospel ministry, as may be suited to their cases, and to the wants of the churches."

The friendship between Basil Manly and Eldred Simkins II at South Carolina College was a contributing cause of the interest taken by the latter's uncle, Eldred Simkins, distinguished lawyer of Edgefield, in establishing a Baptist church and a Baptist school at Edgefield. The ground for both institutions was given by the elder Simkins after Manly had visited the Simkins family in Edgefield and preached in the courthouse, serving then as pastor of the Little Stevens Creek Baptist Church.

The Board of Agents held a meeting, September 18, 1826, and elected Rev. Joseph Andrews Warne as principal. He was an Englishman, living at that time at Newbern, North Carolina, and had wanted to go as a missionary, but having been prevented by ill health, he was devoting himself to teaching. Mr. Warne accepted the invitation to attend the State Convention in Greenville, December 16–19, 1826, and was cordially received.

At the convention announcement was made that the General Committee of the Charleston Association had transferred the library used by Mr. Roberts at his school at the High Hills of Santee to the State Convention, and it was gratefully received for use of the new institution. The amount of $200 was appropriated for the purchase of a library and the committee was instructed to prepare a room for its reception. The convention agreed to apply the legacy of $5,000 left to the denomination by Thomas Gillison to educational purposes, using it as a nucleus for the endowment of the school. Rules for the government of the school, drawn up by a subcommittee and approved by the convention, provided that "this Seminary shall be named 'The Furman Academy and Theological Institution,'" in honor of Dr. Richard Furman; that the institution "shall be under the general direction of the State Convention of the Baptist denomination in South Carolina; who alone shall have the power to alter or amend these rules." The Board of Agents was to exercise the authority of the convention, appointing and dismissing principal and professors, fixing salaries, prescribing courses of study, granting certification, and making rules and by-laws for the regulation of the institution. The board was to appoint an executive committee of three persons residing near the seminary to act with the principal and professors in the management of the students and care of the property. The first executive committee was composed of Eldred Simkins, Sr., Matthew Mims, and Whitfield Brooks. Regulation of the seminary and administration of discipline were to be vested in the principal alone, but the faculty were to constitute an advisory council in cases involving suspension, while the executive committee was to be called in on cases involving expulsion. The principal must be a Baptist minister in good and regular standing in the Baptist denomination, while the professors and instructors must be men of irreproachable morals, competent attainments in science, and, if not Baptists, friendly at least in their feelings and sentiments to the Baptist denomination.

Two sessions yearly were to begin January 15 and July 15. The newspapers of that day carried advertisements relating to the school, with terms of tuition ranging from $5.00 to $8.50 per quarter. Good boarding could be obtained in the village at $25 per quarter, and at the Pottery, a mile distant from the academy, at $20 per quarter. The advertisements were signed by William B. Johnson, president of the Convention and Board.

Furman Academy and Theological Institution opened in accordance with the announcement on January 15, 1827. The occasion must have been an auspicious one, although no account is available. Certainly Dr. Johnson, Basil Manly, and other members of the board were present, and a number of day students in addition to the five ministerial students. Three were Issachar J. Roberts, of Tennessee, Thomas Simons, and James Griffith. Another was probably Samuel Worthington. Simons brought his letter from the High Hills of Santee to the Edgefield Church and took part in the church services. He preached there in September, 1827, according to the church minutes. In January, 1829, a letter of dismission was granted to Brother Simons. Samuel Worthington preached at Edgefield Village Church in December, 1828, and was elected one of the vice-presidents of a temperance society at Sardis.

June 15, 1827, the board met in Edgefield to conduct the first examination of students and declared "that the board are highly gratified with the examination of the students of the Furman Academy."

But the school in Edgefield was not to succeed, as the world counts success.

The Georgia Baptists did not co-operate with the South Carolina brethren in the enterprise; local support seems to have been slight; efforts of the voluntary agents over the territory of the convention were not successful; and the financial difficulties of Columbian College at Washington had a discouraging effect. Principal Warne, whose health was poor, tendered his resignation at the meeting of the board in June, 1828, after only eighteen months of service.

Yet who can measure the results? Perhaps Warne's zeal for the mission cause was transmitted to Thomas Simons, missionary to Burmah; and to Issachar J. Roberts, missionary to China; and perhaps his deep consecration, unable to find an outlet in more active Christian service because of his feeble health, was a challenge to such students as Samuel Worthington, one of the group who carried the torch of evangelism during the great revival of 1831.

However, the seeming failure must have been keenly disappointing to Dr. Johnson and other leaders. At the meeting of the State Convention at Minervaville, December 6–9, 1828, the board reported on the condition of the academy, and passed the following resolution: "That, as there have appeared insuperable obstacles to the success of the institution, on its present plan, and in its present location; to secure the important objects of the convention, as well as to fulfill the part of candour and justice to the trustees of the Edgefield Village Academy, and the inhabitants of that place, it is necessary to abandon at present the classical department of the school, to surrender to the donors the property given with a view to that department, and to make an equitable compromise with subscribers of the same character."

The concrete covered brick building, which was the first home of Furman, was turned back to the donors, and the house bought from Basil Manly was offered for sale. Beneficiaries were placed under the tutelage of Rev. Jesse Hartwell at the High Hills of

Santee, "with a view in future to establish the institution in more strict accordance with the original design of making the theological department more prominent."

Discouraged but not defeated, the convention appointed Brethren Johnson, Manly, Mims, Blanding, and W. A. Lawton to select a suitable site for the school.

Hartwell took the students into his home the first year, 1829, and later built simple huts for them at his own expense. Four ministerial students in 1829 were increased to eight when the term began in January, 1830, and by April four more had entered, the twelfth being James C. Furman, son of Dr. Richard Furman, who was to become the first president of Furman University. The school plant included rooms for fifteen or twenty students, a library to house the books which had been used originally at the Roberts Academy and later at Edgefield, and a commodious chapel.

The State Convention, meeting at Robertville in December, 1830, adopted a scholarship plan advocated by Dr. Manly and recommended by the Charleston Association, which included: the raising of annual scholarships of $30.00 each, to run for five years; the beginning of a permanent endowment; engaging two ministers from each of the three associations affiliated with the convention to raise funds; employing beneficiary students in missionary labors during vacation; and a manual labor plan. The recommendation was adopted with enthusiasm, and the board immediately after adjournment elected Rev. Samuel Furman, son of Dr. Richard Furman, as junior professor.

During 1831 the new financial plan was fairly successful. Dr. Manly, one of the agents, raised more than $7,000 in subscriptions and cash, while the other agents raised about $1,000.

In the summer of 1831 the institution was almost depleted by calls on professors and students to engage in protracted meetings.

In May, 1833, there were eighteen students present, the largest number that had been in the institution at any time; the number of volumes in the library had risen to 1,500, and there was a general atmosphere of progress and optimism.

Dr. Johnson, writing a friend in Boston concerning the 1833 convention in Newberry, felt much encouraged over the progress of the school: "To see very evidently the interests of our convention growing in importance, and sustained, under God, by such able hands as I beheld surrounding me, and taking hold with an energy that seemed to forbid any future paralysis, afforded me the most heartfelt satisfaction, and excited my gratitude and praise to Almighty God. By a letter received from our Treasurer this evening, I learn with much pleasure, that five or six new students have already arrived at the Furman Theological Institution. We hope to embody as many as forty, at least, this year."

But before the close of 1834 both professors had resigned, and the convention found itself with a theological institution without a faculty, with little financial resources, with an unsatisfactory location, and practically without a student body.

The classical department had been abandoned with the removal of the school to the High Hills; but in 1834 the convention declared their willingness to "superintend a classical school, for the reception of students in general, on the manual labor system," and the board was instructed to look into the matter of location and means and to report back at the next meeting. The constitution was amended so as to create a separate board of trustees elected by the convention at the end of every fourth year, who should own, control, and manage the school. The hope of continuing the school where it was for another year failed to materialize when the board was unable to find a suitable principal.

The transplanted tree of Furman had yielded good fruit in the lives of young men who had gone forth to preach, and when fears for its existence were felt, denominational leaders put themselves vigorously to the task of cultivating the soil about it. Nicholas Ware Hodges, appointed financial agent, proved very energetic, and there was much discussion in the religious press and in religious meetings. Much of the discussion centered about whether the convention should support only theological education or combine the theological with classical and introduce manual training. The lower part of the state favored more generally the former plan, while the upper section favored the academic and manual labor features.

Dr. Johnson called the convention in extra session at Barnwell in October, 1835, in order to make necessary decisions and arrangements for reopening the school. A committee composed of Basil Manly, W. B. Johnson, J. B. O'Neall, J. M. Chiles, and J. B. Furman, digested the material obtained and reported their conviction that "a permanent provision for the instruction of young ministers is the great object of this body, and that other things should be undertaken or done, as they may consist with this object, and become auxiliaries to it"; that the manual labor system of education "is but an experiment, yet to be tried," but so popular and promising that "it deserves to be fairly tried in some form that shall not jeopard the funds of the convention, nor make the success of the theological institution dependent on the success of that"; they recommended that all permanent funds then available be used as "a permanent foundation for the support of theological instruction," the annual income of which was to be pledged forever "to the maintenance of a theological professorship," that a general agent be employed to promote a second professorship permanently endowed, and that voluntary agents be engaged to assist in the speedy completion of the task; that arrangements be made as soon as possible to begin again the instruction of theological students, and finally that a committee be appointed to select a site for a "manual labor classical and English school, to ascertain what funds could be raised for such a school and to inquire for teachers and officers and report to the regular session in December." This committee was to consist of I. L. Brooks, Z. Watkins, J. Gary, N. W. Hodges, A. D. Jones, and Alexander Sparks. These recommendations were adopted.

The action of this extra session marked out the lines of the next educational experiment to be made by South Carolina Baptists—the attempt to have an English and classical academy conducted on a required manual labor system along with theological instruction on a voluntary manual labor basis.

The manual labor plan was to enable students to pay their expenses while obtaining an education. Nicholas W. Hodges strongly favored the plan, while Dr. Johnson just as strongly opposed it.

In one meeting of the trustees, it was said, Hodges was arguing in favor of the manual labor plan, and Dr. Johnson said the plan would not last, that it was not suited to Southern dispositions, and closed with the statement: "Ardor, Sir, and not perseverance, is our Southern characteristic." Mr. Hodges finally won his point, but the plan did not last longer than three years.

The school was to go through several other adjustments, first in Winnsboro, and next in Greenville, in 1851, where it emerged eventually into full-blown maturity. Dr. Johnson, it will be recalled, favored Greenville as the original site of Furman thirty-two years before. The far vision of the great leader was at last realized.

Dr. Johnson's feelings for the school are expressed thus by Dr. Richard Furman III:

"That institution was peculiarly the object of his affections, his prayers and his benefactions. He watched over it with fatherly care, commended it to the liberal support of his brethren, and was the moving spirit in all measures adopted to promote its interests, and witnessed with a genuine joy, the tokens of its growing usefulness. Believing that the interests of the ministry and the denomination would be advanced by enlarging our educational plan, and changing the Institution into a University, he favored the change, and did more than any other man towards establishing the Furman University on its present basis. To him it owes a large and lasting debt, for positions it has taken, and for work it has already accomplished. When the project was started for establishing a general Baptist Theological Seminary for the South, it met his hearty approval, and he hailed it as the omen of increased ministerial power."

Chapter X

Edgefield

"In the year 1830, I received an invitation from the Edgefield Baptist Church to become her Minister, & at the same time one from the Trustees of the Edgefield Female Academy to become its Principal. I accepted both invitations, & removing in December, I commenced my labors in January 1831, as Minister of the Church, & Teacher of the Academy."

That was Dr. Johnson's introduction to the twenty-two years he was to spend in Edgefield, during which period religious and political upheavals were to cast their shadows over the nation.

Edgefield at that time was a neat little village in the head fork of Beaverdam Creek, in the western part of South Carolina. The houses were scattered and numbered forty or fifty. They were neat, commodious, and generally painted. About forty families resided there in 1830, and the population was estimated as 300. There were also seventeen houses at Pottersville, one mile north, where a newspaper was published. There was a male academy as well as the female academy. The principal denominations were Baptist and Methodist. Within a few years, in 1836, the Episcopalians were to erect their beautiful little brick church. In that year, too, the *Edgefield Advertiser* was to begin publication.

W. W. Ball, journalist and author, describes Edgefield as having had "more dashing, brilliant, romantic figures, statesmen, orators, soldiers, adventurers, daredevils, than any county of South Carolina, if not of any rural county in America." He further asserts that "an artist drawing the typical Edgefieldian would use stronger colors, make bolder lines, than if he were drawing the composite man, or woman, of another county. They had polish, refinement, education (or their leaders had) and they had humor and wit. Withal some of them could be more extreme in manner and ways than is conventionally acceptable to the politer circles. They were impetuous, dashing people, and sometimes they rode roughly over persons tardy in getting out of the way. Perhaps their good quality of courage sometimes rather suddenly heated made them peculiarly fit for the emergencies of war and the Reconstruction period."

But men of God who made Edgefield their home have given to it a luster that time cannot dim nor the future attainments of her sons outshine. The ground of Edgefield is holy because mighty men of God have left their footprints upon it.

The recurrence should cause no wonder that in 1849 the president of the Southern Baptist Convention, William Bullein Johnson, was pastor of the Edgefield Village Baptist Church, and that one hundred years later, in 1949, the president of that same great body, Robert G. Lee, was once the honored pastor of this people. Edgefield's historical pattern, century by century, seems woven by the master Craftsman.

Some Baptist churches in Edgefield Association had been in existence for half a century before the church in the village was constituted in 1823. Then was the simple frame structure dedicated with due ceremony, the presbytery including William T. Brantly, Robert Carson, James M. Scott, and Basil Manly.

When Manly left Edgefield to become pastor at Charleston, the Edgefield church was without a regular minister until Rev. Joseph Warne accepted a call and served until April, 1828. He supplied at intervals until he left Edgefield, and Rev. N. W. Hodges then supplied until the coming of Dr. Johnson.

The church passed the following resolutions in April, 1830:

"Whereas, the citizens generally of this place having called and invited the Rev. W. B. Johnson of Greenville to take the charge of the Female Academy in the place:

"Resolved: That we as a church highly approve of that measure, and also invite the said W. B. Johnson to supply our pulpit as a minister of the Gospel and that we will pay a proportionate part, according to our means, of the sum of five hundred dollars per annum for such a service."

The deacons were requested to forward to Dr. Johnson a copy

of the resolutions, awaiting his consideration and answer, and in May the deacons reported having heard from Dr. Johnson, and his reply was read. The minutes fail to give the text of his reply, but perhaps he was merely considering the call, for at the August meeting the acceptance was read.

Dr. Johnson began his pastorate in Edgefield in October, 1830, at a Saturday service. According to the church minutes:

"In October 1830 the church met. Preaching by the Rev. Mr. Johnson. Opened a door for the reception of members, whereupon the Rev. W. B. Johnson presented his letter of dismission from the Brushy Creek Baptist church, requesting membership with us, and was received with great cordiality. . . ."

"Brother McWhorter requested that Rev. Mr. Johnson be appointed to take his place as delegate to the association. A collection was taken for minutes and for the State Convention. Communion was observed on the Sabbath."

The association was held at Salem Church, Edgefield District, Saturday, October 16, with the sabbath devoted to preaching, and the sessions of the association continuing on Monday, October 18. Attending as representatives from the Edgefield Village Church were Rev. W. B. Johnson and Matthew Mims. Forty churches formed the association at that time, with a total membership of 2,829. Dr. Johnson's church at Edgefield had the comparatively small membership of 79, including 44 whites and 35 colored, although some of the other churches had an even smaller number of members. Churches of larger membership were Little Stephens Creek, with 250, and Gilgal, with 225. Church contributions for missions and education were at a low ebb, with nothing listed for domestic missions; only $5.25 for foreign missions, of which Gilgal gave $5.00 and Horn's Creek, 25 cents; and $23.87 for Furman Academy, of which Edgefield church gave $8.00, Bethany $10.00, Dean Swamp $2.88, Siloam $1.00, and Sardis 50 cents.

Dr. Johnson at once became a recognized leader and was elected moderator, a place he was to hold for about fifteen years.

According to the minutes: "On Sabbath morning the Charity Sermon was preached by Brother R. M. Todd, after which a public collection of $58.12½ was received from the congregation. The balance of the day was employed in preaching, notwithstanding the interruptions from the inclemency of the weather, to a vast concourse of people, who appeared anxious to hear the word."

The public collection was divided equally for foreign missions, domestic missions, and for educational purposes.

At the Monday session the Mount Gilead Church, constituted in December, 1829, prayed membership with the body, which was granted, and their delegates, Thomas Morris and John Cloud, received the right hand of fellowship, and an invitation to a seat.

Messengers from sister associations present were Wilson and Hodges of Saluda, Elbert Lindsay of Reedy River, Joiner and Dunkin of Bethel, and James Furman of Charleston Association.

Elected to the State Convention at Robertville were Dr. Johnson and twelve others.

"Heard with great pleasure the Report of the Chairman of the Edgefield Domestic Missionary Society. . . . Whereupon the Association proceeded to appoint a Domestic Missionary Board, to co-operate with the above Society, consisting of the brethren W. B. Johnson, N. W. Hodges, Jesse Blocker, J. G. O. Wilkerson and M. Mims. . . . Heard the Reports of the various Ministering brethren on their Missionary tours, during the past year, which were quite encouraging. . . ."

The committee on religion reported that some of the churches were holding evening meetings in private homes, and a few of the churches kept up Sunday schools regularly on Lord's Day for the instruction of the rising generation. "We regret to state that some of these useful institutions that were in operation last year have since declined and entirely come to nothing; while, on the other hand, we learn with pleasure, that a few still continue in successful operation, and some new ones have been established. We believe, however, the principal reason why many Sunday Schools fall through, after a prosperous commencement, is, that so few persons can be found with suitable qualifications to conduct them in a proper manner, and who, at the same time, are willing to give themselves up to the work on Sabbath days."

The report further stated that there were in the District of Edgefield two Bible Societies, namely: the Edgefield Village Bible Society and the Ridge Bible Society, both of which were auxiliaries to the American Bible Society. They were engaged in supplying destitute families with copies of the Holy Scriptures as gifts if they were unable to pay the purchase price. Five Auxiliary Bible Societies had been formed in aid of the object. There were five Temperance Societies in the association; and the Edgefield Domestic Missionary Society was continuing its operations. Three "respectable Female Societies, auxiliaries to it," and a majority of the churches contributed to its support.

The report continued:

"While we make this favorable report of the state of Religion amongst some of our Churches, we are compelled, though reluctantly, to state the fact, that a great many of the Churches of our Association seem to be nearly, if not quite asleep, doing nothing either for themselves or others, and having little if any increase in numbers. We hope, however, that they are not entirely insensible of their state, and that there are some of their members who are awake themselves and are striving to awake their brethren. . . ."

There were 20 ordained ministers and eight licentiates belonging to the association.

The Association adopted the resolution passed by the preceding State Convention, recommending that the churches in the convention observe the first Monday in the three years following the convention as a day of fasting and prayer "that God would crown with abundant success their efforts to spread the blessings of the Redeemer's Kingdom."

Dr. Johnson was appointed to prepare the next Circular Letter, from a subject of his own choice, and that was included with the minutes of the meeting. It dealt with the new birth as presented by our Saviour to Nicodemus, and following a detailed discussion, Dr. Johnson summarized:

"From the view, therefore, which we feel ourselves at liberty to take of the new birth . . . our conclusion is simply this: That as God beheld man morally dead in trespasses and sins, without hope and without God in the world, He was pleased in mercy to provide a way of recovery according to which the Holy Spirit restores the lost creature unto his merciful Creator. . . . Wherefore the mysterious working and perfecting of the new creature may be considered simply this: The implantation of the spirit and disposition of Christ in the soul, giving that moral cast to the affections and will, which, in its operations, assimilates the whole man into the moral likeness of the Divine Redeemer, till he shall attain 'unto a perfect man, unto the measure of the stature of the fulness of Christ.' "

"Permit us, Brethren," he wrote, "to remind you, that regenerated souls are conformed to the likeness of God's dear Son. They partake of his nature, and shall share with him in his future glory. They are, therefore, honored with being co-workers with Him. On them, as favored instruments, he devolves the great duty, and confers the high privilege of advancing his glorious kingdom in the earth. Then should we enter with readiness and delight, into every plan for ameliorating the condition of man. . . . We should manifest our devotedness and zeal to the cause of suffering humanity and of God, by our liberal contributions to the treasury of the Lord, by our fervent prayers for his blessing on a lost world, and by our uniting efforts to promote his kingdom. . . . And nothing but the termination of our pilgrimage on earth should abate our ardour or cool our zeal in that cause in which we have embarked our all, and which is dearer to us than life. We may often exclaim, 'who is sufficient for these things?' But let us be animated to renewed vigor by the gracious answer, 'my grace is sufficient for thee'; cheering prospects, sustained by recent events, lead the spiritual mind forward in the promotion of plans for promoting the Redeemer's kingdom. . . . Ethiopia is stretching forth her hand unto the Lord, and the Isles of the sea are rejoicing in the brightness of their Lord's coming. Light and truth are bursting from the mountain and the valley, pressing forward on the right hand and on the left, with invincible influence upon the kingdom of error and darkness. . . . The palace and the cot, the noble and the slave, drawn by a kindred spirit, unite in advancing Missionary, Bible, Tract, and Sunday School Societies. All these, with Institutions of similar designs, are so many tributary streams rolling on their mighty waters, which shall ultimately cover the whole earth with righteousness and peace. . . . May we all be engaged as faithful servants to do our part in the work of faith and labor of love, which our God requires at our hands. . . ."

While Dr. Johnson's pastorate in Edgefield and his service in the association began in October, he did not move his family to that place until December. The late Miss Claudia Townes, his granddaughter, related that she had seen in his own handwriting the statement: "I arrived at Edgefield C.H., S. C., on Thursday evening the 30th of December, 1830, with my family to settle as preacher of the gospel and teacher of the Female Academy."

Dr. Johnson had purchased a residence from A. B. McWhorter for $1,800, the deed dated, August 7, 1830, and into this house he and his wife and their seven children moved when they came to Edgefield. The location was on what is now Simkins Street, adjoining property known as the Edmund Bacon place, just off Main Street. In 1833 he acquired three lots fronting the property on Main (then Jefferson) Street.

Members of his household included, besides his wife, his two older daughters, Claudia Coddington Johnson, age 19, and Elizabeth Bellinger Johnson, age 17; his sons, Charles Kelsall, 15; William Bullein, Jr., 13; and Francis Cleveland, 8; another small daughter, Henrietta Ann, who was almost 7; and the youngest child, Thomas Hornby, 3. Dr. Johnson's stepmother, Mrs. Elizabeth Bellinger Johnson, was probably a member of the household also.

Mrs. Johnson brought her letter from Brushy Creek Church to the Edgefield Church in April, 1831, and during the same year Claudia and Elizabeth united with the church on profession of faith.

Occasionally mention was made in the minutes of a servant of the family joining the church: "Grace, servant of Bro. Johnson . . . Fillis . . . Jacob. . . ."

In January, 1831, Dr. Johnson preached from Proverbs 27:1, "Boast not thyself of tomorrow," etc. In February he lectured on the first chapter of the First Epistle of John; in March he preached from Luke 12:32, "Fear not, little flock; for it is your Father's good pleasure to give you the kingdom." He was absent in May on other denominational matters, and there was preaching by Brother Mallary, according to the minutes. The pastor was present, however, in June and July. Then came the month of August, 1831, with its great spiritual awakening.

Chapter XI

The Revival of 1831

The spiritual revival of 1831 was like an earthquake, its rumbles felt in far removed places, its memory awakening thoughts and feelings never before experienced, never repeated exactly.

While the political world was in the throes of nullification and abolitionism, the men of the church were proclaiming another doctrine of nullification and abolitionism: The debts of sin are null and void, paid by the Lamb of God: ". . . though your sins be as scarlet, they shall be as wool." . . . "If the Son therefore shall make you free, ye shall be free indeed."

Edgefield District shared largely in this great awakening, and the ministers of the association were supplemented by students from Furman Theological Institution in leading many to a saving knowledge of Christ. Seventy-five years later men were still living who traced their conversion to the great revival of 1831.

James C. Furman was one of the ministerial students who assisted in the revival, and in describing it years later he said that every day immense congregations gathered, and through the day meetings were held in the open air. "Not only a marked decorum but an almost awful solemnity prevailed," he wrote. "The fallow ground of hearts long indifferent to divine things was effectually broken up, and the seed of saving truth fell from the sower's hand, quickly to germinate in the prepared soil."

Referring to the revival, Dr. Johnson wrote in his "Reminiscences": "In August of the same year, it pleased our Heavenly Father to grant us a spiritual revival, accompanied with the addition of many redeemed souls to the church. I have been present at many such meetings, but none, that I have ever attended, were [was] equal to this. So extraordinary was this, that at its close, I

[73]

wrote a full account of it to Dr. Brantly, who then lived in Philadelphia, & edited the Christian Index, which he published under
the caption of 'Animating Scenes in Zion.' And which letter I now
incorporate with the reminiscences I am writing."

In his account Dr. Johnson stated that a camp meeting in Virginia in 1830 had inspired the Baptists of the Edgefield Association
to turn their July union meeting at Sardis Church into a camp
meeting. That was the beginning of the revival that swept the
association. Twenty-eight persons had been brought to the knowledge of the truth, eight were baptized, and it was supposed that
not fewer than five hundred souls had received deep awakenings.

"Those of us from our church, who were present at the camp-
meeting," wrote Dr. Johnson, "were desirous that the ministers
visit us, and the request was made that they should do so, but we
hardly indulged the hope that they could. To our surprize and joy,
however, several of them came to see us in the evening of the day
on which they left the camping ground. Notice was soon given
that there would be preaching in the meeting house, the bell was
rung, and a goodly number of precious souls attended. After
preaching, a short address was made to the audience, and the
church with all Christians present were requested to approach the
area in front of the pulpit, and kneeling, united in prayer for the
blessing of God upon the coming of his servants. With alacrity,
as if moved with one harmonious spirit, all were presently pros-
trated before the throne of grace. It was a solemn moment: Prayer
was made: God was present to hear: the people felt his presence,
and were prepared to expect the blessing so fervently supplicated.
And from that evening for ten successive days and nights, have
we been engaged with the servants of the most High in spiritual
labors for the good of souls, and the glory of the Lord.

"On each returning morn, a sunrise meeting ushered in the
duties and delights of the day. At ten o'clock, at four o'clock, and
at candle-light, we have waited upon the preaching of the Gospel
followed by impressive exhortations. Invitations repeatedly given
on the same day, and reiterated day after day to those who desired
prayer to be made for them, were accepted by numbers, who with
terrible groans hastened to prostrate themselves before God. With
these the ministers and private Christians were afterwards en-

gaged in conversation, directing them to the Lamb of God who taketh away the sin of the world. At private houses in the intervals of public worship, prayer, praise, and exhortations were constantly going on. And so deeply was the population of our town impressed with the presence of the descending God, that with a few, very few exceptions, they believed that what they beheld was the work of the Lord. The meeting house was scarcely ever empty from sunrise till ten or eleven o'clock at night, and indeed on one night, it was occupied after the meeting was over, till near day, by one poor stricken soul and his friend, who accompanied him there to pray for his relief. Long before the bell would announce the arrival of the hour for preaching, the streets and ways leading to the meeting house would be covered with those who were hastening to obtain seats. The news of these amazing scenes reached the neighboring regions and drew great numbers to come and see the Lord's doing, so marvelous in our eyes. And so much were the hearts of the inhabitants of our town opened by the Lord, every house, even the public houses, threw their doors open to receive and entertain the visitors, waiting on the extraordinary occasion. A partial suspension of business with some, and a total cessation of it with others was demanded and cheerfully acquiesced in from the wonderful scenes constantly passing before their eyes. The male and female Academies, embracing about a hundred scholars, were at first partially suspended, and finally dismissed: Teachers and pupils being found in the house of God. . . .

"Such was the effect of divine truth upon the hearts of the people, and so manifest did the power of God appear to be present to heal, that on Saturday a door was opened for hearing experiences, when fourteen persons, mostly in the bloom of life, related the dealing of God with their souls, and were received for baptism. On Monday the door was again opened for the same purpose, when seven more recounted the mercies of the Lord in bringing them from darkness to light, and were received for the solemn ordinance.

"On this day after the first sermon, we proceeded to the baptismal water. The scene was imposing. For the accommodation of the multitude in attendance, those who rode in carriages were requested to leave the house in the first place and to take their stations on the opposite side of the stream convenient for witnessing the solemn ceremony. The administrator, supported by one of his ministering brethren, then preceded the audience, who succeeded in the following order: the ministers of the Gospel, five or six deep, the candidates for baptism in the same manner, the females first, dressed in white, the males next; after them the members of the church, and then the congregation. Commencing one of the songs of Zion at the meeting house, the air resounded with the praises of the most High God, whilst we passed through the streets of our town to the baptismal wave. There in the presence of a thousand spectators did your unworthy brother have the exquisite delight of immersing into the liquid grave, twenty-one immortal beings in token of their death to sin, and resurrection to a newness of life. Solemn and sublime was the scene, reminding us most forcibly of that scene more solemn and sublime, in which Jesus, the Son of God, before a countless multitude 'went humbly down from Jordan's shore, to seek a tomb beneath its wave.'

"On Wednesday and Friday the same scene was renewed, ten being baptised on the first and fourteen on the last of those days, making in the whole forty-five immortal beings, who, within the short space of ten days, were translated as we trust, from the kingdom of darkness into the kingdom of God's dear Son, and publicly professed their allegiance to their new Sovereign. Besides these, twenty-five others professed to have received comfort at this meeting. Some of these were baptised at a neighboring church on the following Sabbath, about five miles below this place, and others at one ten miles above. So that the whole number of those who were, according to their own statements, made recipients of a hope which maketh not ashamed at this meeting, was seventy souls. Some of these intend uniting with the Episcopalians, some with the Presbyterians, others have already joined the Methodists . . .

"Among the laborers of our own denomination were students of the Furman Theological Academy, who exhibited a becoming zeal and ability in this their Master's work. To the young people they were particularly useful. I mention this with pleasure, as it shows that in our efforts at that Institution to improve the ministry, the spirit of piety and holy zeal is not quenched. But that with increased ability to work for God, students are owned as his servants in building up his church against which the gates of hell shall never prevail. Let not any of my brethren engaged with us in the late mighty work in this place, who have not enjoyed the advantages of a classical education, think that I mean by this honorable mention of our young students for the ministry to disparage their high worth.—Far from it. With great pleasure did I see their zeal and witness their successful efforts in these marvellous doings of the Lord. Honored men of God! Though destitute of the advantages of human learning, they spoke well for their Master. They did valiantly for the Lord of Hosts. . . ."

After relating several touching incidents connected with the meeting, Dr. Johnson spoke of the continuation of the revival in other churches of Edgefield Association.

"On the morning after the close of the meeting here the servants of the Lord proceeded to Little Stephens Creek church, ten miles above this place. There they found a large audience assembled, it being the stated day for the church to convene. And there for six days have they been engaged in scenes of labors similar to those in which they had been engaged here. Thirty persons have during the meeting been baptised and added to the church. At Horn's Creek five miles below this place the like scenes were presented on Saturday and Sabbath following the meeting here and such was the state of feeling exhibited, that in all human probability, had there been a sufficient number of ministers present to have carried on the meeting, many days might have been gloriously spent in the work of the Lord. Fifteen persons were there baptised and added to the church. At the Red Oak Grove Church sixteen miles below this place, for the last six days, has the work of the Lord been going on triumphantly. And I have just heard that at Sardis Church, where the camp-meeting was held, twenty-five persons were baptised on the last Sabbath. . . ."

In his report for "The Committee on Religion" at the next association meeting in October, 1831, Dr. Johnson said the revival "came upon the inhabitants like the mighty shock of an earthquake, overturning the foundations of skepticism and the self-wrought schemes of salvation, and convincing every one that there was a power and reality in the religion of Jesus Christ. Many will rejoice in Eternity that ever the Lord put it in the hearts of His ministering servants to visit that place. The impulse given here reached to every part of the District of Edgefield and even beyond its limits in certain directions. Meetings of six and eight days continuance were held at several churches in succession and in different parts of the District at the same time, where ministers from four to six or eight in number, united their effort and the people continued to meet day after day, notwithstanding frequent interruptions from heavy rains, and in such numbers that in many instances meeting houses could not accommodate them. The result of these meetings has been a vast ingathering of precious souls into the kingdom of our Redeemer. Upwards of eight hundred have been added to different churches of our denomination in a little more than two months. . . . Nearly a whole district has turned to the Lord, men of the first character and standing in the community have been the subjects of this revival, besides many who from long continuance in the course of sin and neglect of the means of grace had appeared to be beyond the reach of any saving influence."

Mrs. Maria B. Taylor, niece of Dr. James C. Furman, accompanied him to Edgefield District for the meetings and said, "The whole country was ablaze with the wonderful conversions and marvellous work of God's spirit." At the close of one especially moving message "the space between the pulpit and the aisles was crowded with weeping and praying mourners—old grey-headed men, young men, and maidens, and stout-hearted infidels who had persistently and prominently with loud mouths resisted all the previous administrations of divine truth. One of them who had been the subject of conversation at our meals, swung himself from the gallery, the stairway being crowded, his friends all around uttering exclamations of surprise and delight."

Dr. Furman and James M. Chiles were two who preached in the Liberty Hill section of Edgefield District, and among other converts was a young man with whom they prayed long after one of the services had ended at night.

"Long years after," wrote Dr. Furman, "one of the young ministers received a letter from a Dr. Quarles of Mississippi, asking advice as a deacon in a Baptist church, respecting a knotty case of discipline, and identifying himself as the young medical student of Liberty Hill, Edgefield District, S. C., converted in the great revival."

Even persons who professed no religious faith were impressed with the results of the revivals which had spread to other places. One writing from Abbeville, above Edgefield, to a brother elsewhere, said:

"A most extraordinary religious excitement prevails in this Dist. Last Saturday at Mount Maria in this Dist. 15 miles below this town were 62 persons baptised—it is not very far from our race grounds & every racer, groom, & steward has been converted or seriously improved. Col. Griffin who was a great racer & outrageous sinner has quit training his horses—sold one or two & let out his face as long as a yard stick. Strange is it not?"

While Mount Moriah Church, referred to in the foregoing paragraph, was in Abbeville District, it was in Edgefield Baptist Association, and it was there the State Baptist Convention met in December, 1831, presided over by Dr. Johnson. How intently the people must have listened as Rev. Jesse Hartwell in his introductory sermon confirmed their faith as he preached of Jesus Christ, "In whom we have redemption through his blood, the forgiveness of sins, according to the riches of his grace"; and as Basil Manly delivered the missionary message from the text: "But be shod with sandals; and not put on two coats."

From the high hills of holiness the churches descended to the dark depths of despair. The circular letter of the Edgefield Association in 1833 was devoted to the subject of religious declension. Several causes were assigned, among them political strife• and contention. The slavery question was being agitated more and more. But the most pertinent reasons set forth were the failure of the mass of Christians to observe the sabbath day in a proper manner and the failure to support the gospel and the cause of Christ with their material goods. However, by 1838 there was rejoicing again because of the spirit of revival that was again manifesting itself.

Chapter XII

The Johnson Family

The year after the Johnson family established themselves in Edgefield, Charles Kelsall, the eldest son, became a student at Brown University at Providence, Rhode Island. He entered on July 19, 1832, at the age of seventeen. A young man of keen intellect and a student of law, naturally he was interested deeply in the political situation in his home state, which had taken drastic measures to protect its rights. The nullification of the "obnoxious" tariff act was an issue that divided even the best citizens of South Carolina. Men of Edgefield, ever ready for a fight, were almost solidly for nullification.

Eighteen-year-old Charles Johnson, in a letter to his father dated from Abingdon, Massachusetts, where he was spending a vacation, January 9, 1833, refers to his father's position as well as his own, relative to the subject:

"I had the pleasure of reading your last communication to the Editor of the *Index*. The hope which you expressed in its conclusion does indeed appear to me to be the only one which we now have; that is, that the over-ruling hand of Providence may so direct the redeeming spirit of the people of the United States, that our rights and the Union may be preserved. The manner in which this is to be effected appears to me to be yet unknown. . . . It has always been, and still continues to be, my settled conviction that we have acted too precipitately. The State, however, has acted in its sovereign capacity, and I feel it to be my duty, as you observed, to stand by her to the utmost of my ability. Should circumstances require my return, I would do so with alacrity, prepared to encounter any risk in the service of my native State. It appears from some of the papers which I have seen that the Union Party is rapidly gaining ground. Since the statements contained in the newspapers are seldom to be relied upon, I should like to be informed of the actual state of the case. The inhabitants of this part of the country are greatly incensed against the Southern Nullifiers. They do not believe that the Convention expressed the sentiments of even a majority of the people. I heard a gentleman say not long since that after the first of February he would seize upon the first Carolinian he met with. Since the time for the accomplishment of his threat had not yet arrived, it would have been mere bravado to have avowed myself. After that time, however, he will have the opportunity. In the course of an address on temperance which I heard the other evening, the speaker, while expatiating on the dreadful effects of ardent spirits, made use of this comparison: 'The spirit of nullification is the spirit of harmony and peace, when compared with ardent spirits.' Mr. Fickling and myself are the first advocates of Southern principles, which a great part of this [illegible] have seen. . . .''

In the same letter Charles speaks of having written to "Sister Elizabeth" and mentions others in the family: "From the difficulty of finding anything on which to write, I had not intended to write to Grandmother, but since it is my Father's request, I shall write to her soon. . . . It gives me the greatest pleasure to hear of my dear Mother's continued convalescence. Please to give my most affectionate and filial love to her and inform her that I will soon answer her letter."

In 1834, at the age of nineteen, Charles K. Johnson completed his course at Brown, and it is probable that his father was there to share with him that honor, for the minutes of the church state about that time, "Brother Johnson was absent on a visit to the North."

In December, 1834, Charles K. Johnson presented his letter from the Providence Church to the Edgefield Church. Later in the church minutes he is named as a delegate to the next associational meeting.

Other things of interest were occurring in the Johnson family in 1834, also. In October of that year Claudia Johnson was married to William Moore Butler, of Edgefield. William was the son of Stanmore Butler and Patience Youngblood. After the death of William's father, his mother married Allen B. Addison.

In 1835, Dr. Johnson considered seriously leaving South Carolina and going to New Orleans as a missionary of the American Baptist Home Mission Society. Perhaps he was thinking of it as early as January, for in accepting the call of the Edgefield Church to be "the supply for the present year," he wrote: "It is pleasing to me to know that my services are acceptable to the church, and I now inform that body . . . that I accept their invitation, with the understanding that if in the providence of God I should think it my duty to withdraw from the office of supply within the year the church will receive three months' notice of such intention."

Records of the American Baptist Home Mission Society for July 20, 1835, state: "A letter was presented to the committee from Rev. Wm. B. Johnson, of Edgefield, South Carolina, stating that he would go to New Orleans as our missionary if we would give him $1000 per annum. After due deliberation on the importance of New Orleans as a missionary field and on the superior qualifications of Dr. Johnson for that station, the Committee resolved to appoint him at a salary of $1000 per annum."

What caused Dr. Johnson to change his mind is not known, but it may be surmised that the confused state of affairs regarding Furman Theological Institution had as much to do with it as anything else. Perhaps in his discouragement over the prospects of the school, he had thought to seek a new field of labor. One's mind can travel at length over the trail of what might have been or might not have been had the great leader given up his dreams for Furman at that time.

The departure of troops for Florida in 1836 provided an outlet for the energies of many of the young men of Edgefield, and Charles K. Johnson went as 2nd Sergeant in Captain James Jones' company, with Eldred Simkins, 1st lieutenant; Edmund Penn, 2nd lieutenant; John W. Wimbish, ensign; Milledge L. Bonham, 1st sergeant; along with others who composed the three companies of Colonel Marshall Frazier's regiment.

The old Public Square, with the frame courthouse in the center, was teeming with excitement that day in early February. It is easy to imagine that Dr. and Mrs. Johnson and other members of the family were on hand: Sister Elizabeth, assuming even then the protective attitude that characterized her life; William, who at nineteen was wishing no doubt that he, too, were going; Frank and Thomas, the younger boys, whose pulses were quickened with all the emotions that have stirred the hearts of boyhood since time began. Perhaps Claudia was there with four-month-old William Johnson Butler; and Ann, in all the exuberance of gay young girlhood—with eyes on Brother Charles, handsome in his uniform, one of those made by the ladies of the village; hearing the patriotic music played by the band from Hamburg; listening to the silver-tongued Governor McDuffie as he made a short but animated address to the respective companies.

"He told them," reported the *Advertiser,* "that they were charged with the honor of South Carolina and said he had no fears that that honor was safe. We looked at the officers and we looked at the men, again and again, and we venture to say without intending to boast, that the volunteers from Edgefield, come what may, will nobly do their duty."

Soon they were on their way to the southern frontier; but within a few months they were back at home, and life went on as usual. Perhaps an extra note of thanksgiving was added to the family devotions because of the safe return of the son; for the father was a man of warm heart and tender emotions, though outwardly undemonstrative as a general thing. With him the current ran deep, and it was not uncommon for him to weep when engaged in family devotions about his own fireside. As he spoke of the love of Jesus, he was overpowered with the great wonder of it.

The spirit of hospitality prevailed in the Johnson home, and those who visited there found in Dr. Johnson an exhilarating host. His conversational powers were of a high order, and the rich store of knowledge which he possessed found ready utterance, supplemented by a courteous manner and polite address. He delighted in imparting knowledge which he himself had acquired, and was tactful in dismissing or introducing subjects. His clear argument, quick comprehension, and ready repartee assured the close attention of his listeners, and he was usually the center of social groups into which he was placed.

Years later, the Rev. E. L. Whatley, who was then pastor of the Edgefield Baptist Church and occupying the same residence that Dr. Johnson had owned, was seated on the spacious piazza "enjoying the breeze and admiring the fine situation" as Whatley expressed it, when a friend called. In the course of the conversation he remarked, "Well, you are preaching to the Edgefield Church and living in the house famous as the residence of Dr. Johnson."

"Even so," replied Whatley.

"Why, you have completely got into the old doctor's shoes. But I expect it is a good deal like Major Jack Dowling said of Martin Van Buren when he put on old General Jackson's boots—you don't fill them up!"

The school that Dr. Johnson conducted in Edgefield ranked high among schools of that class, and many of the best educated women of South Carolina studied under him. As a teacher he was particular, exact, and thorough, and his pupils were well grounded in the elements of knowledge. They were conducted through a rigid course of mental and moral discipline and generally left his supervision with the adornment of a solid education.

In 1838, Ann Johnson and her friends were studying not only the solid branches of learning under her father but Miss Stark had lately come from the Female Collegiate Institute of New York to teach them the ornamental arts of drawing, painting, and needle work, while Mr. James T. Bacon was teaching them music. Ann was Queen of the May that year at the brilliant festival held in the Bacon grove adjoining the school. Chandeliers and festooned lamps suspended in various parts of the garden "diffused a tempered splendour far around," the local newspaper reported. On an elevated stand the musicians played the harp, violin, and flute as the lovely young ladies came in a processional into the garden. There was Flora, Queen of Flowers, with her attendants, announced by the Herald. Then the Queen of May, accompanied by her Prime Minister, ascended the throne that was enwreathed with flowers and surrounded by green branches. The crown was placed on Ann's head by the Prime Minister, and following the poetic sequence the happy young Queen responded graciously:

> My heart o'erflows, I cannot say
> What bliss has crown'd me on this day!
> Welcome, my subjects, to my sight!
> To see you is the Queen's delight.

[84]

Ann later attended the Albany (New York) Academy for Young Ladies. She married Colonel G. F. Townes, of Greenville, South Carolina, becoming his second wife; and they have descendants living today.

Meanwhile, Dr. Johnson was busy with other affairs of a local nature. Through the press that year he recommended two new school books, an English grammar and a school geography by R. C. Smith. The geography, he commented, "is far removed from anything objectionable, as our domestick institutions are regarded." He took the opportunity of recommending the sermons of Dr. Wayland "on the moral law of accumulation, works of real excellence and worthy of repeated and serious reading."

As chairman of the Publishing Committee of the Baptist Association, he announced that the Association Sermon, "delivered by N. W. Hodges in October last is now ready for delivery at 12½ cents a copy. . . . It is worthy the attention of the churches, every member of which should possess a copy, and reading it with special attention, practice the duties which it sets forth with conscientious care."

The anniversary meeting of the Edgefield Central Temperance Board was held at the Baptist Church, with Dr. Johnson presiding as chairman. He made the opening prayer, after which "a very impressive and elegant address upon the evils of intemperance was pronounced by the Rev. Mr. Suares of Aiken," according to the press account, and a committee was appointed to wait upon Mr. Suares and request a copy for publication.

Another organization that claimed his attention was the "Philosophical and Agricultural Society of Edgefield" for the advancement of agricultural science in the district, of which he was president.

Dr. Johnson was frequently announced as the speaker on patriotic occasions.

But his first thought always was for the church and the work of the denomination.

As a preacher he interpreted and expounded the Scriptures, dwelling with delight upon the discriminating doctrines of Christianity. He was unexcelled in his exposition of the law and the

[85]

doctrines of grace. In solemn and earnest manner he spoke with unaffected simplicity.

After one discourse on the doctrine of the new birth which Dr Richard Furman III heard, a saintly sister remarked to Dr. Furman, "Dr. Johnson preaches today as if he was on the verge of heaven."

Tears frequently came to the eyes of those who heard Dr. Johnson as he dwelt upon the amazing grace of God that found expression in the redemptive death of his Son.

Charged as pastor with the duty of keeping the church pure, Dr. Johnson was unyielding in his demands that church members keep themselves unspotted from the world. The Negro bell ringer who yielded to the lure of liquor, or the young lady who attended a dance felt alike his censure. Nor was his own son an exception.

Several meetings of the church considered the case of Charles K. Johnson for "holding erroneous views of the scriptures," and he was excluded. Writing to his sister, Elizabeth, a few years later from New Orleans, Charles spoke of attending a Unitarian Church, and that was probably the faith he espoused.

Almost immediately after the exclusion of his son, Dr. Johnson was extended the annual call to serve the church as "supply," and he again accepted.

Death ever cast its shadow about the family. Claudia had lost her husband September 26, 1839, and on July 10 of the next year, she herself died a Christian's death.

During her illness she was calm and composed, putting her trust in Christ. Filled with adoring gratitude, she gave utterance to her feelings in the following hymn:

> Ah, I shall soon be dying,
> Time swiftly glides away;
> But on my Lord relying
> I hail the happy day.

Two little daughters of Claudia's grew to womanhood—Anna Patience, who married John Lake Nicholson, and Emmala Simpson, who married General William C. Moragne. Both have descendants.

Claudia's young son, William Johnson Butler, was taken shortly after his mother's death. Also taken was another, designated on the tombstone simply as "The Babe."

William Bullein Johnson, fifth son of his parents, died in New Orleans in 1842 at the age of twenty-five years. He "lived and died universally respected and beloved," his father wrote in the Bible.

His brother Charles, writing to a member of the family about the death of William, said: "He never uttered a profane word. Above all, he forgave every wrong done him, with a perfect charity and gentleness, united with a firm and dignified sense of his own rights, to an extent that I have never seen equalled. Benevolence was his characteristic. I can scarcely restrain a tear (a strange thing with me) when memory calls up a thousand little instances of his magnanimous self-devotion to myself and others. With the holy, the loving, the charitable, the good, he is fitted to dwell. With the hard-hearted, the malignant, the revengeful, the bad, he had nothing in common. I do not exaggerate. I have not done him justice. Every person loved him."

Said the New Orleans *Picayune:* "For his premature decease, the eye of friendship shall oft be dimmed with the tear of regret.— 'Requiescat in pace.' "

Once more within a few short years the father penned words denoting the death of a child, this time the shining mark, Charles: "Died on Saturday evening, 19th June, 1847, Charles Kelsall Johnson, aged 31 years, 9 months and 19 days. He was the 4th son of his parents and possessed of remarkable talents."

Charles was engaged in the practice of law and was one of the most popular young men of New Orleans. One night while he and some friends were taking a ride on a steamboat on Lake Pontchartrain, what promised to be a lark ended in his death by drowning.

Scarcely had the family recovered from the shock than they were called upon to face the loss of the beloved wife and mother— her death hastened by the death of her son. At last the frail body of Henrietta Hornby Johnson yielded its hold on life, and the sorrowing husband had no words to describe his grief. He simply wrote under the section in the Bible entitled "Deaths" the words: "Henrietta Johnson, 5th of July, 1847, at half past 6 o'clock, P.M., in her 61st year (Monday afternoon)."

The church clerk wrote: "Notice is taken of the death of our sister, Mrs. Henrietta Johnson. She died on Monday evening the 5th inst., at the residence of her husband in this place and was buried in the churchyard on Tuesday afternoon. The religious services were conducted by Bro. D. D. Brunson."

Elizabeth, who had been the chief stay of her mother through the months and years of her frail health, now became the main dependence of her father, her sister, Ann, and the two brothers, Frank and Thomas, for the making of the home. If the father's heart was grieved over the death of other sons, it was cheered by the prospects of the useful careers upon which his remaining sons were to embark.

Thomas had united with the church by experience September 10, 1843, and on December 24, 1843, the church "granted a certificate to Bro. Thos. H. Johnson commending him to the care of the brethren of the Furman Institution whither he intends going with a view to the ministry."

Thomas was then only sixteen years old. Two years later, at eighteen, he had entered Brown University, where he was a student for more than two years. He began a career of teaching, and in 1850 was in charge of the Edgefield Male Academy. That same year, May 1, 1850, he was married to Miss Margaret Hibler, daughter of Thomas Jefferson Hibler, of the Liberty Hill section of Edgefield District. The officiating minister was his brother, Rev. F. C. Johnson. Thomas Hornby Johnson moved to Gainesville, Alabama, where he edited a newspaper and taught school. While enlisted in the Confederate Army, he died in Mobile, October 7, 1862, five days after the death of his father. Said the obituary notice:

"The deceased was born at Greenville, S. C., April 14, 1827, and was a younger son of the venerable Dr. Wm. B. Johnson, distinguished as a teacher and preacher in all the States of America. Enjoying in boyhood the personal instruction of such a father, and being naturally grave and studious, he was even in early life distinguished by his attainments in classical literature." Thomas H. Johnson was a member of the Sumter Warriors, 36th Alabama Regiment. For some years he edited the *Weekly Southern Sun,* of Macon, Mississippi.

Children of Thomas Hornby Johnson and Margaret Hibler Johnson were: William B. and Claudia Kelsall, who died young and unmarried; Eloise who married John Sheppard Bealle, and lived in Birmingham, Alabama; Jefferson Hibler Johnson who married Mary Crow, and lived in Columbia, Tennessee.

Francis Cleveland Johnson, four years the senior of his brother Thomas, was the last member of the family to unite with the church. He was twenty-two years of age when he accepted the saving grace of Jesus Christ—the same age his father was when he was converted. The life of this son more nearly paralleled his father's in service, also.

Recording the minutes of February 9, 1845, the church clerk at Edgefield wrote: "On this Sabbath the church did not meet in conference, having assembled by request on the previous evening to hear from Francis C. Johnson what the Lord had done for his soul, whose experience was satisfactory. Whereupon he was baptized, which was fixed for this day after morning service. Immersed Francis C. Johnson this day in the presence of a large assembly." On February 11, Francis C. Johnson was dismissed "to join the church at Hardy's, in the neighborhood of which he is residing at present."

Francis C. Johnson had likewise attended Brown University, from March 1, 1842, to October, 1842. Financial reverses in the family that year probably made it necessary for him to forego further college training, although he must have been a young man of unusual talents. He was teaching a school at Aiken in 1843. Almost at once after conversion he began to take an active part in church work. At revival services which began August 24, 1845, the Edgefield Village Church enjoyed the labors of Francis C. Johnson, along with several other ministers.

He became one of the first Southern Baptist missionaries to China. He went as "Theological Tutor and Missionary," and after making much progress in the written language he returned, broken in health. His home was then in Marietta, Georgia. He continued his ministerial duties and served as chaplain in the Confederate Army.

The Rev. Francis C. Johnson was married to Miss Caroline Hickson, of the Saluda section of old Edgefield County, and they had seven sons: Hickson, Connell, Stewart, Waterman, Call, Owens, and Dawkins.

Ann Johnson's marriage to Colonel Townes took place December 20, 1854. Their children were: Mary Henrietta Townes, William Johnson Townes, Claudia Kelsall Townes, whose births were recorded in the Bible by their grandfather; then later, the births of twin daughters, Katherine Floride Townes and Joanna Lois Townes, known as Kate and Joanna, were recorded by their aunt, Miss Elizabeth Bellinger Johnson.

Mrs. Henrietta Ann Townes died August 20, 1864. And one year later, August 20, 1865, her young daughter, Mary Henrietta, died at the age of nine years and eight months.

Elizabeth went to Florida after the death of her father and sister to make her home with her brother, Rev. F. C. Johnson and his family. Some years later, in the burning of Hickson Johnson's home at Micanopi, Florida, many valuable family papers were destroyed.

Chapter XIII

The Dark Shadow

Above the storm of sectional misunderstanding in the 1840's, the voice of God was heard. He used the whirlwind of animosity to arouse his people. He used the lightning flash of friction as a sword to cut in twain the General Convention of Baptists; and through the magic of divine calculation he multiplied divided forces into legions that marched like two giant armies against the cohorts of sin.

Slavery was the issue that divided many churchmen of the North and the South in their thinking. Honored men in the North, like Dr. Francis Wayland, were not Abolitionists in the strict sense of the word. They believed slavery to be sinful, but the slaveholder was not necessarily a sinner. Leaders in the South, like Dr. Johnson, felt that slavery was a subject with which the denomination as a whole had no need to concern itself. Slavery was sanctioned by the Old and New Testaments, and certain modes of conduct were demanded of both master and slave.

On the other hand, uncompromising Abolitionists like the eloquent and conscientious Rev. Elon Galusha were willing to inject the issue into the machinery of the denomination.

In April, 1840, about the time the Baptist Board of Foreign Missions was meeting in New York, a group of antislavery Baptists, forming what was known as the American Baptist Anti-slavery Convention, held a meeting there, with Galusha as president. Galusha was one of the vice-presidents of the Baptist Board of Foreign Missions, and was the only member of that board to attend the antislavery meeting, according to Dr. Johnson. The Antislavery Convention issued an Address setting forth the sin of holding slaves, the duty of owners to emancipate slaves, and threatening to exclude from their communion tables and pulpits Baptists of the South who persisted in holding slaves.

Baptist churches in Alabama, namely Fellowship in Wilcox County and Carlowville in Dallas, announced in resolutions that "insuperable obstacles to further cooperation in the foreign mission department" had been presented, and recommended to "brethren of the South to adopt measures for opening channels by which our cheerful benefactions may be carried to the perishing heathen, that they may receive the word of life."

Dr. Johnson, anxious over the threatened breach, hastened to explain that Galusha had acted not in his capacity as vice-president of the Board of Foreign Missions but as an individual leader of another group. The press had carried an erroneous report of the situation in the statement that the Alabama churches had withdrawn all connection with the Baptist Home Mission Society on account of the circulation of Abolition papers by that body. In explanation, Dr. Johnson quoted the Preamble and Resolution adopted by one of the Alabama churches and continued:

". . . I now affirm, that neither the Convention nor the Board has at any time written, printed, circulated or given countenance to, any Abolition publications whatever."

The acute state of affairs in the denomination was reflected in the Corresponding Letter and Resolutions of the Edgefield Baptist Association of September, 1840, signed by Johnson as moderator and John Hewitt as clerk:

"A subject of very grave importance now forces itself upon the attention of Southern Baptists, demanding the full exercise of that wisdom which cometh from above, and which is profitable to direct," the letter to Sister Corresponding Associations began. "We refer to the course that a Body of Baptists at the North with whom we have been long associated in the general efforts of benevolence, have recently taken."

Reviewing the main points in the Address of the American Baptist Antislavery Convention, the letter continued: "It is to be presumed that what our Bibles have not taught us to do, the threats of our brethren at the North will assuredly fail to accomplish, and therefore the exclusion will follow as a matter of course. If there existed no general concert of action between these brethren and us, this high handed measure would be painful, mortifying, deeply distressing. But when it is known that for more than twenty years the Northern and Southern Baptists have united in the grand missionary enterprise, and that God's blessing has been most manifestly shed down upon our united efforts, such a measure is appalling, and most sincerely to be deplored. What the result will be as to farther connexion between Northern and Southern Baptists generally, in the grand schemes of Missionary, Bible and Tract efforts is known to Him only, who 'sees the end from the beginning.' "

Speaking of the stand the Alabama churches had taken, and their advice to other churches of the South to seek a different channel for the transmission of their benevolent contributions to the heathen, the letter stated: "If this course shall be generally adopted, we are at once a dissevered people. But before this shall be adopted let us ponder well upon its propriety.

"The President of the Anti-Slavery Convention acted in his individual character and not as the Representative or exponent of the Board of Missions or Convention. Now as the Baptist General Missionary Convention will assemble at Baltimore next April would it not be more prudent and more in accordance with the spirit of the Gospel to wait until that Body shall assemble, and know whether it will sustain the views and principles of the Address or not? If that body shall disavow those principles and views, though an individual officer maintain them, why should we separate, and seek a new channel for our contributions to the heathen? If they shall sustain them, our course of action will be clear and unavoidable. We must separate and form a new Missionary Body.

"Permit us then, brethren, respectfully to suggest that no action be had on this subject before April next: that the Southern Delegation to the Missionary Convention be there in full, and that they take such steps as they may deem proper for obtaining an expression of the sentiment of that Body on this matter, and on their return, inform their constituents of result, that they may then act, as the nature of the case shall require."

In the resolution appended, the Edgefield Baptist Association instructed its delegates to the next General Convention to obtain from that body an expression of its approval or disapproval of the views and threats contained in the Address of the Antislavery Convention "to the end, that if that Body shall approve of the views and threats contained in that Address, the Southern Baptists may take measures for forming a separate Missionary Body."

Dr. Johnson, as president of the South Carolina State Baptist Convention, sent a communication to the *Edgefield Advertiser* in reference to the "deeply interesting" State Convention which met at Sumterville in December, 1840, when resolutions drawn by Dr. Johnson were passed, recommending that Southern brethren hold a meeting prior to the General Convention in Baltimore, which was to convene in April, 1841. The resolutions spoke of the general disquietude among churches in the South and Southwest produced by the Abolitionists at the North, "a disquietude that threatens a division of the Baptist Triennial Convention," and because of the "magnitude of the Missionary enterprise and the importance of united action for its advancement, such division is to be deprecated, and if possible prevented; the manner of adjusting the difficulty so as to remove the disquietude and prevent a division was conceded to be "one of delicacy and importance, requiring deliberation and mutual counsel."

A recommendation was made by the South Carolina State Baptist Convention that the preliminary meeting be held in the meeting house in which the Triennial Convention was to assemble, "at 10 o'clock on Monday before the last Wednesday in April next, that they may deliberate and determine upon the manner in which they shall act on the subject. . . . That they be requested, after the rising of the Triennial Convention, to give information to their constituents of the result of their doings."

Brethren Kingsford and Wilcox, representing respectively the American and Foreign Bible Society, and the American Baptist Home Mission Society at the South Carolina Convention, alluded to "the exciting subject produced by the conduct of the American Baptist Anti-Slavery Convention. . . . The statements made in reference to the numbers and influence of the abolitionists of our denomination in the Northern States, show that they are small and feeble: that the great body of our brethren in the North of standing and influence, have no sympathies with the Abolitionists, and they have no desire to interfere in the smallest degree with the

[94]

institutions of the South, and that they will be ready to give an expression of disapprobation . . . at the next meeting of the Triennial Missionary Convention in Baltimore."

Other resolutions expressed confidence in the "integrity, Christian temper and true-heartedness" of Kingsford and Wilcox; reiterated the convention's attachment to the Bible cause and missionary interests, and recommended the brethren "to the churches that they be well received and liberally aided in the collections for the respective objects."

Rev. A. Rice from the American and Foreign Bible Society was likewise cordially recommended to the churches.

The idea of a preparatory meeting of the Southern delegates seemed to be general, with only such details as the exact time and place to be worked out by Southern leaders.

Dr. Basil Manly, then president of the University of Alabama, suggested through the *Christian Index* that all Southern delegates meet in Richmond on the Wednesday preceding the Triennial Convention, for the purpose of consulting on the slavery question and determining the position proper to be assumed. He had reached this agreement in consultation with Dr. John L. Dagg. Dr. J. B. Taylor and Dr. J. B. Jeter, both of Richmond, Virginia, eventually cooperated with Dr. Johnson and the South Carolina Baptist State Convention in arranging for the convention to be held by Southern delegates at the Calvert Street Church in Baltimore.

In a communication to the *Biblical Recorder and the Southern Watchman*, Dr. Johnson went into details about arrangements for the place of meeting and continued:

"I avail myself of this opportunity to express my strong hope of a scriptural and amicable adjustment of the difficulty which has grown out of the unwarrantable course that the Abolitionists have pursued. From personal interviews with the esteemed Treasurer of the Triennial Convention and the worthy Agent of the E. Com. of the A.B.H.M. Society [Education Committee of the American Baptist Home Mission Society] and from letters read from leading Brethren in Boston, New York, Baltimore and other places, I am satisfied that our principal Brethren in the North are far from being Abolitionists. They recognize the toleration of slavery in the Scriptures and they readily leave their Southern Brethren to the exercise of their liberty in this matter.

[95]

"It is true, that the Boards and Executive Committees of the Convention and General Societies of our denomination have, in answering the calls made upon them to 'define their position,' declared themselves neutral. And so far as they confine themselves to this point they have done right. For they are only the agents of the bodies, by whom they are appointed. Their authority is limited to their specified objects. In prosecuting these, they have acted with integrity and prudence, and are above reproach and suspicion. Their reports will be made in April and their powers will cease. I regret, therefore, that they have been called on 'to define their position.' For it is not with *them* that we have to do, but with their principals, viz.: The *Convention* and Societies. . . . Something must be done in April at Baltimore by these bodies for future amicable movement. But a general disclaimer with a general welcome, such as is suggested by my Brother Fuller, will, with all deference to his opinion, fail to satisfy the South. Something more definite will be required.

"At the request of the Agent of the A.B.H.M. Society I gave him in writing, my views of what I thought would satisfy the South, and might be acceded to by the North. Altho he did not speak positively on the subject, yet he expressed himself favorably in relation to the plan proposed. A copy of the same views was given afterwards to other respectable Brethren from the North, who unhesitatingly expressed their willingness to accept the plan. These views will be presented at the preparatory convention in Baltimore and will afford, with what others may suggest, a foundation for profitable conference, out of which I trust, will be formed the plan of adjustment that will be satisfactory to the North and to the South."

The above communication appeared in the *Edgefield Advertiser,* which carried accounts of the preparatory meeting and the General Convention.

The preparatory meeting was held on the 26th of April, when T. Stocks, of Georgia, was named chairman and Crane, of Virginia, secretary, J. B. Jeter, of Virginia, was secretary pro tem.

Dr. Johnson presented to the meeting a Preamble and Resolution which had been offered by the brethren of the North "as expressive of their views of new tests of Christian fellowship. These so entirely accorded with our own, that the delegation agreed to wait the action of the Convention in reference to the election of its Board of Managers before any further proceedings" were entered upon.

The "Preamble and Resolutions on Tests of Church Fellowship" that apparently turned the tide at that crisis read:

Whereas, the Scriptures constitute the only rule of conduct for Christians and the Christian Church; and whereas, it is evident in the Scriptures that churches are independent bodies, having no Head but Christ, no law but His revealed will; whereas, they have no right or authority to censure or excommunicate any but their own members; and whereas, the Constitutions of the Baptist General Convention of the United States, the American Baptist Home Mission Society and the American Foreign Bible Society require officers and managers of those institutions to be "brethren in good standing of Baptist Churches in general union with the Denomination"; and whereas, a disposition has been manifested to introduce new tests of good standing and fellowship unknown to the denomination generally when said constitutions were adopted; and whereas, announcement of disfellowship on the basis of such *new tests* is now creating embarrassment and alienation among those who have been united in the bonds of fraternal love for many years, and hitherto have delightfully cooperated in the holy enterprise of disseminating the truth of God through these organizations; therefore—

Resolved, That the undersigned deem it their duty and privilege to record their full conviction, that *no new tests* unauthorized by the Scriptures, and by established usages of the great body of our churches, should be suffered to interfere with the harmonious operation of these benevolent Associations, as originally constituted; and therefore they embrace this fitting occasion to express their decided disapprobation of all such tests, believing them to have a direct tendency to part asunder those who have "one Lord, one Faith, one Baptism"; and above all, they invade the prerogative of Jesus Christ, the one and only Legislator of the churches and of the Saints; to whom be glory forever. Amen!

Eighty names of Northern and Southern brethren were signed. The convention proper met in the First Baptist Church, of Baltimore, and was attended by about 250 delegates—261 according to the official table—a larger number than had ever attended a Triennial Convention. Dr. Johnson was elected president; Dr. Rufus D. Babcock, Jr., of Poughkeepsie, New York, secretary; and Dr. James B. Taylor, of Richmond, Virginia, assistant secretary. The elections were by ballot.

Dr. Johnson was welcomed to the chair by Dr. Spencer H. Cone, retiring president, and on taking the chair, Dr. Johnson expressed his gratitude to Almighty God because he had thus been favored by the convention. "A sense of deep responsibility fills my spirit," he said, "in approaching a chair, which was first adorned by the sainted Furman, of my own State, and successively occupied by the estimable Semple of Virginia, and the honored Cone of New York. . . . The President of this body is not called to preside over the Legislature of a Nation, or the destinies of an earthly kingdom. The affairs of such bodies relate to *time*. The deliberations of this body relate to *eternity*. The members of this body, redeemed from sin and hell, are associated together for the purpose of disseminating the blessings of eternal life to the perishing millions of the heathen world. In such an assembly there is no place for strife or vainglory. The fear of God, a singleness of eye to His honor, a regard for the spiritual and eternal welfare of man must predominate and guide the counsels, and form the decisions of its members. . . . That its deliberations may be conducted 'decently and in order,' the Convention places itself representatively in the President. The members, therefore, in sustaining him, preserve their own dignity. I, therefore, confidently look to you, beloved brethren, under God, for an obedience to your own rules, and assure you, that whatever ability I possess, shall be cheerfully exerted in aid of your efforts for the accomplishment of our weighty concerns. May the God of Grace add His blessing to our labors."

Motions were passed that "the fervent thanks of this Convention are due to our Heavenly Father, that throughout the deeply interesting discussions and transactions of this session, *He* has caused to prevail so large a measure of Christian affection and harmony"; and "That the thanks of this Convention be presented to the President, for the able, impartial, and courteous manner in which he has performed the arduous duties of his station, during the present session."

The report of the board for the preceding year showed $56,-948.42 received and $61,860.27 spent, a condition which made it necessary to limit expenditures. This procedure was felt at the mission stations, and there were numbers of expressions of disappointment. Rev. Durlin L. Brayton wrote from his Tavoy Mission a typical note of sorrow: "Shall I then send my little band of scholars back to the jungle, disappointed, cast down and dismayed?"

The fields were ripe, the laborers were few, and funds were being withheld, awaiting the outcome of the Convention.

The *Baltimore Weekly Sun,* reporting the meeting of the Board of Foreign Missions, stated:

"The election of officers for the Board of Foreign Missions was held yesterday, and quite an animated debate took place in anticipation thereof. Several of the Northern gentlemen assumed the somewhat novel position of inquisitors, and demanded to know whether certain individuals representing various portions of the South had not come into that Convention, instructed to proscribe particular delegates, for the particular principles entertained by them, referring of course to the question of slavery. The distinct disclaimers of the South, while they were made in manly and Christian spirit, under this unusual ordeal, seemed to appease the very unnecessary excitement into which the interrogators had been wrought. The effect of this conduct eventually appeared at the close of the day, when upon counting the ballots it proved that each of the persons alluded to, supposed to be obnoxious in consequence of their ultra opinions, had been left in a minority, and the abolition influence pretty thoroughly eradicated from the Board, a work in which the Northern Delegation, doubtless displeased with the unseemly course of their brethren, must have essentially aided. The Rev. Daniel Sharp, of Boston, was elected President of the Board.

"At the adjournment, the Rev. W. Colver, of Boston, asked permission to retire from the Convention in consequence of what he was pleased to term the proscription of that body, and the Rev. Elon Galusha requested his name be removed from the Committee on Agencies from the same motives. . . ."

The letter from the Southern delegation to their constituents stated: "In our intercourse with our Northern brethren generally, we found a most delightful spirit. They received their Southern brethren with utmost affection and confidence. A very few were led as they declared, by a sense of duty to require as a test of fellowship the course which has been heretofore prescribed by some of them for their Southern brethren to pursue. On the Lord's Day hundreds of brethren from the North and South, the East and West, sat down at the same communion board. The season was refreshing. We sat together in heavenly places in Christ. In the close of the service the overflowings of the full heart were indicated in the flowing tear, friendly grasp of the hand, and the Christian salutation, while all felt and many said, 'It is good to be here.'

"The election of the Board of Managers resulted agreeably to our wishes. The usual appointment of a committee to nominate the list of officers and Managers of the Board was dispensed with and a general ballot was adopted.

"On this board will appear the name of Bro. Baron Stow as Recording Secretary, who has for some time past stood before the public in an equivocal position. But in a letter which was committed to Bro. Johnson's hand to be read before the meeting, we were fully satisfied that this Brother has not thrown his Southern Brethren from his heart, his pulpit or his communion table. As this is a private letter it might be indelicate to publish it, but copies have been put into the hands of Bro. Sands of Virginia, Bro. Meredith of North Carolina and Bro. Stocks of Georgia.

"We can therefore say to all our Southern brethren, that we are fully satisfied with the spirit and sentiment of the great body of our Brethren at the North, and take pleasure in assuring them that the Foreign Mission Board, the American and Foreign Bible Society, Publishing and Sunday School Board, and the Executive Committee of the American Home Missionary Society are all satisfactory to us. We would, therefore, most affectionately entreat you, brethren, to continue your cooperation with all these bodies and to increase your contributions for the furtherance of these objects."

Dr. Johnson reviewed the situation and wrote to the *Edgefield Advertiser:*

"With these evidences from our Northern brethren that they

were not Abolitionists, the question with the South, as it appeared to their Delegation, was: Can we remain in the convention with the few Abolitionists there, though their treatment of us has not been of the kindest sort? Can we, for the sake of the noble cause in which we are embarked, and which has received such blessing from God, bear with Christian fortitude such unkindness from these good but mistaken brethren? Can we remain with them in Convention to carry, without division, the GRAND MISSIONARY ENTERPRISE? The answer was plain. We can.

"And now is not the character of the removal of the difficulty a good one? It involves in it no concession of principle, or of right. It is not calculated to offend any one, even the Abolitionists themselves. Some few were not pleased with it. But these were very few, for, as far as my knowledge extended, there were not, out of 250 members of Convention, 15 Abolitionists present. Some of these were conciliated and went home with altered views of their slaveholding brethren, and of Abolitionism. Brother Galusha endeared himself to the Convention by his mild pacificatory conduct. The tone of the Abolitionists who were in the Convention has been, since our meeting in Baltimore, moderated. The manner in which the removal of the difficulty was effected, led to such intercourse between the Northern and Southern members, as to endear them to each other in closer bonds. 'Brotherly love' was not only seen to 'continue', but to prevail. He, who had left on record the encouraging words, 'Where two or three are gathered together in my name, there am I in the midst of them', graciously fulfilled it on this occasion. His presiding influence, the breathing of His own blessed, peaceful spirit, bowed the heart in submission to His will, and happily prepared the brethren to submit themselves to one another in the Lord. . . . And now in conclusion, let me entreat my brethren at the North and South, to help with their prayers, that the adjustment of the difficulty may not be disturbed. My firm conviction is, that the manner in which it was effected was of God, and that no other mode of adjustment was consistent with the preservation of the union of the Denomination. In this view of the matter, let us thank God and take courage."

Chapter XIV

Johnson the Conciliator

Following Dr. Johnson's election to the presidency of the Triennial Convention, his role of peacemaker was even more pronounced if possible than before.

Preceding and during the convention of 1841, he had sought to bring about a better understanding between the slaveholders and nonslaveholders, and his efforts were largely responsible for averting a separation at that time. But the conciliatory tone of the preamble and resolutions from the Northern brethren assuring those from the South that no new tests of fellowship would be required, failed to satisfy some of the Southerners.

While neither the words slaveholder nor abolitionist were mentioned, there was no question in the minds of those tendering and accepting the olive branch as to the implication. Some in the South, however, were as determined to denounce the Abolitionists of the North as the latter had been to force their opinions.

The Rev. H. D. Duncan of South Carolina expressed his dissatisfaction in a communication to the *Recorder and Watchman:*

"But it will perhaps be told us that the compromise made at the Triennial Convention has removed every difficulty; and that we of the South have no further reason for complaint. . . . Is that compromise such as we had reason to expect? It contains no disclaimer against Abolitionists or their principles, *thereby leaving untouched the main subject of difference.* Will such terms of confederacy be subscribed to by us down South? For one I think not."

Addressing a letter to the Rev. Mr. Duncan through the same medium, Dr. Johnson explained the matter, stating that the general principles set forth in the resolutions were preferred to any specific designation of a given test. He took the liberty of making the explanation "in this public manner, because your dissatisfaction is publicly made, and because, if *your* judicious mind has a doubt of the propriety of the adjustment, the minds of many others may be likewise disquieted."

Dr. Johnson pointed out the unconstitutionality of the stand taken by the Abolitionists who had demanded the emancipation of slaves as a new test of fellowship and showed the counteracting effect of the Preamble and Resolutions. He then suggested that probably Duncan would be satisfied with the exclusion of Abolitionists from the convention, in conformity to resolutions passed by Duncan's own association.

"Permit me to assure you," wrote Johnson, "that such an adjustment was absolutely impracticable because unconstitutional." He quoted from the rules of the constitution to prove his point. Exclusion of Abolitionists would be just as unconstitutional as the demands of the Abolitionists against slaveholders had been. "Hence it is evident," he concluded, "that the disclaimer is complete, and that it does not 'leave untouched the main subject of the difficulty.' . . . And I trust that He, who helped so manifestly in bringing about the adjustment will conciliate all hearts in its maintenance, and render it productive of great good."

In secular life also Dr. Johnson sought to prevent dissension.

His high regard for Dr. Francis Wayland, president of Brown University, is noted in Dr. Johnson's recommendation of Wayland's *Sermons* to the churches whenever opportunity afforded. The Edgefield Association had purchased 400 copies in 1839, and they were widely distributed. Wayland's *Moral Science* was used by Dr. Johnson in his classrooms, and it had been in general use in other schools as a philosophy textbook. In November, 1842, *Moral Science* was under fire because of its antislavery teachings, and the teachers of Edgefield District in Dr. Johnson's absence held a meeting and voted to delete the work from the list of textbooks recommended. That book was condemned as a work containing doctrines "inimical to the institutions of the South; sentiments which should not appear in a work on Moral Science. . . . The opinions set forth we conceive to be erroneous, dangerous in the extreme, and meriting the condemnation of Southern Teachers and Parents," read the statement of proceedings.

Dr. Johnson himself seemed to be the person against whom a communication signed, "A Parent," was aimed:

"Should there be found Teachers hardy enough still to use it [Moral Science] as a class book, they ought to be held up to public view, to enable those parents who wish their children brought up in the Southern faith, to know them, so that they may guard against the evils of having their children taught whilst young, doctrines which they themselves know to be obnoxious and unsafe towards our free institutions."

Wayland was being prominently mentioned as president of South Carolina College, and the editor of the *Advertiser* expressed in no uncertain terms his disapproval: "We have been credibly informed that Mr. Wayland is at present a prominent candidate for the President's chair of the college, of which we are extremely sorry; his work on 'Moral Science,' at present in use in some of the schools, was on Monday last, at a meeting of School Teachers of this District, pronounced as being an improper work to be placed in the hands of the youth of Southern States on account of its possessing too much of the doctrine of Abolition. We hope our wise Legislators will examine into this, and at all events, place at the head of our flourishing institution one whose heart and soul is Southern, and whose character is beyond doubt as regards Abolitionism."

Dr. Johnson, in a courageous Christian spirit, sought to pour oil on the troubled waters. *Moral Science* caused the Abolitionists to raise a cry of triumph and to hail the author as their champion until his later publication, *Limitation of Human Responsibility*, gave the Abolitionists to understand he had no sympathy with their cause. They then denounced him with severity, and on a trip to England Dr. Wayland had been received coldly by the Abolitionists in that country.

Dr. Johnson quoted *Moral Science* as declaring, "The Gospel *neither commands* masters to manumit slaves, *nor authorizes* slaves to free themselves from their masters." It goes further and prescribes the duties suited to both parties.

"It is true that the Professor teaches that slavery is wrong, and he is thus an anti-slavery man, but not an Abolitionist. Nowhere does he denounce the slaveholder as a *thief*. . . . Immediate abolition would result in the greatest possible injury to slaves who are not competent of self government."

A good textbook, he argued, should not be discarded because of one exception. Other works used in the classical department of schools contained unwholesome teachings. The *Iliad* of Homer, for example, has as its chief goddess Revenge; Gibbons' *Rise and Fall of the Roman Empire* is an insidious attack on the Christian religion, yet it is put into the hands of youth as an important link in the chain of historical writings; Paley's *Moral and Political Philosophy* was tainted with abolitionism, yet it was used in South Carolina College. Dr. Johnson suggested that offensive chapters be cut out of an otherwise excellent work, or let the pupil meet the error and refute it under competent instruction. "Let us be prepared to defend slavery if we are right."

He had found Wayland's *Moral Science* superior to other works on the same subject and therefore had used it in the academies over which he presided, "not only without injury but with manifest advantage. From the abridgment for use of Schools and Academies, I cut the section on 'Domestic Slavery' so the younger class which uses the work will have nothing to do with that section." His older class used the complete volume.

The teachers in removing the work from the list had recommended no work to take its place. He himself had included it in the suggested list but, in his absence, it was removed, he said. If he knew of another work, he would readily adopt it, he stated. "Nay further, much as I prize the *Moral Science,* if I knew that the community would be disquieted by its use in my School, I would discontinue it."

A further note of conciliation was added when he expressed the opinion that, although he had known Dr. Wayland for eleven or twelve years and had the highest regard for him, he thought a native of the State of South Carolina or a graduate of South Carolina College should be elected president.

The board of trustees of the South Carolina College, meeting soon after, elected Professor Henry as president.

Dr. Johnson continued his role of conciliator in a larger sphere, also.

In March, 1842, he admonished the Rev. James C. Furman in

regard to a pending lawsuit involving the two Baptist churches in the city of Charleston:

"I have understood since I left town that some thought of a suit against the First Church for some money, has been entertained by some of the members of the Second Church.

"I hope that this will not be done, my brother Furman. Christians should not go to law before the unjust. And surely Christian churches ought not to be found doing what their members should not. I am sure you would not favor such a course of proceedings."

Dr. J. L. Reynolds, senior professor of Furman Institution, resigned in December, 1844, as the result of friction with the faculty, the board, and his subordinates. Harmony in the educational enterprise was probably in Dr. Johnson's thoughts when he wrote Dr. James C. Furman:

"In looking around for his successor, my mind fixes on no one for the office but yourself. And I write to you at this early period to ask you to think seriously of it. I have a particular desire for you as the Senior Professor."

Dr. Johnson's opinion of James C. Furman was justified by the progress of the institution under his leadership. For more than a quarter of a century Dr. Furman led South Carolina Baptists in their educational and much of their denominational work, and with singular devotion the rest of his life was given to Furman Institution. His coming to the faculty resulted in new vigor and more order in administration. The name was changed to Furman Theological Institution, and four departments were planned, with a professor to preside over each as soon as resources warranted a faculty of that size.

With the burden of local, state, and national affairs of the denomination upon him, it is not surprising that Dr. Johnson's strength was almost depleted during 1843. For several months he was ill and unable to take part in church or secular affairs.

From August until December of that year Dr. Johnson was unable to preach, but the church continued to function with supplies. The Female Academy at Edgefield was closed for several months because of his illness, but a notice in the *Advertiser* stated:

"The health of Rev. Dr. Johnson, Rector of this Institution, being restored, he will, by divine permission, resume its duties, *in person,* the first day of January, 1844."

But the year 1844 was to bring forth a number of changes in Dr. Johnson's orderly life. He was to sever his connection with the school he had supervised for thirteen years, and he was to ask his church to choose a successor to him as pastor; for the eddying currents of denominational unrest were about to call forth his utmost efforts to hold the craft in a steady course; efforts that seemingly failed; and in the following year he was to make the significant statement: "I . . . am ready for the event."

* * * * *

William Bullein Johnson, in the vigor of young manhood, had gone to Philadelphia to help organize Baptists of America into a Convention. And thirty years later, in April, 1844, as a man of 62 years, ripened in the service of the great Head of the church, he attended the last meeting of that body, held again in "The City of Brotherly Love." He went alone from the state of Georgia as its only representative to the first meeting, driving his horse through the country. He probably went by steamer to the last meeting in company with other brethren from South Carolina. According to Dr. Johnson, thirty-two of the "elite" attended the first meeting, and 458 attended the last. Of the men who composed the first meeting, only seven were living in 1844. Dr. Johnson had consistently attended the triennial sessions and had taken an active part in the proceedings.

Of the meeting in 1844, the Philadelphia correspondent of the Charleston *Courier,* under date of April 30, wrote:

"The Baptist Triennial Convention is in session here and more than five hundred ministers are in attendance. The proceedings have been of an interesting character, and especially so upon one point, that of slavery. This occasioned a vigorous debate, but the matter was finally settled by the adoption of a declaration to the effect that, however much individual members might feel themselves at liberty to promulgate their views concerning slavery, yet the Convention itself did not stand in any manner either for or against it."

[107]

The matter was not settled so easily in the American Baptist Home Mission Society, which held its meetings between sessions of the General Convention. A conciliatory resolution offered by Dr. Richard Fuller, of South Carolina, eventually obtained. Dr. Johnson, reporting the meetings to his association, said: "But before the Society reached that desirable point, another was offered, to the following effect, viz.: 'That it is inexpedient to employ, as Missionaries of the Cross, those who hold property in man.' When the question was taken on this motion, it was lost in the negative. And had the Society . . . stopped on the high ground, which they had reached, when brother Fuller's motion was adopted, they would have done well. But another motion soon followed and carried, viz.: That a Committee be appointed, consisting of nine members, three from the North, three from the South, and three from the West, with the President of the Society as Chairman, whose duty it should be to report at the next meeting of the Society in April, 1845, an amicable dissolution of the Society, or such an adjustment of the Constitution, as will admit of the co-operation of Northern and Southern brethren in the conduct of its affairs. . . ."

That committee held a meeting before leaving Philadelphia but came to no definite conclusion. Dr. Johnson told the members of the committee that the South, to a man, would refuse to continue in the society on any other principle than that of equal immunities and privileges, and that they would never concede the right of having men holding slaves appointed to the missionary service by the society. The ultimate decision as to union or separation rested, he felt, with Northern brethren who were not Abolitionists.

"If they shall choose to work with the Abolitionists, a separation will take place. But if they shall choose to work with us, the union will continue, and the Abolitionists will go off to themselves, which I think they ought to have done some time ago."

During the business meeting of the main body of the Convention, Dr. Johnson requested that he not be re-elected president. He observed that he had been the subject of protracted indisposition and had not fully recovered when he suffered a relapse just before leaving for the Convention. The experiment of presiding the first two days of the Convention satisfied him that he did not have the strength to perform the arduous duties of the office throughout the session. He felt that as the South had furnished the presiding officer for twenty-one years and the Middle States for nine years, it was desirable for some other section to furnish the president.

The Abolitionists nominated Dr. B. T. Welch, of Albany, New York, and the conservatives, Dr. Francis Wayland, of Providence, Rhode Island. Dr. Wayland was elected. Although an antislavery man, he was said to be eminently liberal in his views, conservative in his spirit, and conciliatory in his manners.

Dr. Johnson must have exercised infinite tact in presiding over the Convention the first two days, and in appreciation the following resolutions were unanimously adopted by that body:

"Resolved, That the thanks of this Convention be cordially presented to the Rev. Wm. B. Johnson, D.D., for the able, impartial, and conciliatory manner in which he has performed the arduous and responsible duties of President of the Convention. And that, as he declines to be considered a candidate for re-election to the office, we tender to him the assurance of our unfeigned respect and affection."

Chapter XV

The Widening Breach

The Alabama Baptists, at their State Convention in 1844, propounded the query that precipitated the breach. Resolutions signed by Rev. Jesse Hartwell, president of the Alabama Convention, asked the direct question of the Board of Foreign Missions: "Are slaveholders eligible and entitled to receive any agency, mission, or other appointment" from the board?

The reply of the board, signed by Daniel Sharp, president, and Baron Stow, recording secretary, dated, Boston, December 17, 1844, included the following statement: "If, however, any one should offer himself as a Missionary having slaves, and should insist on retaining them as his property, we could not appoint him. One thing is certain, we can never be a party to any arrangement which would imply approbation of slavery."

Naturally that decision was received by the slaveholding brethren as a direct challenge, and further co-operation was deemed impossible. A called meeting of the General Board of the Triennial Convention was held at Providence, Rhode Island, to confer on the proper action of that body. After a free and full consultation a separation was thought best. If the Baptists of the South did not withdraw, it was foreseen that the Abolitionists and conservatives of the North would be rent asunder, according to Dr. J. B. Jeter's account of that conference. The Southern brethren returned home with the assurance of the wisest and most conservative of the Northern brethren that the formation of a Southern convention would meet their approbation and secure their earnest prayers for its success.

Dr. Johnson, writing of that period, said: "Several of our churches cherished the hope that by means of remonstrance and expostulation, through the last Annual Meeting of the Board of Managers at Providence, the Acting Board might be brought to feel the grievous wrong they had inflicted. The Managing Board was therefore affectionately addressed on the subject, and was entreated to revise and reverse the obnoxious interdict. Alas! the results were—contemptuous silence as to the application made; and a deliberate resolve, expressing sympathy with the Acting Board, and a determination to sustain them."

Leaders of the denomination in the South thereafter turned their thoughts to the organization of a separate convention.

The church at Edgefield, following Dr. Johnson's announcement in June, 1844, that it would be necessary for them to choose another pastor, had called Rev. J. M. Chiles, who began his pastorate in January, 1845. At the first service in the year, Dr. Johnson preached a parting sermon, and Mr. Chiles was present to receive words of counsel from his honored predecessor. "The season was one of a pleasant and affecting character," the minutes state, "on account of the earnest and sincere interest exhibited by our beloved Brother Johnson for the welfare of the church and the usefulness of her new pastor in his parting interview."

Within another week Dr. Johnson was off on a journey through Georgia to Tallahassee, Florida, where he spent several weeks, and on the return he met with brethren in Alabama and Georgia. His heart was burdened for the fields white unto harvest; his feelings sensitive to the reaction of Baptists in the states through which he traveled; his mind busy with the solution of the great problems that confronted them.

In Tallahassee he was entertained in the home of Hon. James E. Broome, later governor of Florida and Baptist leader who was instrumental in organizing the First Baptist Church in Tallahassee. There was no Baptist church in that city when Dr. Johnson was there, but he preached in the Presbyterian and Methodist churches several times and also to the Baptists in a church some miles out of Tallahassee. Kindness he found to be a universal characteristic of the people, and the labors of pious ministers of the gospel, aided by the efficient police force and the Temperance Society, were powerful instrumentalities for good. He saw only two persons intoxicated and heard only one oath while there. He asked the prayers of the brethren everywhere for the blessing of God upon the sheep in that city, that "the little one may become a thousand and the small one a strong nation."

He visited the counties of Jefferson and Madison and found the same good order and intelligence as in Leon. They had organized a Baptist association, with twenty-one churches and seventeen ministers. The Rev. John Broome, formerly of Barnwell, South Carolina, had shared largely in the organization of Baptists in those places.

"Florida presents a large field for missionary efforts which the Methodists have cultivated with characteristic diligence," Dr. Johnson wrote. "The Baptists entered the field with some spirit and the Presbyterians and Episcopalians have not been idle. The harvest is ripe and waits for the sickle. Who will thrust in their sickle and reap this harvest?"

Returning home, Dr. Johnson spent one night at Quincy; then going into Georgia, he went through Bainbridge, Blakely, Fort Gaines, and Georgetown, where he crossed the Chattahoochie and visited Eufala and Glenville, in Alabama. He re-crossed the Chattahoochie at Columbus, where he spent two days. From there he went to Hamilton, then to LaGrange, where he spent the sabbath. In the evening he had "an agreeable and profitable interview with the church and the pastor, Brother Dawson, on the subject of the reply of the Boston Board of Missions to the Alabama Baptist State Convention."

He reached Penfield for the two-day session of the Executive Committee of the Georgia Baptist Convention. "Church order and the delicate subject of our relations to the Northern brethren, which were likely to assume a new form as the consequence of the late decision of the Baptist Board of Foreign Missions, engaged our deliberations," he wrote. "It was peculiarly delightful to me to see our brethren so calm and judicial under the exciting state of things caused by the unconstitutional action of the Board of Missions."

The Georgia committee had considered particularly a letter and resolutions which had been sent out by the board of the Virginia Foreign Mission Society. The letter stated that the decision of the Acting Board was unconstitutional; was a violation of the compromise resolution passed at the 1844 General Convention; was unjust to Southern supporters of the foreign mission cause; and was an unwise step. "It is an outrage to our rights," the Virginians stated. "We have been injured by the decision of the Board. What shall we do? To remain united with the Board is impossible. Self-respect forbids it. No redress from the Convention can be expected. To abandon the Foreign Mission enterprise we cannot. It has a strong hold on our affections. Instead of diminishing, let us augment our contributions; let us increase the fervency of our prayers for the conversion of the world. Towards our Northern brethren, let us cultivate feelings of kindness."

In view of the considerations presented, the Board of the Virginia Foreign Mission Society adopted resolutions to the effect that "all farther connexion with the Board of the Triennial Convention is inexpedient and improper"; that the treasurer of the Virginia board deposit in a savings bank any funds in hand, to be disposed of as the Virginia Foreign Mission Society should direct; that a convention be held in Augusta, Georgia, on Thursday before the second Lord's day in May, 1845, to confer on the best means of promoting the foreign mission cause, and other interests of the Baptist denomination in the South; that churches and associations appoint delegates to the proposed convention wherever it might be held. They expressed willingness to have the convention meet in Richmond or in any other place that might be selected.

The Georgia Executive Committee accepted the proposal of the Virginia Board to meet in Augusta on May 8.

Leaving Penfield, Dr. Johnson went by Washington and Lincolnton, Georgia, and arrived at his home in Edgefield, April 2, 1845. He had been away two months and three weeks, had traveled 900 miles, and had been received "as a minister of Christ far beyond my merits," he reported. He had obtained in cash contributions to the Bible cause more than seven hundred dollars, "and have returned home with my constitution greatly invigorated and my health good." He had found his family "in comfortable health."

Back at home, Dr. Johnson turned his attention solely to the part South Carolina would play in the great drama that was about to unfold. In fact, realizing the shortness of time and the urgency of the situation, he had written from LaGrange, Georgia, to the

Board of Agents of the South Carolina Baptist Convention "to obtain their approbation of an extra call of the Convention." The board consisted of eight members, and while he had heard from only four, each of whom concurred in the necessity of an extra session, he felt the matter to be so important that he took the liberty of calling the convention to meet in Edgefield on May 3, 4, 5. Shortly afterwards he received affirmative replies from the other members of the board.

In his circular addressed to members of the State Convention of the Baptist denomination in South Carolina, Dr. Johnson quoted the reply of the Baptist Board of Foreign Missions and said in part:

"This declaration of the Board will assuredly go far to the drying up of the streams of pecuniary contributions to benevolent objects by the Southern Baptists in the present channel—streams, which have been fast diminishing. Funds are already withheld by Alabama and Virginia because of the extraordinary and unconstitutional action of the Board of Foreign Missions. . . .

"The propriety of your assembling at an early period is obvious from the fact that our brethren of Virginia have proposed and our brethren of Georgia have accepted the proposal, that a Southern Baptist Convention be held at Augusta, Georgia, on the Thursday before the second Lord's Day in May. The time and place for such Convention being thus settled, it will necessarily be held, and the propriety of our being represented there is too apparent to need remark.

"Under these circumstances I invite you to assemble at Edgefield Court House at 11 o'clock on Saturday before the first Lord's Day in May, to deliberate on the course to be pursued, and to appoint Delegates to the Convention to be held in Augusta. And I am happy to add that the Baptist church here unanimously concur in the invitation. I indulge the pleasing hope then, of seeing you here at the time appointed and that we may finish our business in time for our Delegates to the Convention in Augusta to take their seats in that body. Allow me to close with one strong reason for your coming together, viz.: *The necessity of union among ourselves.*"

Dr. Johnson's circular was dated April 14, 1845.

Meanwhile, other Baptist groups in the state had taken action.

Rev. J. M. Chiles complied with the request of a Ministers' and Deacons' Conference held at Dry Creek Church to call a meeting of the Edgefield Baptist Association in order to plan for the meeting in Augusta. It so happened that the meeting was scheduled for the Monday that was included in the State Convention, and therefore the Association meeting as such was canceled and merged with the state meeting.

The Wentworth Street Baptist Church at Charleston was one of those protesting the action of the acting board and addressed a communication to the board of managers of the General Convention on the eve of their annual convention, requesting them to revise the reply of the acting board.

H. D. Duncan, moderator of the Savannah River Baptist Association, called upon all churches in that association to hold meetings and elect delegates to attend the meeting in Augusta.

The Incorporated Baptist Church of Charleston passed resolutions favoring the election of one or more delegates from individual churches to the meeting in Augusta, rather than representatives from larger groups, such as associations and state conventions. They preferred meeting Tuesday before the third Lord's Day in June, but elected delegates to represent that church whenever the Convention should assemble.

The Edgefield Church passed resolutions and elected delegates to attend the associational meeting as first announced before Dr. Johnson's plans were known.

Conforming to Dr. Johnson's judgment, the Edgefield church on April 13 invited the State Convention to hold the called meeting there, and appointed a committee composed of N. L. Griffin, G. L. Penn, A. B. Addison, R. T. Mims, and M. Frazier to receive the convention.

The South Carolina State Baptist Convention met accordingly on Saturday, May 3, 1845, and remained in session until Monday, May 5, observing the Lord's Day with religious devotions.

As Dr. Johnson left his home that Saturday morning in May to go the short distance to the church where he was to meet his brethren from other parts of the state, he passed the grounds of Mrs. Edmund Bacon, the Episcopal Church in its mellow setting, the Female Academy; then turned into the lane that led to the unpretentious frame church of the Baptists. He probably was not thinking of the beauty and fragrance of the roses that ran in reckless abandon over fence and arbor; nor of the mighty oaks that seemed to breathe a benediction upon him; nor yet of the long-leafed pines that reached their glistening boughs heavenward as though in supplication to One who gives to his creatures all things needful. Perhaps he was not even aware of the sweet-throated redbirds, thrushes, and mockingbirds that kept their mid-morning trysts in leafy retreats—unmindful of the slender, dignified man, immaculate in black broadcloth suit, his white stock neatly arranged; his thin, frosty locks, wavy at the ends, showing beneath his high-crowned hat; his brow furrowed; his lips compressed; his expression sorrowful yet determined.

Entering the pulpit where he had stood so many times, he called the Convention to order. Voices of the assembly were raised in song, and the Rev. J. Grisham invoked the blessing of Almighty God upon the deliberations of the body.

Then the venerated president stood and looked upon the brethren who made up the Convention over which he had presided for twenty years—since the great Dr. Richard Furman had cast off his garments of flesh.

He addressed them in detail as to the situation confronting Baptists of the South and Southwest following the decision of the acting board relating to the appointment of missionaries. The board's decision to withhold appointment from slave owners was unconstitutional, and he quoted in particular the article which requires that "such persons only as are in full communion with some church in our denomination, and furnish satisfactory evidence of genuine piety, good talents, and fervent zeal for the Redeemer's cause, are to be employed as missionaries."

"Adoption of this article by slave-holders and non-slaveholders proves the Convention made not ownership of slaves a disqualification in one who should offer for a missionary appointment," said Dr. Johnson.

It was natural that funds of the South and Southwest should be withdrawn, Dr. Johnson told them, as these sections no longer reposed confidence in the body as a whole. . . . "Something therefore must be done. . . . A new channel must be created, through which the liberality of the Southern and South Western Baptists shall flow, that its streams may go forth to evangelize the world. . . . I have been brought to this conclusion by slow and painful steps. It was my privilege . . . to be associated with that noble band . . . who organized the General Missionary Convention. . . . But now . . . there comes an awful irruption upon us, cleaving the body in twain. Its indications were at first small, but they have enlarged and multiplied. What it was in the power of our feeble efforts to do in arrest of their progress, and in prevention of the catastrophe, has been done, but all in vain. I, therefore, bow submissively to the overruling Providence of Him who maketh darkness his pavilion and the thick clouds his chariot, and am ready for the event. There is no doubt in *my* mind that the time has arrived when we . . . should withdraw our connexion from our Northern brethren in the missionary enterprise at home and abroad, and form a separate organization for the prosecution of this noble work."

Dr. Johnson reviewed the biblical grounds on which he stood. God gave the Jews authority to purchase bondmen and bondwomen of the heathen as an inheritance for them and their children for a possession forever. No statute on their records revokes this authority. It was of force in the days of the Saviour who gave teachings along many moral lines, but "he touched not the subject of slavery." When slavery is part of a settled policy, one may hold slaves innocently and without crime. It is a matter of opinion and not of faith, Dr. Johnson contended.

The separation, he believed, would result in two lines of service instead of one, and the Kingdom program would go forward more quickly; just as the dissension between Paul and Barnabas lent impetus to the early Christian church by providing two teams instead of one; and just as Joseph was sold into bondage in order that later the lives of his brethren might be preserved.

"Let us not indulge in hard thoughts. . . . God's hand is in it. 'The wrath of man worketh not the righteousness of God.' "

Inviting the attention of the Convention to two plans, he stated that the first was similar to that of the existing General Convention, with separate and independent bodies for the prosecution of each objective.

The second proposal on which he enlarged as his preference was one Convention embodying the whole denomination, together with separate and distinct boards for each objective of benevolent enterprise, located at different places and all amenable to the Convention.

"Judicious concentration is of the first moment in all combinations of men for important enterprises. The plan just suggested proposes such combination. In its successful operation, the whole denomination will be united in one body for the purpose of welldoing, with perfect liberty secured to each contributor of specifying the objectives to which his amount shall be applied."

Article I would read: "This Body shall be styled, the Convention of the Baptist Denomination in the Southern and South Western Portions of the United States of America, for Missions and Other Benevolent Objects."

Some of the Southern leaders with whom Dr. Johnson said he had communicated felt that a theological institution of a high order should engage the deliberations of the Convention to be held in Augusta, but he felt the time was not yet ripe for this step.

Dr. Johnson expressed the opinion that the Southern and Southwestern states should continue to contribute to the treasury of the General Convention in sufficient amounts to enable them to be represented at the convention of that body to be held in Cincinnati in 1847. It would be the courteous thing to do, he said, in order to inform the General Convention of the steps taken by the South and Southwest. Some financial matters would have to be settled also.

Closing his address, Dr. Johnson said, "May the God of wisdom and grace preside in your counsels and direct you aright."

The Committee on the President's Address made their report:

"The committee, to whom was referred the President's Address, report, that they have had the same under prayerful consideration, and recommend,—

"I. That it be approved, and that a copy of it be requested for the press.

"2. That, in their opinion, the recent action of the Acting Board of Foreign Missions in Boston, and other events of like character, occurring among our Northern brethren, demand of the Churches in the South and South West, a separate and distinct organization.

"3. That delegates be appointed to attend the meeting of the Convention to be held in Augusta, Georgia, on the 8th inst."

Twenty delegates were named to represent the South Carolina State Convention at the meeting in Augusta.

It was then Monday, and the brethren shook the parting hand, to meet three days later with others from different Southern states in the Georgia city across the Savannah River from Edgefield District.

The First Baptist Church of Augusta, Georgia, as it appeared when the delegates met here in 1845 to form the Southern Baptist Convention. Courtesy First Baptist Church, Augusta.

Chapter XVI

The Event

The Baptist Church of Augusta, on the corner of Greene and Eighth Streets, stood like a grand lady in her impressive dignity, awaiting The Event.

Before the hour of eleven on Thursday, May 8, 1845, the brethren had begun to gather. Most of them probably had reached the city the day before, coming by water, by rail, by stagecoach or private conveyance. There was subdued excitement as one brother clasped the hand of another; there were whispered bits of conversation as one brother greeted another; there were understanding glances as brethren from one state looked across the church at brethren from other states, and a feeling of holiness pervaded the atmosphere.

The Spirit of the living God breathed upon the assembly, and the Southern Baptist Convention was born.

Dr. William T. Brantly, pastor of the church, calls the meeting to order. Dr. J. B. Taylor, of Virginia, moves that Hon. Wilson Lumpkin, of Georgia, be called to the chair. Hon. Thomas Stocks, of Georgia, seconds the motion.

It is in keeping with the importance of the occasion that so honored and distinguished a Christian layman as the excellent Lumpkin, accustomed to the halls of Congress and to the gubernatorial chair, should be called to preside over the opening phases of the convention. With beneficent mien he announces a hymn, a prayer, a scriptural passage. He states the purpose of the meeting. He names a committee to ascertain the number of delegates and religious bodies represented; and shortly thereafter they report some 300 delegates present, from the states of Maryland, Virginia, North Carolina, South Carolina, Georgia, Alabama, Louisiana,

Kentucky, and the District of Columbia. Because of the shortness of time, Mississippi, Arkansas, Tennessee, and Florida were unable to send representatives, but letters have been received from them, the chair states. The delegates having been ascertained, the committee proceeds to the appointment of officers:

Rev. W. B. Johnson, D.D., of Edgefield, South Carolina, president.

Hon. Wilson Lumpkin, of Georgia, and Rev. J. B. Taylor, of Virginia, vice-presidents.

Rev. J. Hartwell, of Alabama, and Mr. J. C. Crane, of Virginia, secretaries.

Let us watch the events with the mind's eye:

Dr. Johnson, called to preside, arises from his seat and goes to the platform. He is given the hand of Christian fellowship by Lumpkin. Does the body rise to its feet as those two honored contemporaries stand face to face, eye to eye, heart to heart? And when President Johnson stands before the audience, is it a sudden burst of Augusta sunshine that dims his eye and blurs the faces before him? Or does the mental vision of that small group who formed the first General Convention of Baptists in the United States thirty-one years before glorify the present? Do the long-familiar words, "elicit, combine, direct," form themselves once more in his consciousness as he hears again the Great Commission: "Go ye, therefore, and teach all nations"?

But the work of the meeting must proceed, and Dr. Johnson gives earnest attention as Dr. Richard Fuller, of South Carolina, arises to move that a committee of sixteen be named to prepare a preamble and resolutions for the action of the body. With his knowledge of the men present and his seasoned judgment, Dr. Johnson names them: Rev. Dr. Fuller and Dr. M. T. Mendenhall, of South Carolina; Rev. J. A. McKean and W. Crane, Esq., of Maryland; Rev. T. W. Sydnor, of the District of Columbia; Rev. J. B. Jeter and Rev. T. Hume, of Virginia; Rev. R. McNabb, of North Carolina; Rev. B. M. Sanders and Rev. C. D. Mallary, of Georgia; Rev. A. Travis and Gen. E. D. King, of Alabama; Rev. Isaac T. Hinton and Rev. R. Holman, of Louisiana; Rev. Isaac McCoy, of Kentucky.

With the organization complete, a respite is taken for lunch and in order to give the committee time to prepare their report. It is completed and presented by Dr. Fuller, chairman, shortly after the opening of the afternoon session.

The editor of the *Augusta Chronicle & Sentinel* has hastened to his office to write his opinion of the body, "which for intelligence and respectability of numbers and appearance, numbering as it does among its delegates, some of the first men in the connexion in the South, reflects the highest credit upon the denomination."

The report of Dr. Fuller's committee is the subject of considerable debate; there are many verbal amendments, and some are acted upon and adopted. Too much haste is inadvisable, and the Convention adjourns for the day.

Friday morning the Convention meets and resumes its unfinished business. Amendments are considered at length, a phrase here and there is changed; the utmost good feeling prevails.

The report, then, in its revised state, is ready, and the handsome and eloquent Fuller reads in resonant tones:

"The committee to whom it has been referred to report a preamble and resolutions, cannot but express their profound sense of the responsibility resting upon your body, at the present eventful crisis, as the integrity of the nation, the interests of truths, the sacred enterprise of converting the heathen, are all involved in your deliberations. That this convention was imperiously demanded must be apparent to all. . . ."

Here follows a rehearsal of the decision of the Boston Board with all its grave significance, and the speaker concludes:

"Amidst such circumstances your committee esteem it absolutely necessary that the friends of the Triennial Convention and the lovers of the Bible shall at once take their stand, and assert the great cathedral principles of that constitution and of the Word of God.

"Your Committee therefore submit the following resolution, as embodying all that they are now prepared to suggest to your body; therefore,

"Resolved unanimously, That for the peace and harmony, and in order to accomplish the greatest amount of good, and the maintenance of the Scriptural principles on which the General Missionary Convention of the Baptist denomination in the United States was originally formed, it is proper that this Convention at once proceed to organize a society for the propagation of the Gospel."

A vote is taken on the Preamble, and a unanimous consent is given.

The Convention now proceeds to the consideration of the resolution.

The Rev. J. B. Jeter, of Virginia, has the floor—with none to question his right.

"I have never addressed a deliberative assembly under a deeper sense of my responsibility," he commences, "and without consuming the time of the house I shall proceed at once to the discussion of the question. There are but three courses to be considered by the Convention. The first is to submit to the action of the Acting Board at Boston and co-operate. The second is to await the action of the Triennial Convention at its regular meeting two years hence, and the third is to withdraw and form a separate organization. . . . I have been a conservative, so much so, indeed, as to be considered by some of my friends as leaning to the North. I am now in favor of a separate organization, and the more I reflect upon the subject, the difficulties which at first presented themselves to my mind vanish, and I believe the cause of God will be promoted thereby. . . . May I read the following extract from a letter from Dr. Wayland:

" 'You will separate of course. I could not ask otherwise. Your rights have been infringed. I will take the liberty of offering one or two suggestions. We have shown how Christians ought not to act, it remains for you to show us how they ought to act. Put away all violence, act with dignity and firmness and the world will approve your course.' "

Mr. Haynes, of South Carolina, speaks: "I am desirous to define my position. I am the delegate of two bodies; one has instructed and the other has not; I, however, feel perfectly at liberty to act upon this question, and I most heartily concur in the spirit of the resolution, and shall vote for it from a firm conviction that it will result in good. I, therefore, go hand, heart and soul for the resolution."

Says Mr. Duncan, of Virginia: "There is one difficulty in my mind. I desire some of the Committee to state why it should be called a society. If that difficulty is removed, I will vote for the

[123]

resolution. What relation would we sustain to the Triennial Convention?"

Mr. Fuller explains: "I prefer the term *society,* because the Baptist *Church* could not, in this way, be divided; it is separate, independent, republican. The churches of the denomination are not under any general head, they have only been associated for a distinct purpose . . . As to what relation we would sustain to the Triennial Convention: We should occupy the old ground; the North has departed from the original Constitution, to which the South was willing to adhere. . . ."

Now stands a noble and graceful representative of the Middle States, Dr. Lansing Burrows, of Pennsylvania:

"It is with pain I contemplate the objects of this assembly—not because I regret the necessity of a separation from those to whom we of the Middle States have been so long bound by the ties of a common brotherhood. The Middle States were opposed to the action of the Boston Board, and have been at a loss what course to pursue. We have, therefore, waited for the light. . . . Still, I rejoice, and we might all rejoice, that amid all our dissensions Jehovah reigns! And I doubt not that the greatest good will result. . . . As you cannot stop in your efforts to convert the heathen, neither will we. . . . Whether we of the Middle States shall cooperate with the North or South, I know not, but we are unwilling to submit to a severance of those cords which bind us together. I have loved the Baptist Church, and I love it now amid the difficulties which surround it more than ever. . . . A separate organization must be had, and I hope a separation will result in imparting a new and increased zeal in the cause. . . . I bid you, therefore, God speed—you can do no less than to thus act—promptly and efficiently."

Mr. J. S. Tinsley, of Virginia, is the next speaker:

"Mr. President: I am among that minority in this Convention, who came to this place without having made up any opinion as to the course I should take in regard to the main question before us— *I mean a distinctive Southern organization at this time.* I confess, Sir, I had my fears as to the propriety of such a measure. As no appeal has been made to the Triennial Convention, I was apprehensive such a course might present us to the world in the attitude of seceders from the great body of American Baptists. . . . I had determined, when I came to this place, that I should act with the majority of this Convention; that to whatever point the South should be drawn by the threatening elements. . . . I should be there, if among the living. . . . I shall go heart and hand for an immediate organization. And, Sir, in this I believe we shall be entirely united—not merely united one with another, but that the will of Christ will form the bond of our union. . . . With the voice of our ascending Lord, in His last command, still sounding in our ears —with a swelling and expansive benevolence of heart which, like connecting seas, shall begirt the globe, and with an eye single to the glory, resting upon the platform of this sin-darkened world, our great concern will be to be used as the instruments for spreading the light of life over the dark expanse of human desolation."

Mr. Nichols here arises and moves that prayer be made by the Rev. Mr. Mallary, which is adopted. In chaste language, the Rev. Mr. Mallary fervently and eloquently invokes the Supreme Ruler so to guide their steps as to justify them to the world and redound to his own glory and the salvation of mankind. "It is an imposing and solemn scene, to witness the gray-headed patriarchs of the Church, bow in humble submission before their Lord and Master, solemnly invoking His counsels to direct their footsteps in the path of rectitude."

Rev. John Culpeper, of South Carolina, proposes a verbal amendment, which is accepted. Then there is a call for the question, but some are not yet ready. Rev. Thomas Hume, of Virginia, feels that all who desire to say anything upon the question should be heard.

The Rev. Jonathan Davis, of Georgia, speaks: "I deprecate haste in the discussion of this important question, which is more important than any that has ever before been agitated by the Baptist church. The truth is, a portion of the North, who were opposed to the action of the Boston Board, have waited too long. They could have averted a separation once, but it is now too late. . . . Will there be harmony in the South and Southwest? I observed an editorial in the *Christian Index,* in which fears were expressed that Tennessee and Kentucky would not act with us. I believe they will, and thousands all over the Union, who have not heretofore reflected upon the question, will also harmonize with us. I think a separation will be productive of good, because agitation will cease, and I therefore favor the resolution."

Mr. Joseph S. Baker, of Georgia, editor of the *Index,* obtains the floor: "Brother Davis's allusion to the article in *The Index* imposes upon me the necessity of saying that he has misapprehended its import. I only contended in that article that the brethren of Tennessee might be passive for a season. I have in my possession a letter assuring me of the fact that they would be with us; as also those of Kentucky. I had doubted what position Kentucky would assume, but that doubt is now removed, and I believe Kentucky will occupy the front rank. Mississippi, too, who at first hesitated, is now openly for separation, and I have assurances that many north of Mason's & Dixon's line will justify the action of this Convention, aye, even the more moderate throughout the North and the world, will sympathize with and justify us. I think," he added, "the instructions given to delegates were inexpedient, because this body is only primarily advisory."

Mr. McNab, of North Carolina, next speaks: "I desire to say a few words in reference to my State. Since I came here, I have had more light, and I heartily approve the resolutions and I believe my State will also."

Rev. Isaac McCoy, of Kentucky, apostle to the Indians, speaks for that state: "I had supposed that Kentucky was above suspicion," he remarks, "and was astonished to hear that any doubts had been entertained as to how she would demean herself. I feel satisfied she will sustain the action of this Convention."

Dr. Jesse Hartwell, of Alabama, to whom the reply of the Boston Board had been addressed, gives the final word of approval: "I have for several years acted as agent of the Boston Board," he concludes, "and from the many opportunities of knowing the people of that State, I have no doubt that Alabama is in favor of action."

A general call is now made for the question, and when Dr. Johnson puts it, the resolution is unanimously adopted.

It is now moved that the following names be added to the committee of sixteen, who shall prepare and report a Constitution for a Southern Association: Messrs. W. B. Johnson, J. C. Crane, Dr.

Curtis, Dr. Dagg, Samuel Furman, Baker, Stringfellow, and Hartwell.

Prayer is made by the Rev. Mr. Fuller. The Convention adjourns, to meet again at 4 o'clock P.M. But when the members reassemble at that hour, adjournment is had without the transaction of any business. The committee will need the remainder of the day to consider the proposed constitution.

Saturday morning at 8 o'clock the body meets to consider adoption of the constitution. The preamble and constitution as recommended stated in Article 1: "This Body shall be styled the Southern and Southwestern Baptist Convention." When that article was taken up, a motion was made to strike out "Southwestern," which gave rise to a protracted debate, in which several gentlemen expressed their views, the *Chronicle & Sentinel* reported. It was urged on the part of advocates of striking out, that "Southern" was more definite, shorter, and was sufficiently expressive to cover the whole ground. They meant no disrespect to their Southwestern brethren but preferred the shorter and more expressive term.

On the other hand, those opposed to striking out, expressed their fears that some constituents would take exception to a term so sectional and might think their feelings had been disregarded. The gentlemen who engaged in the discussion enlarged and enforced their views with much earnestness, though in the kindest feelings.

("Of this debate we took ample notes," commented the editor, "but at the time of writing out this notice we have not time to prepare them for the press, nor indeed is it important.")

The motion to strike out the word "Southwestern" prevailed by a decided majority, and the article was then adopted.

The remaining articles were considered *seriatim* and were adopted, generally without alteration or objection, as they came from the committee.

Having gone through the several articles, the assembly adopted the preamble and constitution by a unanimous vote. . . .

The preamble read:

"We, the Delegates from Missionary Societies, Churches, and other Religious bodies of the Baptist denomination in various parts of the United States, met in Convention, in the city of Augusta, Georgia, for the purpose of carrying into effect the benevolent intentions of our constituents, by organising a plan for eliciting, combining and directing the energies of the whole denomination in one sacred effort for the propagation of the Gospel, agree to the following rules or fundamental principles."

Styled "The Southern Baptist Convention," and designed to "promote Foreign and Domestic missions and other important objects connected with the Redeemer's Kingdom," the Convention made provision for membership, based on contributions, for officers and boards.

Article 10 stated: "Missionaries appointed by any of the Boards of this Convention, must, previous to their appointment, furnish evidence of genuine piety, fervent zeal in their Master's cause, and talents which fit them for the service for which they offer themselves."

Meetings were to be held triennially, but extra meetings could be called by the president with approval of any of the boards of managers.

After adoption of the preamble and constitution, Dr. Johnson suggested that the Convention unite in prayer to return thanks to the great Disposer of events for the unanimity and good feeling which had characterized their deliberations.

Dr. Carty moved that a committee of three be appointed to prepare an address to the public, setting forth the reasons which had led to the formation of the Southern Baptist Convention, the necessity of such an organization, and giving an exposition of its principles and objects, which should be published in connection with the minutes of this body and in such public prints as would allow it a place in their columns. The resolution was adopted, and Drs. Curtis, Johnson, and Fuller were appointed a committee.

The Rev. Mr. Jeter moved that provisional officers and boards be elected to continue in office until the regular meeting set for May of the following year. After much discussion the resolution of Mr. Jeter was adopted, and the Convention proceeded to organize a provisional government, electing as officers:

Wm. B. Johnson, president; Wilson Lumpkin, vice-president; J. B. Taylor, 2nd vice-president; A. Dockery, 3rd vice-president; R. B. C. Howell, 4th vice-president; J. Hartwell and J. C. Crane, secretaries; M. T. Mendenhall, treasurer.

The Foreign Mission Board was to be located at Richmond, Virginia, with Jeremiah B. Jeter as president, and the Domestic Mission Board was to be located at Marion, Alabama, with Basil Manly, D.D., as president. Vice-presidents were named from the constituent states; other officers were corresponding secretary, recording secretary, treasurer, auditor. There was a board of managers for each board.

Resolutions were passed, thanking the citizens of Augusta for their kind hospitality, and providing for a collection for foreign and domestic missions during the Sunday services.

The sabbath was devoted to worship, and the final business session was held on Monday, May 12. Resolutions were passed to affiliate with auxiliary societies; to turn funds in hand over to respective boards; that the churches sustain the Indian Mission Association "with zeal and liberality"; that the Board of Domestic Missions be instructed to take "all prudent measures for the religious instruction of our colored population"; that claims be adjusted with the Baptist Triennial Convention; that application be made for a charter of incorporation; that the Domestic Mission Board "direct their effective attention to aid the present effort to establish the Baptist cause in New Orleans"; that "with profoundest gratitude to the Great Head of the Church, this Convention do recognise the harmonious action to which it has arrived and that we do regard the exhibition of the Christian Spirit which has governed its deliberations as a proof of the divine presence in the origin and prosecution of this organization."

"And the Convention adjourned sine die."

Baptists of the South had entered upon a new era of Christian evangelization under the leadership of Dr. Johnson, whose justness, impartiality, dignity, and urbanity in presiding, together with his unquestioned Christian integrity, qualified him supremely for the task.

Chapter XVII

Leader of Southern Baptists

With the organization of the Southern Baptist Convention, Dr. Johnson began with even greater zeal than before, an active program of service for Christ—leading Southern Baptists in their missionary and ministerial education efforts. He did not succeed in carrying out all the ideas he advanced at the time, but he had sown the seed that grew and ripened to maturity and brought forth an abundant harvest.

A few days after the formation of the Convention in Augusta, he went to Forsyth, Georgia, where a convention of the American Indian Mission Association was being held at the same time the Georgia State Baptist Convention met, May 17–19, 1845. Dr. Johnson supposedly went directly to Forsyth from Augusta, and presided over the Indian Mission Association.

He evidently was not successful at that time in having the work of the Indian Association absorbed by the Domestic Mission Board, as he desired, as it was not until 1854 that the Indian Association transferred its work to the Southern Baptists, forming in 1855 the Domestic and Indian Mission Board.

Dr. Johnson advocated a continuance of support of the Bible Society, Publication, and Sunday School Societies, organizations that were already in successful operation.

He was invited to accept the post of corresponding secretary of the Foreign Mission Board, a position that would have required his residence in Richmond, but he was unable to accept. As he wrote Dr. J. B. Jeter: ". . . My physicians have forbidden me to take up my abode in a climate more severe than the one in which I now reside. . . ."

He had, however, consented to act as agent for the Foreign Mission Board, and set forth almost at once on his labors, visiting churches in South Carolina and North Carolina. He collected money for the work and wrote Dr. Jeter: ". . . . I have the satisfaction to inform the Board that I find a cordial approbation of our recent movements in Augusta." He found that "the appalling drought has blighted the prospects of the planter in our state in the articles of rice and cotton. . . . So I fear that our collections will be very limited."

After a tour of seven and a half months, he wrote Dr. Jeter: "But we need a higher state of piety, of self-denial, of *New Testament Religion* than exists at present among us. . . . Conformity to the world monopolizes the time, the thoughts, the talents, the money of Professors, so that very little remains to be given to God & His cause. . . . I have, therefore, in my efforts to excite attention to the mission cause, not so much attempted to rouse their feelings for the present occasion, as to lay a foundation for more enlarged, consistent, liberal & persevering exertion in support of the Kingdom of Christ. . . ."

A perusal of *The Gospel Developed,* a volume written by Johnson, reveals the secret of his successful ministry: his strict adherence to the Scriptures for the government of a church of Jesus Christ, with Christ as the head. The Bible gives regulations as to government of a church of Christ, deacons or servants, evangelists, ordinances, ordination, discipline, mode of sending the gospel to every creature, stated times of meeting and plan of giving, reading of the Scriptures, and other observances for the proper functioning of a "Christocracy." Churches are independent of each other in point of government and are amenable to Christ alone as the one supreme Head. The Lord designs that such churches should "dot the world as oases in a desert."

He preached to the churches, awakening them to a sense of the magnitude of the task Southern Baptists had undertaken.

* * * * *

Dr. Johnson and other leaders of the denomination went to Richmond, Virginia, for the first regularly scheduled Triennial Convention of Southern Baptists, which opened June 9, 1846, at the

Second Baptist Church. There was a song of praise in their hearts and a prayer upon their lips for a harmonious session. It was to be expected that Baptists of the South, uniting for the organization of a separate convention in Augusta the preceding year, would be of one mind as to the principal form the body should assume; but with a year's operation under the new setup and sufficient time having elapsed to allow Baptists of the different Southern states to form divergent opinions as to details, there was need for caution and special divine guidance lest the harmony of the new organization be disrupted.

There were 152 delegates present from the several states. And from Canton, China, had come Rev. J. Lewis Shuck and a native Chinese preacher, Yong Seen Sang. Rev. Thomas Simons, missionary to Burma, was also present.

The *Richmond Republican* said of the gathering: "The appearance of this body . . . is attractive to the spectator, as well from the general decorum of its members, as from the high reputation acquired by many of them in the discharge of their public functions. The venerable President, Dr. Johnson of South Carolina, presides with a dignity, grace, and promptitude, which ensure general respect, and the eminent order which prevails, shows that there is an absence of much of that ambition for personal distinction which too often mars the harmony of public assemblies. . . ."

Dr. S. H. Ford, editor of the *Christian Repository,* was present and eager to see the president of the Convention about whom he had heard much. Dr. Johnson had visited Governor Graham in Ford's city of Raleigh, North Carolina, the preceding October, and the high regard felt by the governor for the president of the Convention was evident.

"To say that he presides with more than common dignity, were only to repeat a well-known fact," Dr. Ford wrote later in describing Dr. Johnson. "He possesses all the requisites of a good chairman, quick discernment, promptness, and decision in taking the sense of the house, with a clear, open, pleasant voice. . . ."

He further described the president as being "one of the neatest and most tidy gentlemen I met with. . . . His face is thin and long, and is made to appear longer, by wearing his spectacles on the tip end of his nose. The hair thin, frosty, and long behind, disposed to curl; mouth wide, lips thin, frequently compressed, Lavater would say that Dr. Johnson was precise, regular and methodical in all his affairs. . . . In his intercourse with others, the Doctor is amiable and kind; of manners most courteous, he holds the heartlessness of the Chesterfieldian code in utter contempt. Emphatically a peacemaker, he seeks every opportunity to banish discord and to promote harmony. He witnessed the efforts of Northern fanatics to sunder the ties that bound together the old Triennial Convention, with deepest regret. And no man probably has done more to prevent Southern churches from withdrawing from the A. & F. Bible Society than has Dr. Johnson. May his useful life long be spared!"

The proceedings opened with the reading of a hymn by the president, which was sung, "and a most fervent and truly appropriate prayer offered up by the Rev. J. B. Jeter, invoking a blessing upon the work in hand, and upon all who have in charge the cause of the Divine Master."

Divine guidance was invoked in a resolution that the body look to God for abundant and powerful influence of his blessed Spirit, "that we may prosecute deliberations with Christian courtesy, gentleness and love, that nothing may be done through strife and vainglory."

A high moment of the Convention came when Dr. Jeter conducted the Rev. Mr. Shuck and his native Chinese preacher to the platform and they were received by President Johnson.

Who can measure the joy of Southern Baptists as they beheld the living representative of their missionary labors, the 65-year-old Yong Seen Sang: his blue-robed figure erect, his manner unaffected and easy as he waved a large fan back and forth?

Dr. Johnson very affectionately addressed both Mr. Shuck and the Chinese. He spoke of the wonderful dispensation of Providence by which a country so extensive, so strange in the character and pursuits of its people, so benighted, so long shut up, had been at last opened to us, and we had been permitted to send missionaries there to occupy that important field. He had read, he said to Mr. Shuck, with deep interest the accounts of his labors and trials in his missionary pursuits. To the Southern division it was peculiarly pleasing to have him there and to regard him as a missionary under their auspices. In behalf of the body, he gave Mr. Shuck the right hand of fellowship and Christian recognition and invoked the blessing of God on him and his labors.

Mr. Shuck responded briefly. His feelings did not allow him to express more than gratitude in mingling in the devotions and deliberations of so many distinguished and pious men. It was pleasing to him to communicate any information he had of the great land of darkness which had so lately been and soon again would be the scene of his labors.

Yong Seen Sang then responded, his words carefully translated by Mr. Shuck: "He had formerly worshipped idols and knew nothing of the true God. He was thankful to those whom he addressed for sending the Gospel to China. Their ministers of the Lord Jesus Christ had evinced so much interest in China, that it would cause him, when he returned home, to devote himself with all his ability to preaching the Gospel and instructing the people. He spoke of the harmony that existed among the disciples of Christ. They were one here and would be one in Heaven. He had one request to make of the ministers of the Gospel, and that was, in their prayers, night and morning, to *remember China!*"

Never were hearts more touched. Eyes were dimmed with tears as brethren came forward to shake the hands of the missionaries. And through the auditorium of the church resounded the new missionary hymn:

> Hail! sweetest, dearest tie that binds
>   Our glowing hearts in one;
> Hail! sacred hope, that tunes our minds
>   To harmony divine.
> It is the hope, the blissful hope,
>   Which Jesus' grace has given!
> The hope when days and years are past,
>   We all shall meet in Heaven.
>
> From Burmah's shores, from Afric's strand,
>   From India's burning plain;
> From Europe, from Columbia's land,
>   We hope to meet again.
> It is the hope, the blissful hope,
>   Which Jesus' grace has given.

Prospects were bright to send other laborers out into the vineyards of the world. S. C. Clopton and George Pearcy were to sail for China later that month, and one evening during the Convention Clopton was set apart as a missionary. Special need was felt of "a suitable individual to devote himself chiefly to the Theological training of such native converts in China as may be employed in the Christian ministry." More missionaries for China and Africa were urged.

When the venerable president left his chair for a few moments one member of the body arose and remarked that when the heart speaks, its words are few, simple, and plain. He therefore offered resolutions that "the thanks of this body be tendered to its presiding officer, the Rev. Wm. B. Johnson, D.D., for the dignity, courage, and kindness with which the duties of the chair have been fulfilled. . . . No mere human mind . . . can estimate the extent to which the manner in which the duties of the chair, with the blessing of Heaven, had been discharged, contributed to the harmonious and delightful feelings which have prevailed in the deliberations of the Convention. For himself he trembled when he thought of the consequences which might have flowed from a different manner of fulfillment of those duties by a different man."

The resolutions were unanimously adopted, and when they were handed to Dr. Johnson by the vice-president, Hon. Thomas Stocks, the president said no thanks were due him. They were due from him to the Convention for the honor conferred upon him by putting him in the chair. If thanks were due for the order which had prevailed, it was due to the members, to whose assistance and prayers he was indebted for any success in his efforts to administer properly the duties of the chair.

President Johnson made his valedictory address of the session on Monday, June 15. He had been impressed with the presence and influence of God's Spirit last year at Augusta, but now at the present session he had felt that Presence even more deeply because of the difficulties that had been anticipated in bringing the whole body to unite on topics that would engage their attention. He bade them put their hands with increased zeal and energy to the work. It was time to make great sacrifices of comfort and worldly advancement. They must be ready to give up members of their families to the mission work. He himself might be called on to make the sacrifice. He had a dear son at college whom he had educated for the ministry, and it was probable he would become a missionary to China or some other distant land. He had yet another son whose feelings and education tended to the ministry. He might have to give up both, but he was ready to do so when it pleased God he should. It was an honor to lift the standard of the cross where it had not been raised before. If he and his son should not meet again in this world, then they would meet in a better world as shining stars in the firmament.

The Lord's Supper on the preceding sabbath had been to him a blessed occasion, and to see Brother Shuck bringing his sheaf with him afforded such joy that it was worth a journey from South Carolina, or from across the ocean even, to witness it. He invoked the blessings of God upon the Convention, its churches and ministers. May the blessed gospel be to them not as water spilled on the ground which cannot be gathered again but as the water of life! There would be a final meeting, a Grand Convention which would never adjourn and where there would be no more parting.

The president offered a devout prayer to the throne of grace, and the Convention sang the hymn beginning,

> Blest be the tie that binds
> Our glowing hearts in one,

as with a general shaking of hands the Convention adjourned, to meet the first Wednesday in May, 1849, in Nashville, Tennessee.

* * * * *

The "suitable individual" selected to devote himself to the theological training of native converts in China was Francis Cleveland Johnson, Dr. Johnson's son.

In a letter to Dr. Taylor, July 30, 1846, Dr. Johnson spoke of his son's qualifications: ". . . In my conversations with him, Francis, on the subject of going to China, I found his mind open gradually to the importance of the Theological Department for native preachers, & finally he felt satisfied, that such a position would enable him to do the most good. And at length he resolved on accepting it. And although, my brother, parental affection & declining years would lead me to detain him here, yet a sense of duty obliges me to consent to his going to China. . . . For I am satisfied that God has admirably fitted him for the office of theological instructor. He has a remarkable talent for acquiring language, for mastering profound & difficult subjects, & for illustrating & making plain what he does know."

Writing from China a year later, Francis Cleveland Johnson told his father:

". . . I would your eyes could see their houses, their cities, their numerous arts, and the manifold proofs of their advanced civilization. You must not dream of any man's being fit to publish tracts here, who is not deeply imbued with the spirit of the Chinese literature—whose mind has not cast off its foreign style, speech, and thought, and put on the Chinese. By God's blessing, I myself intend to endeavor so completely to strip myself of the English language, that when I pray in private, when I meditate, I shall naturally and mechanically do it in the Chinese language, and not in the foreigner's language."

But the eternal conflict was going on: good against evil; right against wrong; light against darkness. It was a hard task, and at times the forces of unrighteousness seemed to prevail or to make harder the task of the righteous.

In 1849, Francis C. Johnson returned home because of failing health.

In the same year an epidemic of cholera raged in the southern and central portions of the United States. Dr. R. B. C. Howell, in Tennessee, received first one message and then another from different brethren suggesting a change in place of meeting of the Southern Baptist Convention because of the cholera scare. He replied that there was no necessity for alarm as there were very few cases in the city of Nashville. Then from Edgefield Court House came a letter from Dr. Johnson under date of April 3, 1849, apprising Dr. Howell of the feelings in that section, and suggesting that the Convention be held in Charleston: ". . . Such is the panic on this side of the mountains that I am persuaded you will have but few of us to be with you in May. I am very anxious when we go to the West that we go in large numbers to get acquainted with you all there. . . ."

Dr. Howell and others in Tennessee agreed to the change, and Dr. Johnson sent notices to the press, notably the *Edgefield Advertiser,* explaining the change, with the proviso that the next Convention be held in Nashville. He had the concurrence of the Board of Foreign Missions and the Board of Domestic Missions, and his circular would appear in a few days. "Meantime I inform you of the change as constitutionally made, and affectionately urge upon you the importance of a large attendance as the state of our missionary affairs, and the proposed conference on the subject of a General Theological Institution for the South will require your presence in full meeting."

In spite of all that was done to notify members, some appeared in Nashville on the originally scheduled date, May 2, and held a convention, accounts of which were carried in Tennessee papers. And when the meeting was called to order in Charleston, the question arose as to the authority under which that convention was holding the session. The situation was duly explained, but Dr. Johnson, in a letter addressed later to Dr. Taylor, felt that posterity would blame him for the confusion without adequate explanation.

At the Charleston convention Dr. Johnson read Philippians, second chapter: ". . . For it is God which worketh in you both to will and to do of his good pleasure. . . ."

He also made "an interesting and masterly discourse" on the success of the missionary enterprise, according to the press account.

Once again he was elected to head the Convention, and the time of the next meeting was set for the second Friday in May, 1851, at Nashville, with a change to biennial sessions becoming effective.

The need of a central theological institution in the South was claiming his particular attention, and immediately after the close of the Convention in Charleston a conference was held to consider the matter of theological training. A resolution pointed to the need in the South for a more efficient and well-directed system of ministerial education, and a committee composed of Culpeper, Jeter, and Dagg was named to correspond with theological schools with a view to combining two or more of them into one institution.

The communication received by the Furman trustees in South

Carolina was referred without recommendation to the State Convention when it met in Edgefield in 1849. A called meeting of the South Carolina State Convention in April of that year had considered the matter, and that State's willingness to co-operate had been expressed then and later at the regular convention the latter part of the year.

Resolutions adopted stated "that this Convention will unite with our brethren of other States, in the founding of a Theological Institution, to be located at such place as may be determined upon by a Convention of all the States willing to co-operate in the enterprise."

When the Convention met in Nashville in 1851, the Committee on Ministerial Education reported that no reply from the theological schools with which they had corresponded contained anything to lead the committee to believe the funds of the several institutions could be united in any one of the existing institutions or in the organization of a new one. There was willingness to co-operate in establishing one institution of high order, yet it was invariably connected with certain conditions and reservations relating to their peculiar obligations, the report stated. The committee were convinced that it was not expedient for them to take any further steps in the matter, and they referred the subject back to the denomination.

The South Carolina Institution, combining theological and classical departments, was incorporated as Furman University in 1851 by act of the Legislature, and Greenville was fixed upon as the location. The theological department was separated from the college and made an independent Southwide Theological Seminary in 1859, and less than two years later the Civil War swept over the country, almost destroying the institution.

The leadership of Dr. Johnson in the educational efforts of Southern Baptists extended from the one modest building in the little village of Edgefield in 1826 to the magnificent expanse of buildings that a century later comprised the Southern Baptist Theological Seminary in Louisville, Kentucky, although the sainted leader had been gathered to his fathers fifteen years before the final move was made to the location in Kentucky.

Chapter XVIII

Last Years in Edgefield

Although Rev. J. M. Chiles was pastor of the Edgefield Church during the year 1845, Dr. Johnson preached there at intervals during the year, and when Chiles declined on September 28, 1845, to serve another year, the church "resolved that during the week they would make the call of a pastor the subject of prayer and postponed further action on the subject until next Lord's Day," the minutes state.

On October 26 the church invited Dr. Johnson to become pastor for the year 1846 at a salary of $800, and Dr. Johnson accepted. On January 4, 1846, he assumed the duties of pastor, and that was observed as a day of fasting and prayer.

Regular services were carried on, with morning preaching service for the white members of the congregation and the teaching of the Scriptures to the Negroes in the afternoon. The church clerk occasionally referred to Dr. Johnson as "the Bishop."

The church frequently made contributions to denominational enterprises. When "Brother Huckins, missionary from Galveston, Texas," preached, he received a collection of $100 towards a meetinghouse in Galveston.

On March 7, 1847, Dr. Johnson, in compliance with a request from the congregation, preached a sermon "in reference to the suffering population of Ireland," and a collection was taken for that cause.

On April 4, 1847, "the church heard a letter addressed to the churches of South Carolina from the Corresponding Secretary of the Board of Foreign Missions on the subject of simultaneous collections for missions." And the following Sunday the church "resolved in reference to the circular addressed by the secretary of the Board of Foreign Missions, that Brother Johnson be requested to preach a sermon on the subject of Missions on the 4th Lord's day in May and that the Saturday previous be observed as a special day of prayer in reference to the objects contemplated in that circular."

Accordingly Dr. Johnson preached a sermon on missions, and a committee was appointed consisting of "Brethren Johnson, Griffin and Penn . . . to see the members and others and take up subscriptions on such plan as they think best to aid the Foreign and Domestic Boards of Missions under the control of the Southern Baptist Convention."

Dr. Johnson continued his service as moderator of the Edgefield Association, and at the meeting in 1850 Dr. James C. Furman was present to speak in behalf of Furman University. Reports of institutions under Baptist patronage included Furman Theological Institution, which "calls for our unwearied and united support; especially as it is proposed to connect with it a Classical Institution of high order"; the Hodges and Fuller Institutes at Greenwood; the Johnson Female Seminary at Anderson, which "is in a very flourishing condition."

Brother W. P. Hill, agent of the Domestic Mission Board of the Southern Baptist Convention, was present at the association meeting and reported that he had received within the limits of the association for domestic missions the sum of $316.95.

After hearing the address of Dr. Furman, the association passed a resolution "that they cordially approve of the establishment and endowment of the University, and commend the enterprise to the Churches, as worthy of their hearty approbation and liberal support."

Denominational matters, especially in the educational realm, were claiming more of Dr. Johnson's attention, and he was frequently away from Edgefield. In June, 1851, he was taking an active part in the transition of Furman Institution to the University status, and its relocation in Greenville. It opened in Greenville the first Monday in February, 1851. Necessary funds for a $70,000 endowment had not been secured, and Dr. Johnson was one of fifteen men pledging to raise or give $1,000 each to secure the $15,000 needed. Furman became a university, and final legal details were completed in 1852. Dr. Johnson continued as chairman of the board of trustees of the newly incorporated university.

On November 2, 1851, Dr. Johnson resigned as pastor of the church at Edgefield because of the feeble health of a daughter, and because his service with the denomination would take him more frequently into the upper part of the state. He was spoken of as "the esteemed and beloved supply."

His letter of resignation, read to the church on May 16, 1852, is preserved in the minutes of the church and reads as follows:

To the Edgefield Village Baptist Church:
Dear Brethren:
In pursuance of my vocation in the service of our mission boards and of our university, I have not the opportunity of being present at your meetings and as I shall shortly be for the most part in the upper country, where I purpose to fix my abode, I write to ask a letter of dismission for my daughter, Elizabeth, and my servant, Maria. In thus closing my connexion with you, I commend you to God and the word of His grace, which is able to build you up and to give you an inheritance among the saints in lights.

Yours in the Gospel,
William B. Johnson

Edgefield C.H., S. C.
May 12, 1852.

But Dr. Johnson did not leave Edgefield until January, 1853, and before his departure an unfortunate matter arose involving Rev. C. A. Raymond who had been invited to take charge of the Female Academy at that place. Raymond had been connected with the Fuller Institute at Greenwood, and the trustees of that school claimed that he had broken his contract with them. Other charges were made, reflecting on Raymond's character. By October, 1851, the affair had called for an adjustment by a committee of ministers headed by Dr. Johnson, who conducted a hearing in Greenwood. Most of the charges against Raymond, particularly those relating to his veracity, were sustained. The trustees of the Edgefield Female Academy, which was then headed by Raymond, conducted their own investigation and announced that their confidence in his moral character was unshaken. The Gilgal Baptist Church which Raymond was serving as pastor became divided, and at his own request another pastor was secured.

After Dr. Johnson had moved from Edgefield, the Baptist church at that place invited Raymond to supply as preacher until other arrangements could be made. Raymond and his wife had been received into the membership of that church March 6, 1853, by letter from the church in New Orleans.

At the meeting of the Edgefield Baptist Association that year, the circumstances surrounding the Raymond case were reviewed and resolutions were adopted withdrawing fellowship with the Edgefield Village Church. It was stated that the church, "with a full knowledge of the report of said committee [which had considered charges against Raymond], without any adjustment of said charges, or reconciliation of the parties aggrieved, have received C. A. Raymond into their fellowship and recognized and set him forward as a minister of the gospel. . . . Therefore, resolved that this body, having long known the brethren composing said committee as ministers and brethren in good standing and unimpeachable moral character, have entire confidence in their Christian integrity. . . . Resolved that the above named act of the Edgefield Village Baptist church, is a departure from the purity and simplicity of the Gospel, calculated to disturb the peace and harmony of this body, and for which this body has no fellowship."

This affair caused disquietude not only in the Edgefield Association but also in the South Carolina State Baptist Convention. Forces were arrayed on two sides: those feeling that the rights of a church had been invaded, on the one hand; and those who recognized the right of an association to withdraw fellowship from a church considered to have departed from the purity and simplicity of the gospel, on the other.

Dr. Johnson, recognizing the independence of Baptist churches, yet felt the association justified in this instance, and even though he was no longer living in Edgefield, his influence was felt strongly. Dr. Johnson and Rev. J. M. Chiles both considered the charges against Raymond to be "grave and serious," and Dr. Johnson proposed that Raymond acknowledge to the Board of Trustees of the Greenwood schools the truth of the charges against him and ask their forgiveness—a proposal that was not acted upon by Raymond.

Dr. James C. Furman felt, with Dr. Johnson, that Raymond by his attitude had forfeited any favorable consideration, and that so long as the Edgefield Church continued to have him as minister, the association should remain withdrawn from that church.

Dr. Johnson publicly expressed his views in a *Reply* to an address by the Edgefield Church; and Raymond, in a *Statement of Facts,* spoke in no uncertain terms against Johnson, Chiles, W. P. Hill and others whom he considered were seeking to defame his (Raymond's) character.

Dr. Basil Manly, who had returned to South Carolina and was pastor of the Wentworth Street Church at Charleston, differed with Johnson and Furman. Writing Dr. J. C. Furman about the matter in 1857, prior to the meeting of the State Convention in Greenwood, Dr. Manly said:

"I see the Convention expresses its willingness to give advice in matters of difficulty. What think you of the expediency of introducing to the notice and decision of the Convention some of the points involved in the case of the Edgefield Association. . . . Either I am grievously in ignorance and error myself, or they are. . . . I only wish Dr. Johnson were 15 years younger—that he might bring all the power he ever had in defense of the measures into which his influence has plunged the Association. . . ."

At the meeting of the State Convention in Greenwood, at which Dr. Johnson was present, Dr. Manly presented the credentials of the delegates from the Edgefield Church and moved that they be seated. The motion was tabled, but later in the day a committee of reconciliation was appointed to meet at another time with committees from the Edgefield Church and Association. The reconciliation meeting was held in connection with the Edgefield Association meeting at Horeb Church, September 12, 1857, and the matter was at last amicably adjusted. The report of the committee read in part:

"Having been convinced that a detailed examination of the cause of variance between the Greenwood Trustees and Charles A. Raymond is entirely impracticable, on account of their complicated nature and extent, and also rendered unnecessary, on account of the expected removal from the bounds of the Edgefield Association of the person before named, and while we perfectly acknowledge the right of this or any Baptist Association to withdraw fellowship from an offending constituent body, and at the same time while we acknowledge the entire principle of church independence, yet considering the nature of human fallibility and the paramount importance of the great principle of christian forgiveness, forbearance, toleration and charity, and deeming it of the utmost importance in the present crisis of the Baptist cause in this region—that the Edgefield Village Baptist church should resume her place as in former times in this Association, the council recommend that the Edgefield Village church appear at the next meeting of the Association by her letter and delegates as usual, and that the Association receive them with the same cordiality as heretofore."

The report was confirmed by both the Association and the Edgefield Church.

The *Southern Baptist* stated: "The report was adopted by the unanimous vote of the Association, and the result was accompanied by one of the most touching demonstrations of Christian emotions which we have ever seen. Brethren long in a state of suspense and separation from their own stress of conscience, and honesty of feeling, were now brought to greet each other with the hand of fraternal fellowship, and the expression of affection. The delegates of the Edgefield church were invited forward, and received the hand of fellowship from the Moderator, Rev. J. M. Chiles. This was followed by a prayer, most touching and apposite to the occasion, by Rev. Dr. Johnson."

Chapter XIX

Chancellor of Johnson University at Anderson

"In consequence of the feeble health of a member of my family, I removed, by the advice of my physician, in January, 1853, to Anderson C.H., for the benefit of the drier & more salubrious atmosphere of the Upper country," Dr. Johnson wrote in his "Reminiscences."

In a letter to Dr. J. B. Taylor, just before leaving Edgefield, Dr. Johnson stated: "I am on the eve of removal to Anderson, S. C. . . . It is by the advice of my physicians, that I am removing to a higher latitude for the health of my elder daughter. My own constitution suffers, too, in the summer, from the oppressive heat. . . . For the relief of my daughter, I shall go to boarding for the next year at Anderson, to release her from the irritation & anxiety of house keeping. I shall, therefore, as I have this year, be somewhat migratory, & can act for the Boards, & incidentally do something also for the Furman University at Greenville, & the Johnson Female University, recently incorporated at Anderson C.H. . . ."

The school at Anderson had been established in 1848, and the trustees, led by Elias Earle, Judge Reed, Daniel Brown, and others, paid a deserved tribute to Dr. Johnson because of his labors for female education by naming the new school "in honor of the great Dr. Johnson of Edgefield village." Dr. Johnson was invited to become chancellor of the school, and held that position about five years but did not serve as a regular instructor. The records of that school and of the Baptist Church at Anderson were unfortunately destroyed on May 1, 1865, by a raid of Federal troops.

Advertisements in the newspapers of that day stated that "good boarding, including Washing, Fire and Candles, may be had at either the Hotels, or in private families, at from $6 to $7 per month." The curriculum included in addition to the ordinary secondary subjects, some special subjects, such as drawing, painting, embroidery, and music "on piano and guitar."

The original structure was an eight-room brick building which stood on the spot now occupied by the Baptist parsonage. Mrs. Mary E. Daniel, a lady from Maine, was probably the favorite teacher. Mr. J. S. Murray was principal and taught Latin and Greek. William Wagstaff, an Englishman who had been a soldier at the Battle of Waterloo, taught music in the school, as did Miss Emilia Reed. The institution prospered beyond the expectations of its promoters, and in its fifth year Dr. Johnson delivered an address in which he set forth the superiority of the university system of education, and put the question, "If the university system be the better one for boys and young men, why should it not be for girls and young women?"

The trustees of the seminary gave the subject serious consideration and resolved to raise their institution to a university, where females might be instructed and graduated in every branch of learning and science known to the country at that time. An application was therefore successfully made to the legislature of the state in December, 1852, for a charter with powers to carry out the objects desired, and in February, 1853, the university commenced its exercises with an able faculty, under Dr. Johnson as chancellor.

It was said that when Dr. Johnson entered a schoolroom, every student rose to her feet and remained standing in silence until he was seated.

Dr. Johnson and his daughter lived in the house at the head of Manning Street that was still standing almost a century later. It was built with a first floor basement above the street, and a wide flight of steps leading up from the street to the main story in front.

The university system worked exceedingly well and the institution was patronized to a most encouraging extent. In 1853 there were 119 students enrolled and prospects were bright for a greatly increased number in 1854. Accordingly several additional members were added to the faculty, and every arrangement deemed necessary was made for the comfort and convenience of the students.

A new building was erected on University Hill. It was a two-story structure with projecting wings on both sides, the whole surmounted by a cupola. The dormitories were in a large three-story brick house, on one side. That house was burned in 1883 or 1884. The University Sanitarium later occupied the site.

The young ladies of the university gave their college publication the sophisticated title, *Le Bas Bleu,* and the *Edgefield Advertiser,* acknowledging the first number, commented:

"We acknowledge the first number of this petite publication. It is issued under the direction of certain young ladies of the 'Johnson Female Academy' at Anderson C.H. Making its appearance . . . in the Springtime of the year, we should have preferred greeting our fair sister as 'The Blue *Bird*' rather than as 'The Blue *Stocking.*' In spite of her name, however, we wish 'Le Bas Bleu' much success. May she go on her way lightly and cheerily

"Roving forever from flower to flower,
Kissing all buds that are pretty and sweet."

Meanwhile, the South Carolina Baptist State Convention had decided to sponsor a college for the higher education of females, action to this effect having been taken at the meeting of the Convention in Greenville in 1853. Dr. Johnson had declined re-election as president and had been succeeded by Dr. James C. Furman. The new president placed Dr. Johnson, Dr. J. S. Mims, and Rev. Z. Watkins on a committee to report on enlarging the operations of the Convention. Dr. Johnson reported for his committee in part as follows, according to the minutes of 1853:

"The convention has obtained a charter for a university which is in successful operation. By this arrangement, one of the grand designs sought to be accomplished by the organization of the convention is matured into an agency of elevated character. . . . We recommend that the convention become a more thoroughly missionary body . . . that it extend its fostering care to the Bible cause; to the cause of publication; to female as well as male education; and to the promotion and extension of the Sunday-school system."

The report was adopted and a committee, consisting of Rev. J. G. Landrum, T. P. Brockman, and Professor Edwards, of Furman University, was "appointed to take into consideration the subject of female education as a denominational interest, and to report at the next meeting a plan for the action of the convention."

While Johnson University was considered a Baptist institution, with the support of the Saluda Association, it was not controlled by the State Convention. However, with the decision of the Convention to establish a school for young ladies, efforts were made to have it located at Anderson, with the transfer of the University and its facilities to the Convention.

This action was taken at a meeting of Anderson citizens held at the courthouse on June 9, 1854, "for the purpose of soliciting the location of the said college at this place and taking such measures necessary to effect the object."

The citizens of Greenville likewise held a meeting in the courthouse at that place to seek the location of the new college in Greenville. That meeting was held in June, 1854, and it was proposed to transfer the Male and Female Academies to the denomination.

A money gift of $20,000 from Greenville seems to have been the deciding factor, and on December 25, 1854, the trustees of the academies conveyed all their charter rights to the trustees appointed by the Baptist Convention for the purpose of establishing a college for women on the old site. The Greenville Baptist Female College was thus an outgrowth of the old Female Academy of which Dr. Johnson had been principal twenty-five years earlier. His benediction must have rested in a peculiar measure upon this college, which has justified its existence many times over, even to the present day. That school in its new status as a college went into operation the first Wednesday in February, 1857.

Today (1949) it is the Woman's College of Furman University.

Truly Dr. Johnson has been called "father of female higher education in South Carolina."

At the commencement exercises of the Johnson University in September, 1854, appreciation of Dr. Johnson was expressed in the presentation to him of a silver pitcher from the faculty. Rev. J. Scott Murray, in making the presentation, said: ". . . It would be wholly a work of supererogation for me to dwell on the devotion of your life to the advancement of religion and science—for in both these departments of Christian labor, you have made an impression upon thousands of immortal souls which can never be eradicated. None in this State have done more to advance religion and science than yourself, and none are more worthy of the gratitude and gratulation of the friends of both. . . ."

After expressing thanks for "this beautiful article of domestic comfort," and appreciation of the fine co-operation of professors and teachers, Dr. Johnson said: "You have been pleased, Sir, to advert to *my* services in the cause of Female Education. When I engaged in those services it was from a sense of duty for 'the weaker sex', whose proper training had been overlooked by the *stronger*. The State had established a College for her *boys,* but her *girls* were left to acquire knowledge as best they might, from the liberality of private enterprize, or parental affection. The result was, that out of Charleston, no public Academy or High School invited females to its rich store of learning by means of competent teachers with the advantages of apparatus and library. Progress, however, has been making to a higher order of things for females. And now at the distance of nearly half a century, I behold, with unspeakable delight, High Schools, Colleges, and even an University for females, opening, with inviting aspect, their portals for the entrance of the girls, that they may become fitted for the noble stations designed for their occupancy by the common Father of all his children.

"Whatever agency my *poor services* may have had in the progress of events to the present blessed results in favor of Female Education, is all of the Lord. To His name be all the praise and glory."

The Johnson University flourished until the Civil War began, and it is regarded as the foundation of Anderson College of the present day. The 1916–1917 catalogue of that school stated: "The old Johnson Seminary went down in the ruins of the Civil War, but its ideals passed on to another generation and culminated in Anderson College. . . . It was Dr. Wm. B. Johnson, in his day distinguished in the South and the nation as a leader of progress, who planted the ideal of a woman's college in the heart of Anderson."

Dr. John E. White, writing of the "shadowy forms" in the background of Anderson College, states:

". . . Among them 'clarissimum nobilissimum' is the figure of Dr. William Bullein Johnson. When the history of South Carolina and Southern Baptists comes to be written and truth gets a clear hearing, its angel will dip a pen in the blue and write his name among the greatest religious and educational forces of his country in the last century. Some men are fundamental to whatever they touch, tho, alas, for the rarity of minds and hearts that faithfully trace the vital impulse they have imparted, without which the institutions of their pride and glory would never have survived. We have the Saluda Baptist Association, the South Carolina Baptist Convention, the Southern Baptist Convention, and Anderson College: Their walls about us stand, their influences of good around us are flowing, but who sees the naked hands, and among them as large, if not larger than any, this one giant's hand of William B. Johnson. . . . It is interesting and significant that God sends His prophets out, one here and one there. Richard Furman laid the foundations for South Carolina Baptists in the education of men. Dr. Wm. B. Johnson at the same time discerned with equal passion the potency of Christian womanhood and pioneered for the Baptists in a big way in that field which is now our largest field of enterprise in South Carolina."

Chapter XX

"To Thy Name Be All the Glory!"

Dr. Johnson's physical condition was growing weaker, and after a residence of about five years in Anderson, in 1858, he removed to the home of his son-in-law, Col. G. F. Townes, in Greenville. He was then seventy-six years of age.

Concerning the circumstances, Dr. Johnson wrote in his "Reminiscences": ". . . It being the winter season, I was seized by a severe cold followed by a cough that no remedies succeeded in removing. In this state of my case, the physicians advised me to spend my winters in Florida. This advice I determined to follow, and as I intended to take with me a servant only, I accepted the invitation of my son-in-law, Col. G. F. Townes, who had married my younger daughter, to remove to his home in Greenville, that I might leave my elder daughter with her sister during my absence in Florida. I was however prevented, in the first year of my removal, from going to Florida by a spell of sickness, from which I did not recover in time for visiting Florida in the proper season. My physician then adopted a course of treatment for my cough, which relieved me from it. But unfortunately, I was some months after, again afflicted with a severe cold and my cough returned, but with such an abatement of its former force, that I abandoned the intention of trying Florida for its cure.

"Since the sickness above mentioned, I have suffered interruptions in my health, but I thank my heavenly Father that I have not been wholly laid aside from his service. He has permitted me to preach in the Baptist Meeting House of this place, and in the country; and on other occasions to speak for his cause in addresses to the students of the Seminary and the Schools; to assist in the formation of a new Association, called the Greenville Baptist Association; and to write this book of Reminiscences of Departed Brethren and sketches of my own life."

Climaxing the efforts of Dr. Johnson in behalf of ministerial education was the establishment of the Southern Baptist Theological Seminary at Greenville in 1859.

The *Southern Enterprise* of October 6, 1859, reported that the institution opened "on Monday last at 9 o'clock without any formality or public ceremony at the old Baptist church building." The faculty included Dr. James P. Boyce, first president; Dr. John A. Broadus, Dr. Basil Manly, Jr., and Dr. William Williams. Twenty-six young men were present to begin their courses of study, as outlined by the respective instructors.

Dr. Johnson, by invitation of the chairman of the faculty, offered "a solemn and earnest prayer to Almighty God for His blessings on the Institution, its Professors and Students, and the great and important labors upon which they were about to enter."

After the professors "in a brief and lucid manner unfolded the general plan of studies connected with their several departments," the chairman of the faculty, Dr. Boyce, stated that Dr. Johnson would address a few remarks to the faculty and students. He did so in a very impressive and interesting manner. He contrasted the present state of things in the Baptist denomination with the times when he entered the ministry, more than half a century ago. Then, no such institution existed among us in this country, and few, and comparatively inferior, were the advantages and opportunities of education. He spoke of the favorable era in the world's history at which the institution begins, and the vast fields opened, by the providence of God, for ministerial labor, and the great duty of young men, entering into those fields, being prepared and thoroughly furnished with armor for the conflict. He expressed his high appreciation of the faculty and congratulated the students present on the favorable opportunity furnished them, by this "School of the Prophets," for instruction in the knowledge and duties pertaining to their high calling; admonishing them, however, that the Bible alone was the religion of Christians. Dr. Johnson, in the course of his remarks, spoke of the satisfaction and happiness he experienced in witnessing the auspicious commencement of an institution which he regarded of so much value and importance, and which had long been an object of the prayers, hopes, and labors of good men.

"In one thing, an able Faculty, the most material of all human agencies for success and exalted with every Institution of learning, the Theological Seminary at Greenville is indeed fortunate, and most signally blessed. I do not think I speak in a spirit of partiality in saying, that with this Faculty may be found an amount of talents, genius and learning not surpassed by any other, of equal number, in the United States. True, they are comparatively young men, and their Institution as yet unknown in the list of ancient and renowned colleges, but there are the best reasons for expecting its speedy rise to an equal rank with the foremost of its class in any part of the country. No Institution of its kind—it may be said without disparagement—affords better models for preachers. This would be the testimony of the enlightened of all denominations. It is the testimony already expressed by many who have had the opportunity of hearing and judging. Young men of talents and promise, who are seldom slow in discriminating, and who know how to appreciate the merits of teachers, will delight in the advantages offered by the Seminary, and prosperity and usefulness must, with the blessing of God, be its destiny.

"This imperfect estimate of the merits of this new Institution is expressed in no mere commonplace spirit of commendation. There are occasions when candor and simple justice require utterances of approval, and surely this is such."

For the establishment of the Southern Baptist Theological Seminary, Furman University had emptied itself, surrendering its endowment fund of $26,000 for theological education, and its theological library, in addition to its professor of theology, James P. Boyce, under whose magnificent leadership the Baptists of South Carolina had completed the raising of $100,000 as an inducement for the Seminary to be located in Greenville. The sum was matched by a like sum raised elsewhere.

The long dream of Richard Furman, Johnson, and the elder Manly for a central theological seminary at length was realized under the able direction of younger men. Dr. Johnson was one of the trustees of the Seminary.

And so the aged soldier of the cross carried on. On his seventy-eighth birthday in 1860, he sat down to write his "Reminiscences" —and continued his writing off and on for two years, completing them on his eightieth birthday, with the following paragraph:

"And now that I am permitted, in the good providence of my heavenly Father, to bring these Reminiscences and Sketches to a close on this day, the 13th of June, 1862, on which I have reached my eightieth year, I desire to acknowledge with a sincere and grateful heart His favor and mercy in sustaining me through my infirmities in the undertaking.

"I desire also humbly to commit to his benediction this feeble effort to promote His Holy Cause."

He signs his full name: "William Bullein Johnson."

Dr. Johnson had been in comparatively good health that year. His daughter, Elizabeth, writing her brother, Thomas, in March, 1862, told him: "Father sends you word that he is glad you are going [to the war], that he firmly believes in our success. His health is pretty good, but he feels the bad weather—so much rain. Colonel Townes' oldest daughter, Ella, just 17, has been very ill for six weeks, and is now just able to sit up a little. I have been sick with a kind of Neuralgic Rheumatism in my neck and head, but am getting better. The rest are well. . . . Our country is full of distress—but I fear we have not seen the worst. Anna writes me that her husband has gone back, but she hopes he will return. He has recovered, but one leg is shorter than the other."

Anna was Dr. Johnson's granddaughter, Anna Butler, who had married John Lake Nicholson, of Edgefield.

Dr. Johnson's life span was working out with characteristic exactness. He made arrangements for the disposition of his worldly goods, and wrote in meticulous detail to his son, Thomas, on July 12, 1862, his reasons for leaving the bulk of his property to his daughter, Elizabeth:

Mr. Thomas H. Johnson,
My dear Son,
It is a long time since we have heard from, or of, you, & we feel very anxious to have a line from you. Perhaps the Telegraph or mail route is so interrupted, as to render the communication very difficult, or impracticable. I will risk this letter, however, in the hope of its safe transmission, & a like return of an answer.

On the 13th of last month [June] I reached my eightieth year, & have therefore entered my eighty-first year. I am feeble, but not sick, sleep comfortably, & have a pretty good appetite. I take a ride every fair day, but am still troubled with a cough. Its force is very much abated, however.

Elizabeth's health is much improved, & the rest of the family are in comfortable health. We have lately heard from Anna at Edgefield, & that she is in delicate health. She has three children. Before I had written this I was called out to see a young lady from Edgefield, who informed me that Anna was improving in her health.

As I must naturally expect my death will soon occur, I have made my will in which I have made provision for you & your children, besides the legacy to my namesake.

By losses thro your brothers in New Orleans, I am now a loser of about $20,000; so that I have no great amount to leave to my heirs. In the distribution of this amount, I have left the largest portion to Elizabeth, for the following reasons: 1st. For sometime before your Mother's death, the care of the family rested upon Elizabeth, & since that event, *altogether,* notwithstanding her feeble health.

2. Her present state of health is improved, but still she is often afflicted with neuralgic visitations, that confine her to the bed & room for several days at a time. And it is not improbable, that she may be confined to her bed for months & even years by the same disease before she dies. To bear her expences will require, under such circumstances, no small amount of means. And I am sure that none of my children would wish to know that she was dependent upon other resources than her own.

3. I have another reason. None of my children have done well as to this world. And I have confidence in Elizabeth's principles to believe, that if any of her brothers or her sister, or their descendants should be in distress, she would relieve them. These reasons, my dear Son, have determined me to give the largest portion of my small estate to your sister, Elizabeth: one portion during her life, & the other in fee simple.

At my death, you will receive a few hundred dollars, & at Elizabeth's death, perhaps from two to three thousand dollars, & then what she may leave you or your children in her will.

I hope, therefore, that you will be satisfied with my disposition made in my will.

I suppose that you have not yet been called into the action of *fighting the enemy,* but have only been preparing to do so. My daily prayer is that you may be prepared to do your duty to God & your country. Be steadfast in your faith & trust in the God of battles. "The Lord reigneth. Let the earth rejoice. Let the multitude of isles be glad thereof." "Be still & know that I am God!" *We shall triumph,* though severely chastised. . . . I pray for them [the North] as my enemies, that God may have mercy on them, change their hearts, give them new views, that they may turn from their awful wickedness & live.

When you write home, give our love to your wife & the children.

Your affectionate Father,
W. B. Johnson

The letter was written at Greenville, July 12, 1862, and a postscript stated: "I assure you that, in the bequest of the larger portion to Elizabeth, I have acted from a conviction of duty, without the slightest suggestion from her."

Before three months had elapsed, the father and son had both answered the higher summons.

On the first day of October, 1862, Dr. Johnson had gone about his daily routine, perhaps enjoying the drive he was accustomed to take. He had walked about the house and conversed about arrangements connected with his death in the same calm manner in which he was wont to speak of ordinary affairs. He had penned a note to Dr. James C. Furman, who spoke of these details in a tribute before the next meeting of the Southern Baptist Convention.

Now as the day is drawing to a close and he sits on the piazza where the last rays of a glorious autumn sun are gleaming, he talks with Ella Townes, his step-granddaughter. There is an unusual tie of devotion between the two—the one so young, the other so old. Ella has read his "Reminiscences," and they are talking, perhaps, of the long, long past and of the beckoning future.

"How grateful you must be, Grandfather, for doing so much good!" Ella remarks.

Grandfather murmurs very softly, "Not unto me, not unto me—but to Thy Name, O God, be all the glory!"

Does the soft white hair framing the serene countenance take on the glow of a halo? Do the penetrating eyes look far beyond Ella into the mysteries beyond the sunset?

Rising to his feet, the beloved Grandfather walks feebly into the house, to his room. Retiring, he falls into a deep dream of peace—a dream from which he does not awaken until the lengthening shadows of another day close gently about him like a curtain, veiling from even those nearest and dearest to him the glories of the other world into which he has entered.

*　*　*　*　*

A formality befitting him marked the announcement of his death which appeared in the press of the day:

DEATH OF REV. W. B. JOHNSON, D.D—The *Confederate Baptist* announces the death of Dr. Johnson, on the 2d inst., at the residence of his son-in-law, Col. G. F. Townes, in Greenville. He was out and apparently in good health the day before. He was about eighty years of age and was held in high veneration and esteem.

The citizens of Anderson unanimously requested that his body be interred there, and the remains were removed to the house he had occupied there. On the seventh of October the funeral services were held. The casket, preceded by Johnson University students, walking two and two, was borne to the Baptist Church, where services were conducted by Rev. J. Scott Murray. In the church-yard his body rested. Several sermons were preached in his honor, and the seminary professors, associations, and conventions passed resolutions commemorating his service. Dr. H. T. Cook, in an address delivered before the State Convention in 1909, related:

"Judge O'Neall pronounced him the foremost Baptist for 30 years. His ex-pastor, Richard Furman, Jr., affirmed that Furman University was due to him more than any other one man. But it was left to an anonymous pupil to rescue from oblivion her old master in the school room, erect, dignified, lacking somewhat in sympathy and softness but genial and accessible, a terror to evil doers, scathing in rebuke, but whose commendation was something to work for, sweat for, lose sleep and food for, and herself a teacher, laid this wreath upon his last resting place—

"Vacation—long vacation
Has come to thee at last;
Dismissed all cares and troubles,
Things now but of the past.

"Teacher no longer, but learner
Before the great white throne,
Thou sitt'st to hear God's lessons
And make them all thine own."

In conclusion Dr. Cook said:

"Had Dr. Johnson been spared three years longer to see the material and immaterial possessions of his beloved State descending into the bottomless charybdis of a ferocious defeat, he would not have craved exemption from the common ruin and humiliation of his people. For far above the fierce passions of men the stars were still shining and the ancient edict was still in force: They that turn many to righteousness shall shine as the stars of the firmament forever and ever."

In the *Confederate Baptist* appeared a tribute from the faculty of the Southern Baptist Theological Seminary, in which it was said:

"The Faculty of the Southern Baptist Theological Seminary, in view of the death of our esteemed and beloved brother, Rev. Wm. B. Johnson, D.D., deem it their privilege to unite in bearing an affectionate tribute to his memory. . . . A minister of the Gospel since 1805, holding, during a large part of his life, positions of honor and influence among his brethren; one of the earliest and most earnest advocates, both of general and of ministerial education; brother Johnson stood connected, in the public mind, with all the most prominent benevolent enterprises of the denomination in America. In the organization of this Seminary, he took an active part; and, both as a trustee, and by his personal influence, sought to promote its interests. The Professors cherish the recollection of his cordial friendship, pious counsels and unvarying kindness, both to themselves and to their students; and grieve that his venerable form will be no more found in their assemblages. . . ."

In the *Southern Enterprise* of Greenville, it was said:

". . . His great ability, learning, piety, and untiring energy, his long life of devotion to the cause of the Kingdom of Christ, his love of truth and of duty, and uniform adherence to principle, the extent of his labors as a preacher for fifty-eight years, as an instructor of youth, having been for the middle and upper part of South Carolina a pioneer in female education, unrivaled for his success in imparting sound and solid instruction, intellectual and moral, his services in establishing and promoting schools, and in the cause of education generally, his writing—all these, and other considerations, in the life of this truly great man, have conferred on him a fame which will endure with the history and literature of the country."

Said the *Edgefield Advertiser:* ". . . For many long years of faithful duty, Dr. Johnson dwelt in this community, and although other years with their changes have passed since he departed to another field of usefulness, yet we cannot forget in Edgefield to lay a wreath of reverential regard upon the grave that closes over his strongly marked life of Christian beneficence.

"The deceased was a soldier of the Cross who feared not man, nor turned aside from his duties for the love of man. In his pastoral life he dared not dishonor his Master's cause by a complaisant, faltering discharge of his obligations, he ever spoke promptly, and often severely, to error wherever it appeared—whether in the old or the young, the learned or the unlearned, the rich or the poor. The mere garb of sanctimony was no barrier against his searching lessons, and the panoply of sin had no terrors to deter him from the rebuke which it deserved. He was a firm censor under the Gospel's requirements, and, like old John Bunyan, was no respecter of persons in his exposure of wrong and his vindication of right, whether Bible *Truths* or Bible *Duties* were the subjects of his discourses. Perhaps his avocation of teaching the young tended to impart this quality of sternness to the tone of his religious instructions. Whatever produced it, it was perhaps the secret of his long-continued success and acceptableness, both as a teacher and a preacher. Neither was his character at all deficient in the gentler graces of his religion. He was as kind to the poor (though few except his beneficiaries ever knew it) as any who has lived amongst us. He was scrupulously polite in his entercourse with men, setting an example of uniform courtesy, tending to exhibit the lesson that the true Christian is, after all, the true gentleman. As a teacher, he is remembered and beloved to this day by many who feel that they owe their mental improvement to his conscientious care for their advancement, while yet he held upon them the reins of a rigorous but wholesome authority. As a preacher of the Word, there are those in Heaven as well as on Earth who will bear immortal testimony to his faithfulness. . . ."

At the next meeting of the Southern Baptist Convention, held in Augusta, Georgia, in May, 1863, a brief memorial was paid to Dr. Johnson's memory, and in the address delivered by Dr. J. C. Furman, he said: "The traits of his character were very distinctly marked. A clear, logical intellect, fixedness of purpose, promptness and punctuality in the discharge of obligations great or small, transparent honesty (including in this term remarkable sincerity and candor), independence of thought without litigiousness, and a large public-spiritedness; these were some of the traits obvious to all. Whatever he undertook, he did faithfully and thoroughly. During his long life he shared the public confidence as a man of high, unquestioned Christian integrity. . . . Dr. Johnson's death was a scene of tranquility and peace. Surely and quietly he reposed upon the merits of his Redeemer and Lord. As the sun was going down in the close of a glorious autumn day, he sank to his final rest with the softness of an infant's sleep."

The State Baptist Convention, meeting at Darlington in 1863, called for a sermon in honor of the memory of the late Dr. Johnson. At its conclusion, Rev. J. Scott Murray moved that a committee of one from each constituent of the body be appointed to raise funds to erect a monument over the remains of the honored brother. The accomplishment of the plans was delayed because of the stress of war, but in January, 1867, a comprehensive sketch of his life appeared in the *South Carolina Baptist* under the pen of "R. F.," said to have been Richard Furman, grandson of Dr. Richard Furman. It was copied from the *Religious Herald*. The Convention, meeting in Anderson that year, 1867, heard the report of the committee that "in view of the gloomy present and gloomier future they have been unable to devise any plan for carrying out the object entrusted to them, and regard it at present impracticable. They hope in more favorable times it may still be accomplished."

It was not until 1909—47 years after Dr. Johnson's death—that the "favorable time" arrived. It was due to the untiring efforts of Mrs. R. C. Hoyt, a former student at Johnson University that the State Convention erected a monument to his memory. Mrs. Hoyt had private interviews with different members of the Convention and finally made a formal request before the Convention itself. At the meeting of the State Convention in Anderson, December 7–10, 1909, the committee, of which J. W. Quattlebaum was chairman, reported:

"The recently appointed committee on the Johnson monument have brought out and set up in its appointed place, the shaft that had been waiting so many years in its granite bed. . . ."

At the request of the committee, "A Sketch of the Life and Services of W. B. Johnson," prepared by H. T. Cook, was read.

The tombstone is a shaft of classic simplicity with drapery denoting the scholar. The inscription reads:

Wm. B. Johnson
1782–1862

Preacher-Teacher
Patriot, President
Triennial, Southern,
and South Carolina
Baptist Conventions.
Loyal To His Master.
Honored By His Brethren.
Loved By His Friends.

Bibliography

Ball, William W., *The State That Forgot*. Indianapolis, 1932.
Cathcart, William, Editor, *The Baptist Encyclopaedia*. Philadelphia, 1881.
Christian, John T., *A History of the Baptists*. Nashville, 1926.
Christian, J. T., *History of the Baptists in Louisiana*. Shreveport, 1923.
Cook, Harvey T., "Life of W. B. Johnson," in 1909 *Annual of the State Convention of the Baptist Denomination in South Carolina*.
Cook, Harvey T., *The Life Work of James Clement Furman*. Greenville, S. C., 1926.
Garrett, T. H., *History of the Saluda Baptist Association*. Richmond: B. F. Johnson, 1896.
Green, Edwin L., *History of Richland County*. Columbia, 1932.
Hatcher, William E., *Life of J. B. Jeter, D.D.* Baltimore, 1887.
Holcombe, Henry, *Series of Letters*. 1812.
Johnson, Helen, Mss. "William Bullein Johnson."
Johnson, William Bullein. "Reminiscences." Unpublished Mss. in University Caroliniana Library, Columbia, S. C.
Johnson, William Bullein, *The Gospel Developed*. Richmond, 1846.
McGlothlin, W. J., *Baptist Beginnings in Education*. Nashville, 1926.
Mills, Robert, *Statistics of South Carolina*. Charleston, 1825.
Mims, Mrs. J. L., *History of the Edgefield Baptist Church*. Published serially in the *Edgefield Advertiser* beginning Feb. 28, 1923.
Owens, Loulie Latimer, "Early Work of the State Convention." The *Baptist Courier*, March 22, 1945.
Paxton, W. E., *A History of the Baptists of Louisiana*. St. Louis, 1888.
Periodicals: *Annuals of the State Convention of the Baptist Denomination in South Carolina; Augusta Chronicle & Sentinel;* Greenwood (S. C.) *Index-Journal; Minutes of the Edgefield Baptist Association; South Carolina Historical and Genealogical Magazine; The Baptist Courier; The Southern Light,* Edgefield; *The State,* Columbia, S. C.

Raymond, Charles A., *A Statement of Facts,* etc. Edgefield, 1854.
R. F., "William B. Johnson, D.D." the *Religious Herald.* 1867.
Taylor, James B., *Memoirs of Rev. Luther Rice.* Second Edition. Broadman Press: Nashville, 1937.
Townes Papers. Mss. Used by permission of University South Caroliniana Library, Columbia.
Townsend, Leah, *South Carolina Baptists 1670–1805.* Florence, S. C., 1935.
Vandiver, Louise Ayer, *History of Anderson County.* Atlanta, 1928.
Wallace, David Duncan, *The History of South Carolina.* Vol. IV. Biographical. New York, 1934.
W. J. M. author of Sketch of William Bullein Johnson in *Dictionary of American Biography.* Ed., Dumas Malone. New York, 1933.
Woodson, Hortense, *Publish Glad Tidings.* Pageant. Edgefield, 1945.
Much material credited in this work to sources other than here listed was found copied in files of the *Edgefield (S. C.) Advertiser.*

About the Authoress

Miss Hortense Caroline Woodson was born at Edgefield, South Carolina on July 7, 1896. Her father, Tucker Everett Woodson, was a graduate of the Southern Baptist Theological Seminary when it was still located in Greenville, South Carolina. Her mother, Agatha Abney Woodson, was of the family line of Richard Furman.

Hortense Woodson was a granddaughter of the former editor of the *Edgefield Advertiser*, Joseph Abney (1822-1870), which likely accounts for her choice of a career in journalism. After attending Winthrop College, Miss Woodson began working for the *Newberry* (S. C.) *Herald & News*, 1921-1925. She then worked in production and as a reporter for the *Edgefield Advertiser*, 1926-1952, while also serving as special correspondent for the *Augusta* (Ga.) *Herald* in 1930, and the *Greenville News*, 1930-1950.

Miss Woodson took an active interest in civic and historical affairs, serving as a trustee for Anderson College from 1957 to 1961, and as a secretary on the staff of U. S. Senator Strom Thurmond from 1960 to 1968. She was a member of the South Carolina Historical Society, and the South Carolina Baptist Historical Society.

Miss Woodson's life centered around her local church. She was an integral part of the Sunday School, Training Union and Woman's Missionary Society of the Edgefield Baptist Church. She served as the clerk and historian for the Edgefield Baptist Association,* of which her church was a member, and was once state secretary for the South Carolina Women's Christian Temperance Union.

Miss Woodson passed quietly away to her eternal reward on October 20, 1990.

---

* Hortense C. Woodson. *History of the Edgefield Baptist Association, 1807-1957.* Edgefield, S. C.: Edgefield Advertiser Press, 1957.

Appendix A

The
Solemn Covenant
of the
Baptist Church
in the
Town of Columbia, South Carolina.
1ᵗ Octᵃ 1809

Whereas it is the incumbent duty of those who are favor'd with the dispensation of Gospel Grace, to embrace God's Covenant, acknowledge his Government, profess his name, and unite together in the faith and fellowship of the Gospel; We, whose names are hereunto annexed, do now, as in the presence of the Great Eternal God, who knows the secrets of all hearts, and in the presence of Angels and men, acknowledge ourselves under the most solemn obligations to be the Lord's; and we do solemnly covenant and agree:

1ˢᵗ That we will take the only living and true God; One God in three persons persons; The Father, Son, and Holy Ghost, to be our God.

2ⁿᵈ We unreservedly and solemnly give up ourselves, and all we possess to Almighty God; to be ordered, directed, and disposed of by him, according to the counsel of his holy will. And this we do, in an humble dependence on the Grace of the Holy Spirit to aid and support us in these sacred engagements, hoping for acceptance and salvation, through the merit and mediation of our Lord Jesus Christ.

3d We take the Scriptures of the Old and New Testament to be our rule of faith and practice, in the great concerns of religion, and for a general directory in the affairs of Life; and particularly for transacting the affairs of the Church.

Courtesy of First Baptist Church, Columbia, South Carolina

Appendix A

Covenant of the First Baptist Church of Columbia, South Carolina, adopted on October 1, 1809.

The
Solemn Covenant
of the
Baptist Church
in the
Town of Columbia, South Carolina
1st Octr. 1809

Whereas it is the incumbent duty of those who are favor'd with the dispensation of Gospel Grace, to embrace God's Covenant, acknowledge his Government, profess his name, and unite together in the faith and fellowship of the Gospel; We, whose names are hereunto annexed, do now, as in the presence of the Great Eternal God, who knows the secrets of all hearts, and in the presence of Angels and men, acknowledge ourselves under the most solemn obligations to be the Lord's; and we do solemnly covenant and agree:

1st. That we will take the only living and true God; One God in three persons; The Father, Son, and Holy Ghost, to be our God.

2nd. We unreservedly and solemnly give up ourselves, and all we possess to Almighty God; to be ordered, directed, and disposed of by him, according to the counsel of his holy will. And this we do, in an humble dependence on the Grace of the Holy Spirit to aid and support us in these sacred engagements, hoping for acceptance and salvation, through the merit and mediation of our Lord Jesus Christ.

3^d. We take the Scriptures of the Old and New Testament to be our rule of faith and practice, in the great concerns of religion, and for a general directory in the affairs of Life; and particularly for transacting the affairs of the Church.

Appendix A

4th. We promise to maintain communion and fellowship with each other, in the public worship of God, according to the various ordinances of the Gospel; "not forsaking the assembling of ourselves together, as the manner of some is," but embracing all regular and convenient seasons for this purpose, as the providence of God shall permit: and that we will exercise christian forbearance and love, one toward another, praying for, and sympathizing with each other in the various circumstances of life, and using every laudable endeavor to provoke to love and good works.

5th. We promise, individually, to pay a respectful regard to the advice and admonitions of the Church, and to be subject to its discipline, as directed by the word of God, and as conducted in the Spirit of the Gospel.

6th. We promise to contribute in a reasonable manner according to our ability, for the support of public Worship, and the relief of the poor in the Church, and to use our influence to forward and promote the interests of the Redeemer's kingdom in the World. That we will be careful to conduct ourselves with uprightness and integrity, and in a peaceful and friendly manner, toward mankind in general, and towards serious christians, of all descriptions in particular: That we will pay a conscientious regard to civil government, and give it our support, as an ordinance of God.

And this Covenant we make, with the free and full consent of our Souls, hoping through rich, free, and boundless Grace, we shall therein be accepted of God, unto Eternal Life, through Jesus Christ our Lord, to whom be Glory and Majesty, power and dominion everlasting, AMEN.

The signatures of the white members to the above Covenant follow on the next sheet

Courtesy of First Baptist Church, Columbia, South Carolina

Appendix A

4th. We promise to maintain communion and fellowship
with each other, in the public worship of God, according to
the various ordinances of the Gospel; "not forsaking the assemb-
-ling of ourselves together, as the manner of some is," but embra-
-cing all regular and convenient seasons for this purpose, as
the providence of God shall permit: and that we will exer-
-cise christian forbearance and love, one toward another, pray-
-ing for, and sympathizing with each other in the various circum-
-stances of life, and using every laudable endeavor to provoke
to love and good works.

5th. We promise, individually, to pay a respectful regards
to the advice and admonitions of the Church, and to be subject
to it's discipline, as directed by the word of God, and as con-
-ducted in the Spirit of the Gospel.

6th. We promise to contribute in a reasonable manner ac-
-cording to our ability, for the Support of Public Worship, and
the relief of the poor in the Church, and to use our influence
to forward and promote the interests of the Redeemer's King-
-dom in the World. That we will be careful to conduct
ourselves with uprightness and integrity, and in a peace-
-ful and friendly manner, toward mankind in general, and
towards serious christians, of all descriptions in particular.
That we will pay a conscientious regard to civil govern-
-ment, and give it our support, as an Ordinance of God.

And this covenant we make, with the free and
full consent of our Souls, hoping through rich, free, and
boundless Grace, we shall therein be accepted of God, unto Eternal Life, through Jesus Christ our Lord, to
whom be Glory and Majesty, power and dominion everlas-
-ting, Amen.

The signatures of the white members to the above Covenant
follow on the next sheet.

Appendix A

Persons Names	When & How Rec'd	When & how separated from	When Restored
William Bullein Johnson	L. 1st October 1809	Di. 5th Decr 1811	30 Jany 1820
Henrietta Johnson	L. " " "	Di. 5th Decr 1811	12 Feb. 1820
Roling Williamson	L. " " "		These two were re-unitd.
J Alexy Williams	L. " " "		
Patience her mark Williams	L. " " "		
John Good	L. " " "		
Jno Clark	L. " " "		1818 Reunited
Ann Taylor	B. " " "	Dead	
Elizabeth R her mark Hood	B. " " "	"	
Lucy Parker	L. 13. Jany 1810	"	
Ann Dickson	L. 9. March "	"	
Samuel Cobb	L. 11 May "	Dc. 20th Septr 1810	
Mrs Rachel Faust	L. 13. Octr "	Di. 2 Febr 1812	
Nathan White Jun?	L. 12. April 1811	Di. 1811	
Thomas Johnson	L. 12 July "	Di. 5th Octr 1811	
Saml Nettles	L. 3d Novr "		
Tiby Nettles	L. 3d Novr "		
	B 3d Novr "		
John Wilkins		Ex. 28. Aug 1819	
Needham Dudley		Dead	
Strickland	B.		
Nicolas Hoodges	A. 1817		Di 1821
John M Clark	1818		

These Members names were trans-
-ferred to another part of this Book
April 1820.——

Aug 4 1826
J.F.M.

Courtesy of First Baptist Church, Columbia, South Carolina

[170]

Appendix A

Persons Names	When & How Rec[eive]^d.	Ch[urc]h When & how separated from	When Restored
William Bullein Johnson	L. 1st October 1809	Di. 6th. Decr. 1811	30. Jan. 1820
Henrietta Johnson	L. " " "	Di. 6th. Decr. 1811	12. Feb. 1820
Roling Williamson	L. " " "		These two were
Alcey Williamson	L. " " "		reunited
Patience Williams	L. " " "		
John Good	L. " " "		
Jno. Clark	L. " " "		1818
Ann Taylor	B. " " "	Dead	Reunited
Elizabeth R. Hood	B. " " "		
Lucy Parker	L. 13. Jany. 1810		
Ann Hickson	L. 9. March "		
Samuel Cobb	L. 11. May "	Di. 20th. Septr. 1810.	
Mrs Rachel Faust	L. 13. Oct^r. "	Di. 2 Feby. 1812	
Nathan White Junr.	L. 12th. April 1811	Di 1811.	
Thomas Johnson	L. 12. July "	Di 5th. Octr. 1811.	
Saml. Nettles	L. 3d. Nov^r. "		
Feby [Phoebe?]Nettles		L. 3d. Nov^r. "	
	B. 3d. Nov^r. "		
John Wilkins		Ex. 28. Aug. 1819	
Needham Dudley		Dead	
Strictland	B.		
Nicolas Hodges	Ac. 1817		Di 1820
John M. Clarke	1818		

These Members names were trans-
-ferred to another part of this Book
April 1820.

Augst. 4 1820
J. T. M.

Editor's Note:

L. = by letter
B. = by baptism
Di. = dismissed
Ex.= excluded
Ac.= by giving an account, or testimony

[171]

Appendix B

"Various are the modes in which the men of the world use their wealth. Some make a display of it in external pomp; some in debaucheries, excess, and prodigality; wasting, with the greatest extravagance, the bounties of Providence; while others with hypocritical humility, content themselves with mean fare. These, clothed in dress far inferior to their circumstances, and living in a manner unbecoming their sphere in life, indulge reflections on the comparative moderation of their desires, and feast themselves on the exalted opinion which they imagine is entertained by others of their frugality, moderation, and humility.....They are therefore as much influenced by the true spirit of the world, as the first two mentioned characters, and display in their conduct as much if not more pride and vanity. Our concern should be to avoid the errors into which each of these characters have fallen." — William B. Johnson (see page 180).

Appendix B

An Admonition Against Worldly Conformity

The Circular Letter
of the Charleston Baptist Association

written by William B. Johnson
and presented at the meeting of the Association
at Jeffer's Creek, South Carolina, November 3, 1810.

To the churches they represent, send Christian salutation:
Beloved Brethren,

Having stated in the preceding Minutes the business we have transacted at our present meeting, we now call your attention to a solution of the query which contains the important subject appointed to be discussed in the Circular Letter of this year, viz. "What is the precise meaning of that rule of duty mentioned in Romans 12:2, respecting conformity to the world?" This passage is as follows: "And be not conformed to this world; but be ye transformed by the renewing of your mind, that ye may prove what is that good, and acceptable, and perfect will of God."

In the execution of our design, we shall, in the first place, explain the term *world*; then point out the sense in which it is to be received in the passage under consideration; and finally proceed to ascertain and illustrate the rule of duty contained in that passage.

From the poverty, or figurative use of language, a word is often so used as to express different ideas or things. This observation applies strictly to the scriptural use of the word *world*. Among its various acceptations we may observe, that sometimes it signifies the Earth, with its diversified productions and inhabitants; as in St. John's Gospel, 1:10, "The World was made by him." Sometimes it signifies Mankind only, as in Romans 3:19, "That all the world may become guilty before God." And sometimes, it signifies the wicked, or irreligious part of mankind, with their lusts and pleasures, sinful principles and actions, together with the things of time, as they are objects of their attention and regard, as in I John 5:19, "We know that we are of God, and the whole world lieth in wickedness;" and in I John 2: 15-16, "Love not the world, neither the things that are in

[173]

the world. If any man love the world the love of the Father is not in him. For all that is in the world, the lust of the flesh, the lust of the eyes, and the pride of life, are not of the Father, but of the world." This last sense of the word is that which the Apostle appears to intend in the passage under consideration.

From this scriptural sense of the term, taken in connection with the prohibition, you will readily perceive, that as whatever things come within the discription of those lusts the Apostle here discribes, belong to the world, so conformity to it in these is forbidden. By this forbidden conformity we understand, a being so influenced by the spirit and example of irreligious men, as to take a part with them in their sinful pursuits and gratifications, of a worldly nature; so as, in proportion, to forsake, injure, or neglect the cause of God and religion: Or else, to bring the maxims, policy, and spirit of the world into our religious profession, exercises and pursuits, may be intended. Of both we are in great danger; both may exist together; and both greatly injure the soul, and dishonor God.

In forming a correct judgment on this subject it is requisite that we make a clear and just distinction between the actions of men which are lawful, and those which are in their nature sinful. Religion does not require that we should differ from our fellow men in things, either natural or civil, nor yet religious, when their conduct is according to the rule of nature, propriety, and Scripture. In things which are lawful, and left to the free choice, prudence, and opinion of men, it becomes the Christian to avoid singularity. For this must make himself, or his profession ridiculous, and offend others. Even the mistakes and prepossessions of men in things of a neutral kind, or of little importance, may be occasionally conformed to, in perfect consistency with a good conscience, and the honor of God; when our real object in so doing is to avoid offense, and gain men to the knowledge and love of the truth. Thus the apostle Paul was to the Jews, as a Jew; to those who were without law (the ceremonial law seems to have been intended) as without law; and became all things to all men, that he might by all means save some. A greater than Paul also, even our Lord Jesus Christ, appears to have avoided singularity in such things as we have discribed: "He came eating and drinking", made himself easy in his manners to persons and companies of various views, and conditions in life; and while he did not strive, nor cry, nor cause his voice to be heard in the street, to occasion tumult, or draw upon him the public attention, he was accessible and kind to all; where bold impiety, self-righteous singularity, and hypocritical pretension did not provoke His displeasure.

But there are certain principles, and actions, which never can be right, being contrary to moral principles of truth and goodness, and to the genius of the gospel: To these, the Christian never must conform; however they may be countenanced by the example of the multitude, or of those who are in the highest stations of honor and power. To such things we wish to direct your attention in the style of caution.

Gross and scandalous sins, the more refined part of mankind, though destitute of true, vital religion, generally censure and avoid; at least such as are accounted dishonorable in civil life. A Christian therefore, must have departed far already from the line of duty and rectitude, before he can come under very strong temptations, from example, to commit such sins; which are directly contrary to the law of God and only to be found in the practice of men who have given up their claim to decency and respect in civil society. Our chief danger lies in those evils which by the arts of false refinement, delusion and folly, are generally accounted excuseable, if not innocent and honorable. Great danger arises here, from the sympathies of our nature and love of society, as well as from mistakes of judgment, and the vicious inclinations sin has implanted in our hearts. But, should we give way to the spirit of the world, we are in danger, also, after being in the first instance drawn into the practice of sins less obvious and disgraceful, of falling at last into those which are more gross and heinous. Thus many who have been once decent in their manners, of amiable dispositions, and even virtuous principles, by giving way to a fondness for merry, idle company, have become eventually the wretched slaves of drunkenness, profanity, and debauchery, and of every pernicious, shameful vice, and crime. Oh! how many amiable youth, of fine talents and promising hopes, have been thus ruined for ever!

Having mentioned the spirit of the world as an important article in this inquiry; let us before we proceed, endeavor to form our judgment correctly on this subject. It is, we conceive, that disposition of the mind which is proper to a state of sin; and opposite to that which is produced by the "renewing of the mind" of which the

Apostle speaks in the text under consideration: A spirit of selfishness, by which men are disposed to please and live to themselves; which affects independence on God, and disregards His laws, government, and grace; a disposition which leads the mind to contemplate and regard this world as its chief good; and limits our views, hopes, and expectations, to things which are temporal, to the exclusion of those which are eternal.

But to return to the division of the subject made above, and to the account given by the Apostle John of the things in the world which we must not love, let it be observed, that the *lust* of the *flesh* means the sensual appetites and sordid passions of our nature. These are manifested in the world by correspondent actions, and lives of sin – such as excess in eating, drinking, and sleeping; indulgence in ease, effeminacy, and indolence; vain amusements, idle diversions and follies among the lovers of pleasure – excessive exertion in cares and labors, among the sons of ambition and avarice – envy, anger, resentment, malice, cruelty, and oppression, among those who are of a proud, suspicious, unjust, and ferocious temper – the various species of criminal connection between the sexes, among the licentious, with the words and actions which lead to them – and in a word, in a too great indulgence in any animal pleasure,[1] though of a lawful kind; and in all gratifications of inclination and appetite which have not a real tendency to promote the glory of God. — A few explanatory remarks invite your attention:

It is a serious truth, that men of the world too generally provoke their appetites to excess, while enjoying the bounties of providence, to their shame and injury. Such indulgence in eating and drinking, besides other bad consequences, enervates both body and mind; and not only when carried to the extent which would be deemed gluttony and drunkenness; but to that extent which goes beyond the proper demands of nature.

The calls to indulgence in ease, sleep, effeminate softness, artificial delicacy, and indolence, on persons in affluence, are frequent and pressing; but these steal away our precious time, rise in their demands, and if indulged, fix a habit which becomes the

---

[1] In the decades preceding the delusion of Darwinian evolution, the use of the term *animal* in this context meant that which pertains to the physical or carnal nature of man, rather than his spiritual or intellectual nature.

enemy of all improvement, intellectual, moral and religious; and the source of many and sore evils. Non-conformity to the world in these, therefore, is required. You, brethren, are to be diligent in the service of God, redeeming the time, because the days are evil.[2]

The idle pleasures, vain amusements, carnal delights and follies of the world, are often represented by their votaries as neither injurious to men, nor dishonorable to God. But we know, that pleasures which are not directed to some rational end, which consume time unprofitably, dissipate the mind and expose it to temptation, are not of God; and therefore not to be conformed to. The state of the heart which these produce, or rather from which they proceed, should be carefully considered. What is the state of the heart in which men who delight in them, as they are generally conducted, attend on theaters, balls, races, frolics,[3] and games of hazard; and what the consequences to which such attendance leads? Do they approach the places where these pleasures are practiced with a single eye to the glory of God; with a desire to do His will; with humble prayer for His blessing; and with self-dedication to His service? Do they return from them with spirituality of mind, having their hearts inflamed with love to God, and their holiness promoted? Alas! Brethren, far other principles lead men to such places; and very different consequences follow from their attendance on them.

While the Christian is careful to avoid hurtful pleasures, and to improve his time and strength to the glory of God; it becomes him also, to avoid that excessive care and labor about the things of the world, which are to be found with men who are stimulated by the sting of covetousness or ambition. Some who think their conduct highly commendable, and are much approved by others, are so immersed by their own choice in cares and labors of this kind, that they have neither time, nor attention for any thing but their worldly employments; and gravely make this their excuse for neglecting both public and private worship, the care of their own souls, and the souls of their families. Thus many wear out their own strength, and life, as well as of their servants and dependants, in the strenuous pursuits of wealth and eminence. While others, though the silken

---

[2] Ephesians 5:16.

[3] frolics: stated social occasions given only to merrymaking, or playing.

sons and daughters of pleasure themselves, yet, by their plans and agents, pursue the same course of interest, and are equally rigorous, even to cruelty, in exacting the utmost exertions in labor from those under their control, to secure and advance their own luxury, pride and ambition. To these things, however approved by men, the Christian must not be conformed.

The indulgence of envy, resentment, malice and revenge, those fires of hell; and the gratification of sensual, licentous appetites, crimes which are too common in the world, are not only such as you must not be conformed to, in act; but must be opposed to in the first thoughts and temptations which lead to them. All these may be indulged in the corrupt heart, in thought and principle, though concealed from the eyes of men. But as Christians you will recollect, that he who says to his brother "thou fool, is in danger of hell fire;"[4] and that "he who looketh upon a woman, to lust after her, hath committed adultery with her in his heart already."[5] – Thus far on the lust of the flesh.

The lust of the eyes, appears to intend the desires of the carnal mind as exercised on the object of sight; and particularly, on the possessions, decorations and splendors of the world. These are coveted as they are beheld, and especially as hope is entertained of their enjoyment: They include landed estates, servants, rich harvest, store of merchandise and goods, gold, silver, and precious stones; elegant houses, sumptuous clothing, costly furniture and glittering equipages,[6] and to some, crowns, scepters, and thrones; together with every object of sight, which being inordinately desired, or prized, alienates the heart from God. The things may be in themselves good, and to some lawful; the evil consists principally in the corrupt desires of the heart.

Carnal men have universally fallen into this error of laying up treasures on earth, by setting their hearts upon the enjoyments of time, as though they formed man's chief good. To this fatal error you must not be conformed. "Lay not up for yourselves treasures upon

---

[4] Matthew 5:22.

[5] Matthew 5:28.

[6] equipages: carriages

earth," said our divine Redeemer, "but in heaven."[7] You are pilgrims on earth, and your life of short continuance; but you look for a "City eternal in the heavens, whose builder and maker is God"[8] In this city earthly treasures are of no avail. They will neither raise you to its honors, nor prepare you for its enjoyments.

When Christians become conformed to the world in this pursuit of wealth and ambition, though the covetous principle may not gain an entire ascendency, yet, the effects are visible and awful. The importance and value of religious duties, Christian privileges, and devout affections, if not forgotten, are lessened in their esteem. The glories of God the Savior, and the advancement of His cause and kingdom, engage but a small part of their attention – the business, cares and pleasures of the world, gain an increasing ascendency over their mind, and in it the light of truth is greatly obscured. In proportion as exertions are made toward self-aggrandizement, and success attends the pursuit, other views arise; wants multiply, and expenses increase. In the multiplicity of these things, no time is left for serious thoughts, and active exertions in the cause of God. Religious affections die. A contracted mind is the consequence of this; and if at any time an act of liberality is performed, it is rather from ostentation, or some improper motive, than from a regard to the glory of God. The result of all is, that the public interests of religion, as well as its spirit, are neglected. In some congregations ministers of the Gospel, though acknowledged to be faithful, are scantily provided for, if at all; while many members of their churches live in a costly manner. Houses erected for the worship of God are constructed of the roughest materials, and in some places are ready to fall to the ground; while the habitations of the worshipers are, not only comfortable, but in some cases elegantly built and furnished. The pious education of children is neglected; while they are either brought up in all the fashionable follies of the age, and decorated with gay clothing, or are permitted to waste their precious time in forming habits for idleness, ignorance, and vice. The religious instruction of servants is entirely neglected, thought their labor is exacted in full measure.

---

[7] Matthew 6:19.

[8] 2 Cor. 5:1; Hebrews 11:10.

Appendix B

We are aware, brethren, of the excuses which are usually made for such neglects, but we know that they are vain, and without just foundation. They originate in an unfeeling, covetous disposition, which is idolatry. The desire to lay up treasures on earth corrupts, as well as contracts the heart; and for excuse in the neglect of duty, which this desire occasions, the pleas just referred to are advanced, only that permission may be obtained from conscience for seeking and retaining uninterruptedly more ample possessions on earth. Such conformity to the world, the rule of duty under consideration forbids.

Various are the modes in which the men of the world use their wealth. Some make a display of it in external pomp; some in debaucheries, excess, and prodigality; wasting, with the greatest extravagance, the bounties of Providence; while others with hypocritical humility, content themselves with mean fare.[9] These, clothed in a dress far inferior to their circumstances, and living in a manner unbecoming their sphere in life, indulge reflections on the comparative moderation of their desires, and feast themselves on the exalted opinion which they imagine is entertained by others of their frugality, moderation, and humility. Let none deceive themselves by these considerations into a persuasion that they are not in the indulgence of the lust of the flesh, and of the eyes. They as eagerly pursue wealth as others; they with as much exultation survey their store as others; and they retain with more miserly niggardness what they have acquired than others. They are therefore as much influenced by the true spirit of the world, as the two first mentioned characters, and display in their conduct as much if not more pride and vanity. Our concern should be to avoid the errors into which each of these characters have fallen. Earthly possessions, as they are the gift of providence, are not to be rejected, but may, under the Divine blessing on honest exertions, be acquired and enjoyed. They are however to be sought from higher motives than our enjoyment of them: in addition to the supply of our own reasonable wants, the good of our fellow-creatures, and above all, the glory of God should be regarded. This truth we hope you will never forget. Permit us however to suggest a caution to those who are engaged in the acquirement of property. Be not too confident of the good use you

---

[9] mean fare: a state of things inferior in grade or quality·

will make of enlarged possessions; and forbear not to do the good that is in your power now, on the supposition that you will do much more in a future day, when your schemes of interest are accomplished. This often proves a deception: for it is a dictate of reason as well as of Scripture, that he who is unjust in that which is least, will be unjust also in much. Which maxim, in its principle, will apply to our obligations to perform acts of beneficence and mercy, as well as to those which respect common justice. Many therefore who have set out with the plausible intention just mentioned, have awfully deviated from their plan in the execution. Instead of having their hearts enlarged with the increase of wealth, they have become more contracted. Contrast the exertions and contributions ordinarily made by men of wealth, with their means – How comparatively trifling! How insignificant! Men who spend on their persons, families, houses and living, vast sums, can afford but small assistance to the public interests or religion, and relief of the poor. Is not this conformity to the world?

In the pride of life men make a display of what they possess, or think they possess; and all for the gratification of the exciting, foolish and impious passion, *pride*. The lust of the eye seeks out and craves the objects, with which, when obtained, the pride of life is wont to manifest its vanity and presumption. Though it delights to show itself in things great and grand, high stations, power, public authority, sumptuous habitations, dress and equipage; and whatever we have already mentioned as the common objects of covetousness and ambition, yet it is not confined to them; but vaunts in personal accomplishments, beauty, sense, activity, elegance of manners, fine taste, superior understanding, learning and eloquence; or in reputation for virtue – as courage, probity, prudence, zeal, generosity and public spirit, with things of a like nature; and in pretentions to excellence in all kinds of business and professions. As it seeks to be commended and admired of men, so it tends to promote flattery, pretentions, dissembling and falsehood among those it accounts its friends; and in assuming a dictatorial style of conversation and conduct toward those who are considered as persons who should submit to its importance, it either produces a servile spirit of compliance, or excites opposition. As it provokes disgust and opposition, which it rarely fails to do, it forms parties, creates con- tention, intrigue, detraction, reviling, resentment, and all the hateful passions; from whence spring quarrels in families, societies, and neighborhoods, and war and bloodshed among nations; and by filling men with ideas of their own importance, it produces self-will, and contempt of rightful authority. When gratified, the proud mind rests with momentary complacence in the contemplation of its own supposed excellence and worth; when disappointed, it rages with resentment against men, and too often in its discontent, utters blasphemies against God. Such is the pride of life; originating in the delusive passion of sinful self-love, which may be found in the cottage as well as in the palace. To this the Christian must not be conformed.

On the second general branch of our subject, we have to observe that Christians conform to the world when they bring a worldly spirit into religion. This has been one of the greatest causes of injury to the church, and a fatal mean of corrupting it. It is done when an attempt is made to bring the doctrines, ordinances and worship of God to the standard of taste which pleases the carnal mind; when human policy and power are relied on for the support and prosperity of the church; and when our views, principles, profession and conduct in religion, are regulated by the maxims or spirit of the world.

The first of these cannot be effected but by perverting the sacred Scriptures, and by changing or abusing the ordinances of God.

We are chargeable with the second, not only when human establishments are resorted to; when the church so united to the state is governed by the civil magistrate; and when the sword and civil authority are relied on for the support and progress of religion; or when pious fraud is introduced, and pretentions, or mechanical operations are used to impose on the judgment, faith and consciences of men; but also, when our reliance for success in religion is placed on the wealth, number and influence of its adherents; on splendid places of worship, and pompous services; and on the learning, popular talents, enterprise, eloquence and address of its ministers; or on the zeal and exertion of its professors – rather than on the spirit and grace of God. That declaration of Holy Writ should never be forgotten, "Not by might, nor by power, but by my spirit, saith the Lord of Hosts."[10] Correspondent to which are the words of our Lord

---

[10] Zechariah 4:6.

Appendix B

Jesus Christ: "Without me ye can do nothing."[11]

Thirdly, we conform to the world in our religious profession, exercises and pursuits, when a regard to worldly advantage and reputation among men, rather than to the interests of the soul and the honor of God, is our governing motive in making religious profession; and when either in ministers, or private Christians, a spirit of pride and confidence in our own knowledge, gifts, graces, popularity and usefulness in indulged, so that our religious services are done more from a secret desire to manifest their excellence, than to perform the duty we owe to God. When our zeal in religion is more to gain adherents to our particular sentiments, and the interests of our party, than to have the interests of Christ and of souls promoted. It is apparent when a spirit of rivalship prevails, and our great concern is to know "Who of us shall be accounted the greatest;"[12] when attempts are made by individuals or churches to restrain Christian liberty, by imposing regulations on opinion and conduct, in things which God has left to the free choice of His people; when individuals aspire to fill places and perform duties for which they are not qualified, or which belong to the province of another; and when a slavish spirit of subjection to the assumed claims of such men induces us to submit to them. The spirit of the world generally operates in the business of controversy and party, especially when angry disputes and contentions arise: then intrigue, misrepresentation, sophistry and censorious judging take place in the church; and all the violent hateful passions are called into operation; in jealousies, "whisperings, swellings, tumults," and too often in revilings and separation; to the injury of religion, and disgrace of its professors. On this subject an apostle says, "For ye are yet carnal; for whereas there is among you envy and strife, and divisions, are ye not carnal, and walk as men? For while one saith, I am of Paul; and another, I am of Apollos; are ye not carnal?"[13]– If the spirit of the world is called into operation in intemperate zeal, and in the prejudices, partialities, and contention of parties, it is no less so in

---

[11] John 15:5.

[12] Luke 9:46.

[13] 1 Cor. 3:3-4.

[183]

carnal security, and in a cold, formal, lifeless attention to religion. When by our indifference to its most important truths, neglect of its best interests, duties and ordinances, or by conversing of it with levity, we manifest that we, like the world, consider it as a subject of little importance or worth. Or else when forgetting the great concern it has with the affections, conscience and life, we treat it as a subject of mere speculation, for curious inquiry or entertainment: hence "itching ears," fondness for novelty, and critical scrutinizing of subjects, to the neglect of devotion and improvement of the heart, in our own case; and of the works of justice, love and mercy among our fellow men.

In these, and similar ways, as Scripture, observation, and experience prove, the religion of Jesus Christ may be abused among its professors, by conformity to the world. Let it be our serious concern to avoid these dangers! – We shall conclude with some general uses of the whole subject.

As it appears from the fullest evidence, that in things lawful and expedient we are not required to differ in our manners and outward actions from other men, with whom we are connected in civil life; therefore, let us in these things avoid unnecessary, offensive singularity; preserving at the same time decency and moderation. Our chief concern in these is to act from right motives; that whether "we eat or drink, or whatsoever we do, we may do all to the glory of God:"[14] In doing this, we shall in such things differ sufficiently from the world.

As our duty to God, and regard to our soul's interests require, that we should not be conformed to the world in their sins and follies – so let us dare to be singular here.

But especially, let us take care that we do not corrupt the church, disgrace our profession, deceive our own souls, affront the majesty of God, wound our Redeemer in the house of His friends, and grieve the Holy Spirit, by introducing the spirit of the world into our religious profession, exercises, and pursuits.

Let none be vainly confident; all, both ministers and people, are liable to err here. Such is the ensnaring influence of the world; such the corruptions of our hearts; and such the artful temptations of the devil, that if we are not sincerely engaged in self-denial,

---

[14] 1 Cor. 10:31.

watchfulness and prayer, and in looking for help by faith, to Him who, as the Captain of our Salvation, has overcome the world, this sinful conformity to it, in one form or other, will take place and gain an ascendency. Perhaps it is actually the case, at this time, with many who are fond to think that they are of a very opposite character.

Those who are in the habit of conforming to the world, either in its actions or spirit, will probably be displeased at a close investigation of the subject; especially in those branches of it which apply to their own case. But their displeasure so excited, ought to be considered by themselves, as it generally will be by others, as a strong indication of contracted guilt; and of a disposition to continue in their wrong course. Perhaps these very persons will in strong terms censure conformity to the world; and be very severe on the conduct of those they consider chargeable with it, while they freely indulge themselves in their own wrong spirit and conduct; as if they meant to justify the sarcastic observation of the satirist, and "Compound for sins they are inclined to, By cursing those they have no mind to;"[15] while to impartial observers, they may appear to "Strain at a gnat, and swallow a camel."[16] Dear Brethren, these things ought not so to be. One of the best evidences to his own soul which a man can possess of sincerity, sanctified affections, and devotedness to God, and by which he can manifest the truth and excellency of religion to others, is severity to his own faults, united with tenderness to the failings of others. If he is in the spirit of the gospel, he will listen with humility, candor, and meekness, to the admonitions, and even reproofs of truth, as they apply to himself; and be ready to throw the mantle of mild construction, and forgiveness over the weakness of a brother.

If the characteristics exhibited above, of men conformed to the world, are just (and it would be easy to prove them so from Scripture;) then, as reformation is an important use to which this subject should be applied, we would do well, while considering each particular, to ask our consciences in the fear of God, how far it may be applicable to ourselves; and in every case in which it is found so

---

[15] Samuel Butler (1600-1680), *Hudibras*, Part I.

[16] Matthew 23:24.

to be, to determine on such reformation as we have reason to believe a holy God approves. The passage before us furnishes most salutary instruction on this head: "Be ye transformed in the renewing of your mind." Under the operations of grace, the pure, meek, humble, generous spirit of the gospel cherished in our hearts, and exercised in our lives, will destroy in us this conformity to the world.

Would any aspire also to the high honor and happiness of being instrumental in the hand of God to reform others; he must be careful to get his own mind truly enlightened in the knowledge of truth and duty, and divested of partiality and prejudice: he must first pull out the beam from his own eye, drink into the gospel spirit, and get his heart inflamed with love to God and love to men, that he may have a right influence on others. Then may he hope for the blessing of God to crown his endeavors.

It is to be feared, Brethren, that some who wish to promote the general interests of religion, conform too much in a direct manner to the world, in outward things at least, on a mistaken and abused sense of the maxim of becoming "all things to all men." While others who would act as reformers in the very point under consideration, by magnifying trifles, and by an unyielding rigidness in supporting and enforcing peculiarities of their own, in sentiment, speech, dress, and behavior, do not only fail to obtain their proposed end, in the most important sense; but give pain to their best friends, disgust liberal minds in general, and expose religion with its professors to censure and ridicule. Especially, if, as is frequently the case, the conversation of these persons is filled with accounts of themselves, their sentiments, their faithfulness, their intentions and their performances; or with confident assertions, and bitter censures on others: these being with reason, generally considered as indications of a weak, bigoted mind; or of spiritual pride, and an unsanctified heart.

As to avoid mistakes, we have before stated our sentiments respecting the right use of earthly possessions, and the manner and motives with which they should be acquired; so we now as freely declare, respecting stations of civil authority, and public trust, that we who do not consider them as necessarily connected with the pride of life; or as unlawful and improper for the Christian who is qualified for such stations, and called to them in the course of divine providence: but let him not seek them to gratify pride and ambition;

and if he should be called to them, let it be his serious concern to fill them in a manner becoming the faithful servant of God. Let not the Christian also, be backward to engage in plans of public utility, and works of benefience, because in some instances they are patronized and supported by those who appear to be men of the world. Rather let him consider such an undertaking as affording him a favorable opportunity for encouraging his fellow men to turn their attention to the things which are excellent; and for showing them by his example, how to pursue important objects in a proper manner, and from right motives.

Permit us now, in the close of this already long letter, to solicit your serious, diligent attention to the right improvement of the whole subject. We are sensible that human imperfection cleaves to our discussion of it, but the work has been a labor of love. We trust we have your true interests and our Redeemer's cause at heart; earnestly desiring your spiritual welfare. With those of you who rejoice in the divine goodness, we would rejoice; and with such as are in distress we would bear a sympathizing part. Permit us earnestly to call your attention to the state of your souls, and families; and of the churches, and neighborhoods with which you are connected. Be exemplary in your lives. And be not conformed to this present, evil world, whose fashion passeth away. If ever there was a time when the friends of God and religion should put off conformity to a sinful world, arise and shine, a time when they should be steady, firm and persevering in the ways of the Lord – this is the time. What a blow would be given by these means to infidelity and vice, which now boldly stalk among us! And what triumphs might we not expect to witness of the grace of God, over the hearts of those who are now its enemies.

Be intreated therefore, Brethren, by the mercies of God, to present your bodies a living sacrifice, holy, acceptable to God, which is your reasonable service, and be not conformed to this world, but be ye transformed by the renewing of your mind, that you may prove, satisfactorily and comfortably to your own souls, and convincingly to the world, what is the good, the acceptable and perfect will of God, our heavenly Father and Redeemer.

Our meeting has been truly friendly and harmonious: We trust, the gracious presence of our God has been with us, and His blessing

Appendix B

upon us; and on the numerous, attentive audience which
perseveringly attended on the means of grace during our whole
session. Wishing you the best of blessings, and requesting an
affectionate remembrance in your prayers, we remain,
Beloved Brethren,
Yours in Gospel Bonds.
RICHARD FURMAN Moderator.
WILLIAM B. JOHNSON, Clerk.

Appendix C

PROCEEDINGS

OF THE

SOUTHERN

BAPTIST CONVENTION,

HELD IN

AUGUSTA, GEORGIA,

MAY, 8TH, 9TH, 10TH, 11TH, AND 12TH, 1845.

═══

RICHMOND:

H. K. ELLYSON, PRINTER, 176, WEST MAIN STREET.

1845.

[189]

James B. Taylor (1804-1871), an English-born emigrant who became one of the principal founders of the Virginia Baptist Seminary, now the University of Richmond. Taylor was appointed as the first Corresponding Secretary of the Baptist Board of Foreign Missions for the Southern Baptist Convention. See W. B. Johnson's letter to Taylor in Appendix F.

Appendix C

PREAMBLE AND CONSTITUTION

OF THE

SOUTHERN BAPTIST CONVENTION.

We, the delegates from Missionary Societies, Churches, and other religious bodies of the Baptist Denomination, in various parts of the United States, met in Convention, in the city of Augusta, Georgia, for the purpose of carrying into effect the benevolent intentions of our constituents, by organizing a plan for eliciting, combining and directing the energies of the whole denomination in one sacred effort, for the propagation of the Gospel, agree to the following rules, or fundamental principles:

ARTICLE I. This body shall be styled the Southern Baptist Convention.

ART. II. It shall be the design of this Convention to promote Foreign and Domestic Missions, and other important objects connected with the Redeemer's kingdom, and to combine for this purpose, such portions of the Baptist denomination in the United States, as may desire a general organization for Christian benevolence, which shall fully respect the independence and equal rights of the Churches.

ART. III. A Triennial Convention shall consist of members who contribute funds, or are delegated by religious bodies contributing funds, and the system of representation and terms of membership shall be as follows, viz: An annual contribution of one hundred dollars for three years next preceding the meeting, or the contribution of three hundred dollars at any time within said three years, shall entitle the contributor to one representative; an annual contribution of two hundred dollars, as aforesaid, shall entitle the contributor to two representatives; and so, for each additional one hundred dollars, an additional representative shall be allowed. Provided, however, that when application shall be made for the first time by bodies, or individuals, to be admitted into the Convention, one delegate shall be allowed for each one hundred dollars. And provided, also, that in case of great collateral Societies, composed of representatives, receiving contributions from different parts of the country, the ratio of representation shall be one delegate for every thousand dollars, annually contributed for three years, as aforesaid; but the number of representatives shall never exceed five.

ART. IV. The officers of this Convention shall be a President, four Vice Presidents, a Treasurer, and two Secretaries, who shall be elected at each triennial meeting and hold their offices until a new election; and the officers of the Convention shall be, *each by virtue of his office*, members of the several Boards.

ART. V. The Convention shall elect at each triennial meeting as many Boards of Managers, as in its judgment will be necessary for carrying out the benevolent objects it may determine to promote, all which

[191]

Appendix C

Boards shall continue in office until a new election. Each Board shall consist of a President, Vice Presidents, Secretaries, Treasurer, Auditor, and fifteen other members, seven of whom, including one or more of the officers, shall form a quorum for the transaction of business. To each Board shall be committed, during the recess of the Convention, the entire management of all the affairs relating to the object with whose interest it shall be charged, all which management shall be in strict accordance with the constitutional provisions adopted by this Convention, and such other instructions as may be given from time to time. Each Board shall have power to make such compensation to its Secretaries and Treasurer, as it may think right; fill the vacancies occurring in its own body; enact its own bye-laws; have an annual meeting at any place it may appoint, and other meetings at such times and places as it may think best; keep a record of its proceedings and present a report of them to the Convention at each triennial meeting.

ART. VI. The Treasurer of each Board shall faithfully account for all monies received by him, keep a regular entry of all receipts and disbursements, and make report of them to the Convention, whenever it shall be in session, and to his Board as often as required. He shall also, on entering upon the duties of his office, give competent security to the President of his Board, for all the stock and funds committed to his care. His books shall be open at all times, to the inspection of any member of the Convention and of his Board. No monies shall be paid out of any of the Treasuries of the Boards, but by an order from that Board, from whose Treasury the money is to be drawn, which order shall be signed by its presiding officer.

ART. VII. The Corresponding Secretaries of the several Boards shall maintain intercourse by letter, with such individuals or public bodies, as the interests of their respective bodies may require. Copies of all such communications, with their answers, if any, shall be kept by them on file.

ART. VIII. The Recording Secretaries of the several Boards, shall keep a fair record of their proceedings, and of such other documents as may be committed to them for the purpose.

ART. IX. All the Officers, Boards, Missionaries and Agents, appointed by the Convention, or by any of its Boards, shall be members of some regular Church, in union with the Churches composing this Convention.

ART. X. Missionaries appointed by any of the Boards of this Convention, must, previous to their appointment, furnish evidence of genuine piety, fervent zeal in their Master's cause, and talents which fit them for the service for which they offer themselves.

ART. XI. The bodies and individuals, composing this Convention, shall have the right to specify the object, or objects, to which their contributions shall be applied. But when no such specification is made, the Convention will make the appropriation at its own discretion.

ART. XII. The Convention shall hold its meetings triennially, but extra meetings may be called by the President, with the approbation of any one of the Boards of Managers. A majority of the attending delegates, shall form a quorum for the transaction of business.

Appendix C

Art. XIII. Any alterations which experience shall dictate, may be made in these articles, by a vote of two-thirds of the members present, at any triennial meeting of the Convention.

RULES OF ORDER.

1. The meetings of the Convention shall be opened and closed with prayer.

2. No motion shall claim the attention of the President, unless it is seconded, nor shall it be open for discussion, until formally announced by him.

3. When a motion has been made and regularly announced by the chair, no other motion shall be received, except to amend, to substitute, to lay upon the table, to postpone indefinitely, or to postpone to a certain time. But a motion for adjournment shall always be in order, except when a member is engaged in speaking, or the body engaged in voting.

4. When a member wishes to speak on any question, he shall rise in his place and address the chair. If two or more shall rise at the same time, the President shall determine who has the floor, and no member shall speak more than twice on the same question, without the permission of the body.

5. All questions of order shall be determined by the chair, subject to an appeal to the body.

6. All motions offered for the adoption of the meetings, shall be submitted in writing, if required.

[193]

Appendix C

OFFICERS OF THE CONVENTION.

PRESIDENT.
Rev. WILLIAM B. JOHNSON, D. D., South Carolina.

VICE PRESIDENTS.

1. Hon. Wilson Lumpkin, Ga.
2. Rev. James B. Taylor, Va.
3. Hon. A. Dockery, N. C.
4. Rev. R. B. C. Howell, Tenn.

Dr. M. T. Mendenhall, Charleston, S. C., *Treasurer.*

J. Hartwell, Alabama,
James C. Crane, Richmond, Va., } *Secretaries.*

The above officers are also members of each of the Boards of Managers.

BOARD OF MANAGERS FOR FOREIGN MISSIONS.
Located at Richmond, Virginia.

PRESIDENT.
JEREMIAH B. JETER, Virginia.

VICE PRESIDENTS.

E. Ball, Va.
W. Crane, Md.
R. Fuller, S. C.
B. M. Sanders. Ga.
E. Kingsford, D. C.

I. T. Hinton, La.
T. Meredith, N. C.
H. Malcom, Ky.
C. K. Winston, Tenn.

T. G. Blewit, Miss.
W. H. Bayless, Ark.
B. Manly, Ala.
J. McDonald, Fa.
R. Hughes, Mo.

C. D. Mallory, *Corresponding Secretary.*
M. T. Sumner, *Recording Secretary.*
Arch'd Thomas, *Treasurer.*
Cha's T. Wortham, *Auditor.*

MANAGERS.

A. B. Smith,
R. Ryland,
A. Snead,
A. G. Wortham,
W. H. Jordan,

H. Keeling,
J. Thomas, Jr.,
J. Snead,
A. Fleet,
Th. Hume,

E. L. Magoon,
Wm. H. Gwathmey,
W. A. Baynham,
J. Talman, Sr,
T. W. Sydnor.

BOARD OF MANAGERS FOR DOMESTIC MISSIONS.
Located at Marion, Alabama.

PRESIDENT.
BASIL MANLY, D. D., Alabama.

VICE PRESIDENTS.

J. Hartwell, Ala.
Geo. F. Adams, Md.
O. B. Brown, D C.
T. Stringfellow, Va.

S. Wait. N. C.
J. B. O'Neal, S. C.
J. L. Dagg, Ga.
W. C. Crane, Miss.
Jas. Whitsett, Tenn.

J. B. Smith, La.
H. S. Linton, Fla.
W. C. Lincoln, Mo.
W. C. Buck, Ky.

J. L. Reynolds, *Corresponding Secretary.*
M. P. Jewett, *Recording Secretary.*
Thos. Chilton, *Treasurer.*
W. N. Wyatt, *Auditor.*

MANAGERS.

E. D King,
S. S. Sherman,
J. H. De Votie,
W. W. Hornbuckle,
L. Goree,

A. Travis,
D. P. Bester,
D. R. W. McIver,
J. B. Miller,
T. F. Curtis,

E. Baptist,
H. Talbird,
K. Hawthorn,
L. Y. Tarrant,
L. C. Tutt.

Appendix C

PROCEEDINGS.

Pursuant to a call by the Board of Managers of the Virginia Foreign Baptist Mission Society, responded to by various other bodies, a large number of delegates assembled in the meeting-house of the Baptist Church in Augusta.

After a time occupied in devotional exercises, the meeting, at 10 o'clock, A. M., was called to order by Rev. W. T. Brantly, Pastor of the Church, and on motion of Rev. J. B. Taylor, of Virginia, Hon. Wilson Lumpkin, of Georgia, was called to the chair and Jas. C. Crane, of Virginia, and J. Hartwell, of Alabama, appointed Secretaries.

Rev. W. B. Johnson, of S. C., prayed.

On motion,

Brn. T. Stocks. J. B. Taylor, E. D. King, R. McNab, S. Furman, W. Crane, W. T. Brantly, and I. T. Hinton, were appointed a committee to ascertain and report the delegates to this meeting.

All the States and Territories were called in order, and the delegates handed their certificates to the committee.

By request, Bro. J. B. Jeter gave a short statement of the proceedings of the General Board of the Baptist General Convention, at its late meeting in Providence, R. I., which meeting he, with some other Brethren from Virginia, Maryland and Georgia, had attended.

The committee to ascertain who were delegates, presented the following report, which was accepted:

Maryland.

Calvert St. Church, Baltimore,—
  J. A. McKean, Wm. Crane.

District of Columbia.

Ministers' Conference,—
  O. B. Brown,* Th. W. Sydnor.

Virginia.

Norfolk Church,—
  E. G. Robinson.
Emmaus Church,—
  James Clopton.
Shiloh Association,—
  Thornton Stringfellow, Cumberland George.*
Henrico Bethlehem Church,—
  M. T. Sumner.
Bruington Church,—
  R. H. Bagby.

Mattaponi Church,—
  W. B. Todd, W. D. Gresham.
First Church, Richmond,—
  J. B. Jeter, E. Ball, H. Keeling, A. Thomas, Jas. C. Crane.
Second Church, Richmond,—
  Jos. Walker, W. Sands, Miles Turpin, A. J. Crane, J. F. Tanner.*
Grace St. Church, Richmond,—
  J. B. Taylor, T. J. Evans.
Fourth Church, Richmond,—
  A. B. Smith.
Four Mile Creek and Beulah Churches,—
  J. O. Turpin.
St. Stephen's Church,—
  W. Southwood,* T. W. L. Fauntleroy,* Benj. Fleet.

Those marked thus * absent.

Appendix C

Wicomico, Fairfield, Morattico, and Lebanon Churches,—
A. Hall.
Columbia, Fork, and Willis' Churches,—
P. P. Smith.
Salem Union Association,—
B. Grimsley, T. D. Herndon, G. W. Latham.*
Sharon and Nottoway Churches,—
Dan'l Witt.
Taylorsville Church,—
S. S. Sumner.
Shoulder's Hill and Suffolk Churches,—
R. Jones, W. J. Wright.*
Portsmouth Church,—
Th. Hume, Wm. Brooks,* S. Y. Landrum.*
Charlottesville Church,—
I. S. Tinsley.
Farmville Church,—
T. W. Sydnor.

North Carolina.

Kennansville Church,—
R. McNab.
Wilmington Church,—
J. McDaniel,* A. J. Battle.

South Carolina.

Beach Island Church,—
I. Miller, W. J. Hard, H. Mayson.
Steel Creek Church,—
J. J. Wilson, W. S. Johnson.
Pendleton Church,—
Th. Dawson.
Congaree Church,—
J. Scott, J. Williams.*
Good Spring Church,—
D. J. Walker.
Lower Three Runs Church,—
J. A. Wood,* J. T. Furze.
Mount Lebanon Church,—
J. Morris, J. Curry.
Big Steven's Creek Church,—
S. Butler, S. Lenear.
Calvary Church,—
H. W. Mahony.
Swift Creek Church,—
J. Boykin, N. Graham.

New Providence Church,—
J. Culpepper.
St. Helena Island Church,—
W. Hall, L. R. Sams.
Harmony Church,—
C. M. Breaker.
Bethel Church,—
J. B. Miller.
Savannah River Association,—
H. A. Duncan, R. J. Davant, F. W. Fickling,*
Newberry Church,—
J. B. O'Neal,* D. Nance, J. H. Hunt,* W. Harrington.*
Matlach Church,—
G. W. Stalling,* J. Myer.*
State Convention,—
W. B. Johnson, J. Gresham, J. M. Chiles, T. Watkins, A. Simkins, J. O. Nicholson, M. M. Abney, S. Butler, D. D. Brunson, J. Mims, J. G. O. Wilkinson, J. Curry, W. Royal,* J. Trapp, R. G. Mays, W. Fort, L. Hickson, W. Brooker,* W. Watkins.
Camden Church,—
B. W. Whilden.
Willow Swamp Church,—
E. Tyler.
Columbia Church,—
W. Curtis, J. F. Marshall, W. Hooper,* J. Lyles, S. Blanding.
Tyger River Association,—
T. W. Haynes, W. Walker, O. H. Wells.
Barnwell Church,—
N. G. W. Walker, B. H. Brown.
Beaufort Church,—
R. Fuller, W. R. Stancel, L. O. Bannon, L. R. Sams, W. A. Owens.
Beulah Church,—
T. Adams.
Healing Spring Church,—
D. Peebles.
Welch Neck Associatian,—
Sam'l Furman, J. O. B. Dargan, J. M. Timmons.
Welch Neck Church,—
J. F. Wilson, A. Sparks, J. D.

Appendix C

Wilson, R. G. Edwards, J. K. McIver.*
Wentworth St. Church, Charleston,—·
T. Curtis, A. C. Smith, W. E. Bailey, B. F. Smith, C. H. Lannean, T. P. Smith, H. Bailey, W. S. Lawton, J. D. Boyd.
Beach Branch Church,—
A. Smart.
Joice Branch Church,—
H. D. Duncan.
Greenville Church,—
G. F. Townes,* O. H. Wells.
Aiken Church,—
J. Tupper.
High Hills Church,—
L. J. Durkins, W. E. Hughson, A. China.
Anderson Village Church,—
A. Rice, S. McCully.
Black Swamp Church,—
T. W. Rambaut, W. H. Robert, J. S. Lawton, B. F. Buckner.
Sandy River Church,—
B. McBride.
First Church, Charleston,—
M. T. Mendenhall, D. R. Lide, J. D. Debow, S. Howe, W. Troul, A. J. Burke, W. Riley, A. Hobson, J. L. Reynolds.
St. John's, Great Salthetche, Little Salthetche, and Doctor's Creek Churches,—
J. Fant.
Pipe Creek Church,—
J. Nicholas.
Columbia and Philadelphia Churches,—
L. M. Brown.
Union Church,—
J. J. Boyd, D. M. Dunbar.
Mount Olivet,—
D. Sheppard.
Springtown Church,—
B. S. Sweat.
Coosahachie Church,—
R. J. Davant.
Furman Institution,—
J. S. Mims.

2

Georgia.
Eatonton Church,—
J. F. Hillyer.
Millstone Church,—
P. V. Butler,* Z. H. Clark, M. Smith, M. Tiller.
Union Church,—
M. Denerent.
Richland Church,—
J. H. Campbell, H. Bunn.
Apalatchie Association,—
J. Hendrick.
Shoulder Bone Church,—
D. G. Daniel.
Powelton Church,—
C. M. Irwin.
Penfield Church,—
P. H. Mell, J. L. Brooks.
Madison Church,—
T. J. Burney, P. W. Walton.
County Line Church,—
T. R. Morgan, J. Winn.
Executive Committee of State Convention,—
B. M. Sanders, J. L. Dagg, A. Janes, J. B. Waller,* V. Thornton, Th. Stocks, T. J. Burney.
Executive Committee Georgia Association,—
B. M. Sanders, W. H. Stokes, J. S. Baker, D. G. Daniel, C. M. Irwin.
Louisville Church,—
T. Kirklighter, M. Polhill.
Sharon Church,—
L. Steed, J. S. Lasetter.
Hopefull Church,—
W. L. Tucker, B. Palmer, A. Caswell, A. Wiggins.
Antioch Church,—
H. H. Lumpkin, E. M. Gilham.
Damascus Church,—
B. Blanchard,* J. Cartlidge.
Athens Church,—
J. Hillyer, W. Lumpkin, W. Richards.
Shiloh Church,—
C. M. Stevens, W. Handley.
Columbus Church,—
A. Williams, A. M. Walker.
Central Association,—
J. H. Campbell, T. U. Wilkes,

Appendix C

S. G. Hillyer, J. T. Hillyer, T. J. Burnley, J. B. Slack.
Rocky Creek Church,—
J. Polhill, G. W. Evans, J. W. Jones, J. Applewhite,*
County Line Church,—
J. Carter, J. Neal.
Warrenton Church,—
W. J. Harley.
Sparta Church,—
W. H. Stokes.
Palmyra Church,—
J. Davis, B. O. Keaton.
Bethel Church,—
S. Crumb, A. Perry.*
Black Creek Church,—
M. N. McCall.
Little River Church,—
J. B. Slack.
Savannah Church,—
E. F. Winkler.
Freeman Church,—
N. Hill.
Ways Church,—
E. Perryman, W. H. Baldy, M. Brinson.
Rehoboth Church,—
J. Davis.
Clark Station Church,—
J. N. Bolton.
Sardis Church,—
E. Calloway, J. M. Jackson.
Bethesda Church,—
E. S. Hunter, R. Newsom.
Bethany Church,—
J. Davis.
Friendship Church,—
W. Sanders.
Antioch Church,—
J. Davis.
Ruckersville Church,—
A. Chandler, B. Thornton.
Pine Grove Church,—
J. H. T. Kilpatrick, A. Templeton,
Elm Church,—
J. M. Holl.
Sandy Creek Church,—
G. Prior, A. Robertson.
Beard's Church,—
S. D. Durham, W. O. Cheney.
Talbotton Church,—
J. Perryman, C. H. Stillwell.

Richland Church,—
W. J. Harley.
Rocky Creek Church,—
C. D. Mallary.
Suiz Creek Church,—
W. Harris.
Providence Church,—
B. Thornton.
Greensborough Church,—
J. E. Jackson,* V. Sandford.
Sardis Church,—
B. Thornton.
Fishing Creek Church,—
W. Q. Anderson, H. P. Wotton, T. C. Armstrong, R. Joynor.
Darien, South Newport, North Newport and Sunberry Churches,—
J. S. Law, W. H. McIntosh, E. H. Bacon, W. K. Gignelliat, J. Smith,* O. Stevens.*
Augusta Church,—
W. T. Brantley, J. W. Whitlock, M. M. Dye, N. B. Moore, W. H. Starke, M. Hill, J. A. Barnes.
Washington Church,—
N. M. Crawford, W. H. Pope, D. E. Butler, W. F. Baker.
Pennfield Young Men's Missionary Society,—
H. Keeling, J. F. Dagg.
Crawfordsville Church,—
D. S. Anderson, A. Darden.
Reeds Creek Church,—
J. Huff, J. W. Stapleton.
Bethel Church,—
A. Chandler.
Burley Creek Church,—
A. Lewis,* D. P. Smith,* P. Robinson, E. R. Caswell.
Philadelphia Church,—
J. S. Calloway.
Little Brier Creek Church,—
A. Atkins, T. Heart, J. Swint.*
White Plains Church,—
J. B. Thomas, E. P. Jarrell, J. Chapman.
Mercer University,—
J. Devant, B. Brantley.
Carmel Church,—
H. L. Graves, J. S. Bledsoe, J.

Perry,* J. M. Carter, J. L. Graves.

Eatonton Church,—
E. A. Marshall, J. C. Mason.

Providence Church,—
Th. U. Wilkes.

Western Association,—
H. Posey, J. E. Dawson,* J. W. Cooper,* W. P. Burks.

Sweet Water Church,—
W. P. Steed.

Sugar Creek Church,—
J. F. McNeil, B. W. Beard.

Social Circle Church,—
T. A. Gibbs, E. Henderson, J. L. Gresham.

Macedonian Church,—
J. Carter, J. H. Starke, J. H. Fielder.

Mount Zion Church,—
J. J. Pierce.

Ephesus Church,—
R. Tolefree.

Evergreen Church,—
C. D. Mallary, Geo. Walker.

Benevolence Church,—
A. M. Albritton, J. Matthews.*

Antioch Church,—
F. W. Wilkins, J. Swanson.

Horeb Church,—
W. H. Stokes, S. Evans.

Long Creek Church,—
Wm. Harris.

Alabama.

Tuskegee Church,—
A. W. Chambliss, G. W. Gunn.*

Bethany Church,—
K. Hawthorn.

Gravel Creek Church,—
J. C. Jones.

Cuhihatchie Church,—
A. W. Chambliss.

Blackbluff Church,—
J. C. Jones, K. Hawthorn.

Attention & Fellowship Churches,
J. J. Sessions.

Board of State Convention,—
J. Hartwell, B. Manly, D. D.,* E. D. King, D. P. Bestor,* J. H. De Votie,* A. G. McCraw,* H. Talbird, A. Travis, D. R. W. McIver,* T. F. Curtis, S. Henderson,* F. Calloway, W. B. Jones, W. P. Chilton,* K. Hawthorn.

Mount Gillead, Hopewell, Ash Creek and Benton Churches,—
D. Lee.

Union Town Church,—
A. A. Connella.

Montgomery Church,—
H. Talbird.

Tuscaloosa Church,—
Th. F. Curtis.

Siloam Church,—
J. H. De Votie,* E. D. King, Th. Chilton,* M. P. Jewett,* Wm. Hornbuckle,* S. Lindsley.*

Liberty Association,—
W. B. Jones, F. Calloway, J. R. Humphrey, L. Parks:*

Louisiana.

New Orleans Church,—
I. T. Hinton, R. Holman.

Kentucky.

Isaac McCoy.

The meeting then proceeded to organize, by the election of its officers. The following were chosen :

Rev. Wm. B. Johnson, D. D., of S. C., President ;
Hon. W. Lumpkin, of Ga., and Rev. J. B. Taylor, of Va., Vice Presidents ;
And Jesse Hartwell and James C. Crane, Secretaries.
On motion of Rev. R. Fuller,
Resolved, That a committee of two from each State represented in this meeting, be appointed to prepare and report a preamble and resolution for the action of the Convention.

Appendix C

Brethren R. Fuller, M. T. Mendenhall, J. A. McKean, W. Crane, T. W. Sydnor, J. B. Jeter, T. Hume, R. McNab, B. M. Sanders, C. D. Mallary, A. Travis, E. D. King, I. T. Hinton, R. Holman and I. McCoy, were selected as the committee.

Adjourned to 4 o'clock, P. M.   Prayer by Bro. W. T. Brantley.

AFTERNOON, 4 o'clock.

The Convention met.   Prayer by Bro. T. Curtis.

On motion,

Brethren J. Davis, H. Posey, J. L. Reynolds, A. Hall and H. Talbird, were appointed a committee to prepare and present rules of order, for the adoption of the Convention.

Ministering brethren present, were invited to participate in the deliberations of the meetings.

The committee to prepare rules of order presented a report, which was accepted, the rules were adopted and the committee discharged. See page 5.

The committee to prepare a preamble and resolution for the action of the Convention, presented a report, which was accepted, and during the discussion on its adoption, the Convention adjourned to 8 o'clock, A. M., to-morrow.   Prayer by Bro. W. Lumpkin.

FRIDAY MORNING, May 9th, 8 o'clock.

The Convention met.   Prayer by Bro. J. B. Taylor.

Several communications received through the President, were presented and read.

Bro. J. L. Burrows, appeared as a corresponding delegate from the American Baptist Publication Society, and the Pennsylvania Baptist State Convention, and was invited to participate with us.

The report of the committee, under discussion at the time of adjournment yesterday, was taken up, and after a full, free and harmonious discussion, the preamble and resolution were separately adopted, by the *unanimous* vote of the Convention, as follows :

"The committee to whom it has been referred to report a preamble and resolutions, cannot but express their profound sense of the responsibility resting upon your body at the present eventful crisis, as the integrity of the nation, the interests of truth, and the sacred enterprize of converting the heathen, are all involved in your deliberations. That this Convention was imperatively demanded, must be apparent to all. The Boston Board have, in their answer to the Alabama resolutions, most clearly and unnecessarily exceeded their power and violated their trust.

" It is a question admitting no debate, that the Triennial Convention was formed on the principle of a perfect equality of members, from the South and North. And what is all important, the very qualifications of missionaries are prescribed by the original constitution of that Convention,—the fifth article providing that "such persons as are in full communion with some regular church of our denomination, and who furnish satisfactory evidence of genuine piety, good talents and fervent zeal for the Redeemer's cause, are to be employed as missionaries."

"Besides this, too, the declaration of the Board, that if " any one should offer himself as a missionary, having slaves, and should insist on retaining them as his property, we could not appoint him," is an innovation and a departure from the course hitherto pursued by the Triennial Convention,

[200]

Appendix C

(such persons having been appointed.) And lastly, the decision of the Board is an infraction of the resolution passed the last spring, in Philadelphia; and the General Board at their late meeting in Providence, have failed to reverse this decision.

"Amidst such circumstances, your committee esteem it absolutely necessary, that the friends of the Constitution of the Triennial Convention, and the lovers of the Bible, shall at once take their stand, and assert the great catholic principles of that Constitution, and of the Word of God.

"Your committee therefore submit the following resolution, as embodying all that they are now prepared to suggest to your body:

"*Resolved*, That for peace and harmony, and in order to accomplish the greatest amount of good, and for the maintainance of those scriptural principles on which the General Missionary Convention of the Baptist denomination of the United States, was originally formed, it is proper that this Convention at once proceed to organize a Society for the propagation of the Gospel."

The same committee, with the addition of Br'n W. B. Johnson, J. L. Dagg, J. Hartwell, T. Curtis, Jas. C. Crane, T. Stringfellow, S. Furman, and J. S. Baker, were appointed to prepare a Constitution for the proposed organization.

Adjourned to 4 o'clock, P. M. Prayer by Bro. R. Fuller.

AFTERNOON, 4 O'CLOCK.

The Convention met. Prayer by Bro. H. Posey.

A communication was received from the Faculty of the Medical College, inviting the members of the Convention to visit the College Building and Museum; and also presenting 200 copies of an address by Rev. W. T. Brantly, to the graduating class of said College.

Whereupon, the President was requested to reply to the communication, expressing the thanks of the Convention for the copies of the address, and its acceptance of the invitation to visit the College.

On motion,

Resolved, That the thanks of this Convention be tendered to the several Rail Road and other Companies, for the facilities afforded the members in attending this meeting.

Bro. Burrows then addressed the meeting, on behalf of the American Baptist Publication Society.

Adjourned to 8 o'clock, A. M., to-morrow.

Prayer by Bro. J. S. Calloway.

SATURDAY MORNING, MAY 10TH, 8 O'CLOCK.

The Convention met. Prayer by Bro. I. McCoy.

The committee appointed to prepare a Constitution, presented a report, which was accepted.

The Constitution was taken up, and after a free discussion, and amendments during its passage, was, on motion, adopted unanimously. See page 3.

The publishers of the Chronicle & Sentinel, presented a number of copies of their paper, containing reports of our proceedings, for the use of the members. And on motion,

Resolved, That the thanks of the Convention, be tendered to the publishers of the Chronicle & Sentinel.

Appendix C

Resolved, That Br'n W. B. Johnson, T. Curtis, R. Fuller, and C. D. Mallary, be a committee to prepare an address to the public, setting forth the reasons which have led to the formation of the Southern Baptist Convention, and giving an exposition of its principles and objects; to be published with the Minutes, and in such public prints as will allow it a place in their columns. See page 17.

Adjourned to 3 o'clock, P. M.   Prayer by Bro. J. Hartwell.

                          AFTERNOON, 3 o'CLOCK.

The Convention met.   Prayer by Bro. B. Grimsley.

On motion,

Resolved, That the individuals, churches and other bodies, approving the Constitution of the Southern Baptist Covention, adopted by this body, be recommended to meet, according to its provisions, for organiza- tion, by members or delegates, on the Wednesday after the first Lord's day in June, 1846, in Richmond, Va. : And that this Convention now procced to the election of its Officers and Boards of Managers, to continue in office until said meeting.

Whereupon, the officers of the Convention were chosen. (See page 6.)

Resolved, That the Convention appoint a Board of Managers for Foreign Missions, and also one for Domestic Missions, and that a com- mittee be appointed to nominate the members of such Boards.

Br'n E. Ball, H. Keeling, W. Sands, R. McNab, A. J. Battle, S. Furman, J. L. Reynolds, S. Blanding, J. H. Campbell, B. M. Sanders, C. D. Mallary, H. Talbird, A. Travis, T. Curtis, I. T. Hinton, R. Hol- man, W. Crane, J. A. McKean, T. W. Sydnor and I. McCoy, were appointed the committee.

The committee requested the Convention to decide on the location of the Boards of Managers, that the nominations might be made in accord- ance therewith : And it was

Resolved, That the Board for Foreign Missions be located at Rich- mond, Va., and the Board for Domestic Missions, at Marion, Ala.

On motion,

The Secretaries were appointed to superintend the printing and distri- bution of five thousand copies of the proceedings of this meeting.

A special collection towards defraying the expense of publishing was taken, amounting to $98 36.

Adjourned to 8 o'clock, P. M.   Prayer by Bro. J. L. Burrows.

                          EVENING, 8 o'CLOCK.

The Convention met.   Prayer by Bro. J. B. Jeter.

The committee to nominate members of the Boards of Managers, presented a report, and the several Brethren nominated, were chosen. See page 6.

Br'n T. W. Sydnor, W. Curtis and I. T. Hinton, were appointed a committee to nominate a Brother and alternate, to preach the Annual Sermon at the meeting next year : and, after consultation, proposed Bro. B. Manly, as the preacher, and Bro. R. Fuller, as the alternate. And these Br'n were appointed to perform the service.

On motion,

Resolved, unanimously, That the thanks of this Convention are due, and are hereby tendered, to the citizens of Augusta, for the kind hospi- talities, so generously extended to us during our meeting, and we earnestly supplicate that God's mercy may descend in rich effusions, and more than repay in spiritual blessings, the efforts of our friends to render our stay among them so agreeable.

Resolved, That a collection be taken up at the close of the service, in the Baptist meeting-house to-morrow morning, for Foreign Missions, and in the evening for Domestic Missions.

Adjourned to 8 o'clock, on Monday morning. Prayer by Bro. N. M. Crawford.

MONDAY MORNING, 8 o'clock.

The Convention met. Many of the brethren having left the city, only about one hundred members were present. Prayer by Bro. A. J. Battle.

On motion, the following resolutions were severally proposed and adopted, accompanied with free discussion, and harmonious interchange of views and feelings, in regard to the important objects of the Convention :

Resolved, That in accordance with the provisions of the 2nd Article of the Constitution, this Convention will cordially embrace and affiliate auxilliary societies upon its principles, and recommend to the brethren the formation of such societies.

Resolved, That the several State Conventions and other bodies who may be in possession of funds for Foreign or Domestic Missions, be requested to forward such funds to the Treasurers of the respective Boards, as promptly as convenient.

Resolved, That the Aborigines of America, have strong claims on American christians for the Gospel, and as the Indian Mission Association has been organized with special reference to their spiritual benefit, we recommend the churches to sustain that body with zeal and liberality.

Resolved, That the Board of Domestic Missions be instructed to take all prudent measures, for the religious instruction of our colored population.

Resolved, That the Foreign Mission Board of this Convention be instructed to communicate with the acting Board of the Baptist Triennial Convention, in reference to any claim we may have upon that Convention, or any claim which that body may have, or think they have upon us, and that the said Board report fully at the next meeting of this Convention.

Resolved, That our Foreign Mission Board be authorized to enter into any equitable and prudent arrangement, with the acting Board of the Baptist General Convention, to take a portion of its Missions under the patronage of this Convention.

Resolved, That application be made to the proper authorities of the State of Georgia, for a charter of incorporation ; and that Judge J. Hilliyer, Hon. Wilson Lumpkin, Judge Thos. Stocks, Mark A. Cooper, Esq. and Rev. Ch's D. Mallary, be a committee to present a petition for this object.

Resolved, That this Convention recommend to the Board of Domestic Missions, to direct its effective attention to aid the present effort, to establish the Baptist cause in the city of New Orleans.

Resolved, That with profound gratitude to the Great Head of the Church, this Convention recognizes the harmonious and unanimous action to which it has arrived ; and that we do regard the exhibition of the

Appendix C

christian spirit which has governed its deliberations, as a pledge of the divine blessing in the origin and prosecution of this organization.

And then the Convention adjourned.

The President offered the concluding prayer, earnestly supplicating the blessing of Almighty God on the efforts of the Convention and on its members, after which a hymn was sung, and the usual token of affection and fellowship closed this interesting meeting.

WILLIAM BULLEIN JOHNSON,
President of the Convention.

JESSE HARTWELL, } *Secretaries.*
JAS. C. CRANE.   }

The undersigned has found it difficult to arrange the list of delegates, and is still uncertain as to the entire correctness of the names of churches and individuals. The report of the committee was subjected to alterations and interlineations, during the progress of the meetings, and the Chairman was unable to furnish a corrected copy. It is hoped, however, that the list is sufficiently correct to answer the purpose of publication.

JAS. C. CRANE, *one of the Secretaries.*

Appendix C

THE SOUTHERN BAPTIST CONVENTION,

To the Brethren in the United States ; to the congregations connected with the respective Churches ; and to all candid men.

A painful division has taken place in the missionary operations of the American Baptists. We would explain the origin, the principles and the objects of that division, or the peculiar circumstances in which the organization of the Southern Baptist Convention became necessary.

Let not the extent of this disunion be exaggerated. At the present time it involves only the Foreign and Domestic Missions of the denomination. Northern and Southern Baptists are still brethren. They differ in no article of the faith. They are guided by the same principles of gospel order. Fanatical attempts have indeed been made, in some quarters, to exclude us of the South from christian fellowship. We do not retort these attempts ; and believe their extent to be comparatively limited. Our christian fellowship is not, as we feel, a matter to be obtruded on any one. We abide by that of our God, his dear Son, and all his baptized followers. The few ultra Northern brethren to whom we allude, must take what course they please. *Their* conduct has not influenced us in this movement. We do not regard the rupture as extending to foundation principles, nor can we think that the great body of our Northern brethren will so regard it. Disunion has proceeded, however, deplorably far. The first part of our duty is to show that its entire *origin* is with others. This is its history.

I. The General Convention of the Baptist denomination of the United States *was* composed of brethren from every part of the American Republic. Its Constitution knows no difference between slaveholders and non-slaveholders. Nor during the period of its existence, for the last thirty years, has it, in practice, known any thing of this distinction. Both parties have contributed steadily and largely (if never adequately) to those funds which are the basis of its constituency ; both have yielded its office-bearers of all grades ; its missionaries and translators of God's word ; its men of toils many, and of prayers not unavailing, abroad and at home. The honored dead of both these classes have walked in closest sympathy with each other ; anticipating in the Board-room and in the Monthly Concert, that higher, but not holier union now in their case consummated. Throughout the entire management of its early affairs, the whole struggle with its early difficulties, there was no breath of discord between them. Its Richard Furman and its Wm. Staughton, its Jesse Mercer and its Thomas Baldwin, led on the sacramental host shoulder to shoulder, and heart to heart. Their rivalry being only in earnest efforts for a common cause, their entire aversions and enmities were directed with all the strength of their souls, against the common foe. And to the last, did they not cherish the strong belief that they left no other enmities or aversions ; no other rivalry to their successors?

In particular, a special rule of the Constitution defines *who* may be missionaries, viz : "Such persons only as are in full communion with some church in our denomination ; and who furnish satisfactory evidence of genuine piety, good talents, and fervent zeal for the Redeemer's cause." Now, while under this rule the slaveholder has been, in his turn, employed as a missionary, it is not alledged that any other persons than those above described, have been appointed. Moreover, the important post of a superintendent of the education of native missionaries, has been assigned, with universal approbation, to the pastor of one of our largest slaveholding churches.

But an evil hour arrived. Even our humble efforts in the conquest of the world to God, excited the accuser of our brethren to cast discord among us ; and in the last two Triennial Conventions, slavery and anti-slavery men began to draw off on different sides. How did the nobler spirits on each side endeavor to meet this? They proposed and carried almost unanimously, the following explicit resolution :

Appendix C

"*Resolved,* That in co-operating together, as members of this Convention, in the work of foreign missions, we disclaim all sanction, either expressed or implied, whether of slavery or anti-slavery ; but as individuals, we are free to express and to promote, elsewhere, our views on these subjects, in a christian manner and spirit."

Our successors will find it difficult to believe that so important and plain a declaration had become, before the close of the first year of the triennial period, a perfect nullity. In December last, the acting Board of the Convention, at Boston, adopted a new qualification for missionaries, a new special rule, viz : that " If any one who shall offer himself for a missionary, having slaves, should insist on retaining them as his property, they could not appoint him." " One thing is certain," they continue, " we could never be a party to any arrangement which implies approbation of slavery."

We pray our brethren and all candid men to mark the date of this novel rule—the close of the first six months of their three years' power, a date at which the compromise resolution could scarcely have reached our remoter mission stations. If usurpation had been intended, could it have been more fitly timed? An usurpation of ecclesiastical power quite foreign to our polity. Such power was assumed at a period when the aggrieved " thousands of Israel" had, as it now appears, no practical remedy. Its obvious tendency was, either our final subjugation to that power, or a serious interruption of the flow of Southern benevolence. The latter was the far more probable evil; and the Boston Board knew this well. They were from various quarters apprised of it. We, on the other hand, did not move in the matter of a new organization until three liberal States had refused to send northward any more contributions. Our leaders had chosen new rules. Thus came war within our gates : while the means of war on the common enemy were daily diminishing.

By this decision, the Board had placed itself in direct opposition to the Constitution of the Convention. The only reason given for this extraordinary and unconstitutional dictum being—that " The appointing power for wise and good purposes, is confided to the acting Board." On such a slight show of authority, this Board undertook to declare *that* to be a disqualification in one who should offer himself for a missionary, which the Convention had said shall *not* be a disqualification. It had also expressly given its sanction to anti-slavery opinions, and impliedly fixed its condemnation on slavery, although the Convention had said that "neither" should be done. And further, it forbade those who shall apply for a missionary appointment, to " express and promote elsewhere " their views on the subject of slavery in a right " manner and spirit, " when the Convention declared they " were free " to do so. These brethren, thus acted upon a sentiment they have failed to prove—That slavery is, in all circumstances, sinful. Whereas their own solemn resolution in the last Convention, (their's as much as our's) left us free to promote slavery. Was not this leaving us free, and " *in a Christian spirit and manner* " to promote that which in their hearts, and according to the present shewing of their conduct, they regard as a sin?

Enough, perhaps, has been said of the origin of this movement. Were we asked to characterize the conduct of our Northern brethren in one short phrase, we should adopt that of the Apostle. It was " FORBIDDING US *to speak* UNTO THE GENTILES." Did this deny us no privilege? Did it not obstruct us, lay a kind of Romish interdict upon us in the discharge of an imperative duty ; a duty to which the church has been, after the lapse of ages, awakened universally and successfully ; a duty the very object, and only object, of our long cherished connection and confederation?

And this would seem the place to state, that our Northern brethren were dealt with as brethren to the last moment. Several of our churches cherished the hope that by means of remonstrance and expostulation, through the last Annual Meeting of the Board of Managers, at Providence, the Acting Board might be brought to feel the grievous wrong they had inflicted. The Managing Board was therefore affectionately and respectfully addressed on the subject, and was entreated to revise and reverse the obnoxious interdict. Alas ! the results were—contemptuous silence as to the application made ; and a deliberate resolve, expressing sympathy with the Acting Board, and a determination to sustain them.

II. The PRINCIPLES of the Southern Baptist Convention, it remains then to be stated, are

Appendix C

conservative; while they are also, as we trust, equitable and liberal. They propose to do the Lord's work in the way our fathers did it. Its title designates at once its origin, and the simple, firm abiding of the South on the ground from which it has been so unconstitutionally and unjustly attempted to eject us. We have but enquired for "the old paths" of missionary operations; "asked" for, and attempted to restore the practically "good way." The Constitution we adopt is precisely that of the original union; that in connection with which, throughout his missionary life, Adoniram Judson has lived, and under which Ann Judson and Boardman have died. We recede from it no single step. We have constructed for our basis no new creed; acting in this matter upon a Baptist aversion for all creeds but the Bible. We use the very terms, as we uphold the true spirit and great object of the late "General Convention of the Baptist denomination of the United States." It is they who wrong us that have receded. We have receded neither from the Constitution nor from any part of the original ground on which we met them in this work, And if, we ask in parting, the original and broad Bible ground of confederation were *not* equitable, how came it so nobly and so long to be acted upon? If equitable, why depart from it?

We claim to have acted in the premises, with liberality towards our Northern brethren. Thrust from the common platform of equal rights, between the Northern and Southern churches, we have but reconstructed that platform. Content with it, we adhere to it, and reproduce it, as broad enough for us and for them. Have they thrust us off? We retain but one feeling in the case. *That we will not practically leave it on any account:* much less in obedience to such usurped authority, or in deference to such a manifest breach of trust as is here involved. A breach of covenant that looks various ways—heavenward and earthward. For we repeat, THEY WOULD FORBID US TO *speak unto* THE GENTILES. The Jerusalem church, then, must be regathered at the suspected Samaria, or at some new centre of operations, like Antioch. "One thing *is* certain"—We must go every where preaching the word.—"We can never be a party to any arrangement" for monopolizing the Gospel: any arrangement which like that of the Autocratical Interdict of the North, would first drive us from our beloved colored people, of whom they prove that they know nothing comparatively, and from the much-wronged Aborigines of the country;—and then cut us off from the whitening fields of the heathen harvest-labor; to which by cogent appeals and solemn prayers, they have so often protested that, without us, they were inadequate.

III. Our OBJECTS, then, are the extension of the Messiah's kingdom, and the glory of our God. Not disunion with any of his people; not the upholding of any form of human policy, or civil rights; but God's glory, and Messiah's increasing reign; in the promotion of which, we find no necessity for relinquishing any of our civil rights. We will never interfere with *what is Cæsar's.** We will not compromit what is GOD's.

These objects will appear in detail on the face of our Constitution, and in the proceedings, which accompany this address. They are distributed, at present, between two acting Boards for Foreign and Domestic Missions, having their respective seats at Richmond, Va., and Marion, Ala. We sympathise with the Macedonian cry from every part of the heathen world,—with the low moan, for spiritual aid, of the four millions of half stifled Red Men, our neighbors; with the sons of Ethiopia among us, stretching forth their hands of supplication for the gospel, to God and all his people,—and we have shaken ourselves from the night mare of a six years' "strife about words to *no* profit," for the profit of these poor, perishing and precious souls. Our language to all America, and to all christendom, if they will hear us, is "*come over*," and for *these* objects, as ye love souls, and the divine Saviour of souls, "*help us*." We ask help at this juncture for nothing else. We have had more talk than work about these objects too long. We have waited quite too long for the more learned and gifted, and opulent, and worthy, to lead our way toward these objects;

---

*It was not dwelt upon in the Augusta Convention—we do not recollect its being named, but it is too stringent a fact in the case to be here omitted,—that one of the missionaries, with whom the Acting Board, and Board of Managers can sympathise, we presume, and whom they sustain (we hope, however, not in this particular act, but they have in no way openly protested against it)—Brother Mason has actually remitted money to the United States to aid in assisting slaves to "run away from their masters," a felony by the Statute Law of several States.

Appendix C

and we have shortened debate upon them to get to business. Our eyes and hearts are turned with feelings of parental fondness to Burmah and the Karens; with a zeal in which we are willing to be counselled by God and all considerate men, (but by none else,) to the continent of Africa, and *her* pernicious fountains of idolatry, oppression and blood; but yet more, with unutterable hope and thankfulness, to China and her providentially opened ports, and teeming thirsty millions. Among us, in the South, we have property, which we will offer to the Lord and his cause, in these channels—some prudence with which we would have our best wisdom † to dwell; and professions of a piety which we seek to have increased and purified, like that of the first Baptist churches, when they had "rest; and walking in the fear of the Lord, and in the comfort of the Holy Ghost, were multiplied."

In parting with beloved brethren and old co-adjutors in this cause, we could weep, and have wept, for ourselves and for them; but the season, as well of weeping as of vain jangling, is, we are constrained to believe, just now past. For years the pressure of men's hands has been upon us far too heavily. Our brethren have pressed upon every inch of our privileges and our sacred rights—but this shall only urge our gushing souls to yield proportionately of their renewed efforts to the Lord, to the church universal, and to a dying world; even as water pressed from without rises but the more within. Above all, the mountain pressure of our obligations to God, even our own God; to Christ and to Him crucified; and to the personal and social blessings of the Holy Spirit and his influences, shall urge our little streams of the water of life to flow forth; until every wilderness and desolate place within our reach (and what extent of the world's wilderness wisely considered is not within our reach?) "shall be glad"—even at this passing calamity of division; and the deserts of unconverted human nature "rejoice and blossom as the rose."

By order of the Convention.   WILLIAM B. JOHNSON, D. D.

Augusta, Ga., 12th *May,* 1845.

---

† Prov. viii: 12.

Appendix D

Letter From William B. Johnson to William Sprague on the Character of Richard Furman[1]

Edgefield Court House, S.C., May 27, 1848.

My dear Sir: My acquaintance with the Rev. Dr. Furman began when I was a boy, and I well remember the deep and solemn impression which his grave and minister-like appearance made upon my mind, young as I then was; – an impression which was deepened by a more intimate knowledge of his character. As we never lived in the same town or neighbourhood, after I entered the ministry, nor indeed before, with the exception of a few months which I spent in his family, when going to school, – I saw him but seldom, except in the meetings of the general organizations of the denomination; so that my opportunities for observing him continuously were not ample. His deportment, however, was so uniform that his life presented a series of good deeds, without very numerous incidents of striking variety. His regular habits, his conscientious regard for duty, made him observe, with more than ordinary faithfulness, the precepts of his Divine Master. So that, though of Adam's race, he was, by common consent, regarded as not exceeded by any, as a consistent, uniform and exemplary person, in a community of from twenty to thirty thousand, of whom not a few were upright professors of religion in different denominations.

As a man, Dr. Furman was most kind and benevolent. In his family, he was a pattern of conjugal and parental tenderness. To the poor he was sympathizing and beneficent. To the sick, a physician of both soul and body. He was the former by his profession, and to become the latter, he bestowed much attention upon the science of medicine. To this he was led by the benevolence of his heart, from seeing the necessities of the numerous poor in the city, whose streets and lanes he threaded in his pastoral visits. During the sickly

---

[1] William B. Sprague, *Annals of the American Pulpit* (New York: Robert Carter & Brothers, 1865), Vol. VI (Baptists), 163-165

season, in Charleston, sometimes visited by that awful scourge of the sea-ports, – *the Yellow Fever*, Dr. Furman remained firm at his post, and, like an angel of mercy, was found at the bedside of the sick and the dying. In one of the most fatal seasons of this epidemic, he had more than thirty patients, of whom he lost none; and, to the honour of this philanthropist, be it said, these acts of kindness were performed *without money and without price.* In the exercise of the same benevolence, which led to these acts, his manner was to take with him, when he travelled, his lancet and medicines; and, not unfrequently, was it his privilege to minister, on these journeys, to the relief of the sick, especially in the General meetings of the denomination, when some sudden attack of disease upon one or other of the members called into requisition his skill and his kindness.

Dr. Furman was the firm friend of true freedom and of equal rights. As a member of the Convention of this State, in the year 1790, he took part in the deliberations of that Body, assembled to form the Constitution. When the article, which prohibits ministers of the Gospel from admission into the Legislative, Judicial and Executive offices, came up for discussion, he opposed it on the ground of its violating the *right* of the people to elect whom they pleased, and of the ministry to fill any office to which the people should elect them. He repudiated the principle of disfranchising a class of citizens, on the ground of their consecration to a holy office.

As a Christian, the bearing of Dr. Furman was pre-eminently that of a man of God, who set the Lord always before him, ordering his conversation aright, and acting under the solemn conviction, – *"Thou God seest me."* The religion of this good and great man was truly a spiritual, practical religion, under whose influence he was careful to maintain good works, thus letting his light shine before others, with no false or doubtful lustre. Indeed, so eminent was he for exemplary piety and holy living, that the whole city held him in veneration. The ungodly stood abashed in his sight, and the profligate carefully hid his inquiries from his view. A member of a bachanalian party once said to his fellows in debauch, – "Suppose Rev. Mr. ―――― should enter the room, would you be restrained?" "No," was the reply. The names of other ministers of the city were mentioned, with the like inquiry, and with the like negative. Last of all, Dr. Furman's name was mentioned in the same way, when the universal exclamation was "Yes, *Dr. Furman* would restrain us – we could not stand *his* presence." It was no unfrequent remark that, if good works could save a man, the good works of Dr. Furman would assuredly secure *him* admission into Heaven.

As a *Minister of Jesus Christ*, the *tout ensemble*[2] of Dr. Furman was more solemn and imposing than that of any other man whom I have ever beheld. When *he* arose to speak in Church-meeting, Association, Convention, or any other assembly, all eyes were turned upon him, with profound attention, and reverential awe. In the services of the sacred desk, such was the appropriate solemnity of his manner, that the audience *felt* themselves to be in the presence of a man of God, who had "studied to show himself approved unto God, a workman that needed not to be ashamed, rightly dividing the word of truth."

As an *Orator* of the grave character, Dr. Furman was pre-eminent. In his preaching, he intermingled doctrine and practice, experimental religion and pathetic appeal. I remember hearing him, more than forty years ago, preach from the text, – "I am set for the defence of the Gospel" – it was truly a masterly effort. Never shall I forget his solemn, impressive countenance, his dignified manner, his clear statements of the Gospel doctrine and precepts, his unanswerable arguments in support of the Gospel's claim to a Divine origin, the lofty sentiments that he poured forth, the immovable firmness with which he maintained his position, and the commanding eloquence with which he enforced the whole argument. Another discourse, two or three years before, is fresh in my memory, from the text, — "They shall ask the way to Zion, with their faces thitherward, saying, come and let us join ourselves to the Lord in a perpetual covenant that shall not be forgotten." In this discourse there was much pathos. The audience was deeply moved. Indeed, the Doctor seemed to reign over them with irresistible influence, melting their hearts into the tenderest frame, and happily preparing them for the Sacramental table.

In the administration of Baptism, and the Lord's Supper, his manner was of the happiest kind; more especially in the latter, when directing the faith of the communicants to their suffering, crucified

---

[2]   tout ensemble: French meaning "all together," or the general effect produced by the harmony of the parts when considered as a whole.

Lord. Deeply affected himself with the remembrance of the scenes of Calvary, he failed not, by their recital, to affect the communicants. Their abhorrence of sin, which had nailed their Great Head to the Cross, was deepened, whilst their gratitude for his condescension, in delivering them from guilt and condemnation, by such sufferings, was heightened, and their love inflamed.

As the Presiding Officer of an Ecclesiastical Body, his administration was in keeping with all the other parts of his character. Intimately acquainted with parliamentary rule, he conducted the movements, and preserved the decorum, of the Body, with ease, propriety, and dignity. Indeed, his very appearance preserved order. The points presented in ordinary business, or in queries from the Churches, which were of difficult solution, met at his hands an easy explanation, so that the facilities of the Body were equal to the exigencies, – a privilege and blessing of no small importance.

The gift of such a man to the denomination, for the period that Dr. Furman lived, was a gracious ordering of Divine Providence, and it is with melancholy pleasure that I present, for the "Annals of the American Pulpit," this tribute of respect to the memory of so good and great a man.

Affectionately yours,
WILLIAM BULLEIN JOHNSON.

Appendix D

RICHARD FURMAN
1755—1825

Appendix E

Acknowledges a letter FCG. **Feb. 8 1850**

Rev. J. B. Taylor,

Cor. Secy of B. w. in Virginia,

When my son Frances arrived at my house in Dec. he was very weak, but he has since very much improved. Yet I am far from thinking he is sound in health or constitution. I proposed to him, for his own relief & comfort, to preach for me occasionally, that I might go out on the Mission for the Board under the Commission you sent me. But he said, that was <u>impracticable</u>, as the excitement in preparation for the pulpit & then the preaching itself were too great for his nerves. So that he did not expect to be able to preach for a year

Talking, however, does not affect him, he says, & he has therefore taken a school, as he wishes not to be a burden. I was not friendly to this course, but as he thinks it will the best, I have assented to it. If it affects his health, I will bring him home.

From the Foreign Mission Board Historical Files, AR 551-8.

[214]

Appendix E

Letter from William B. Johnson to J. B. Taylor
dated February 8, 1850[1]

Acknowledged in letter to FCG.   [Feb. 8 1850]

Revd. J. B. Taylor,
      Cor. Secy. of B. B. F. Missions,[2]

When my son Francis arrived at
my house in Dec[embe]r he was very weak, but he
has since very much improved. Yet I am far
from thinking he is sound in health or
Constitution. I proposed to him, for his
own relief & comfort, to preach for me
occasionally, that I might go out on the
Mission for the Board under the commission you sent me. But he said, that was
impracticable, as the excitement in preparation for the pulpit & then the preaching itself were too great for his nerves. So
that he did not expect to be able to preach
for a year.

Talking, however, does not affect him
he says, & he has therefore taken a school, as
he wishes not to be a burden. I was not
friendly to this course, but as he thinks it
will be best, I have assented to it. If it affects
his health, I will bring him home.

---

[1] Courtesy Mr. Bill Sumners, Director, Southern Baptist Historical Library
and Archives, Nashville, Tennessee.

[2] James Barnett Taylor (1804-1871) was chosen as the first Corresponding
Secretary of the newly-formed Baptist Board of Foreign Missions (now
known as the International Mission Board) in 1846, a position he would
hold until his death 25 years later. See his portrait on page 190.

Appendix E

His views of divine truth in doctrine & experience have deepened very much, & I entertain the hope that God will yet make him.
an agent of much usefulness in his cause.

Before he left China he borrowed
$59. or of the funds for the mission, which
I will refund as soon as I can make
some collections. My son says, as he
has done nothing for the Mission, he intends, as soon as he is able, to refund
to the Mission Board what has been ex-
pended on him. And I doubt not, though
he is not bound to do so, that he will
if he should at any time have it in his
power, do, as he says.

I have received your envelope cover-
ing a letter for Bro. Roberts & I shall be
very much gratified in presenting it to
him personally. Your to Frances,
I have forwarded

From the Foreign Mission Board Historical Files, AR 551-8.

Appendix E

His views of divine truth in doctrine & experience have deepened very much, & I entertain the hope that God will yet make him
an agent of much usefulness in his cause.

Before he left China[3] he borrowed
$50.00 of the funds for the Mission, which
I will refund as soon as I can make
some collections. My son says, as he
has done nothing for the Mission, he intends, as soon as he is able, to refund
to the Mission Board what has been ex-
pended on him. And I doubt not, though
he is not bound to do so, that he will,
if he shall at any time have it in his
power, do as he says.

I have received your envelope, cover-
ing a letter from Bro. Roberts, & shall be
very much gratified in presenting it to
him personally. Yours to Francis,
I have forwarded.

---

[3] Francis Cleveland Johnson was one of the first foreign missionaries
appointed by the Southern Baptist Convention in 1846. He intended to
devote his life to the theological training of converts in China, but ill health
forced him to return to the U. S. in 1849. See pages 89 and 136-137.

[217]

Appendix E

My daughters desire their very respectful remembrances to you, my Brother, & My son Frances would do the same, if he were present.

My personal regard to your lady & family. Yours in the Gospel, my dear brother, with christian regard

William B. Johnson

Edgefield C. H. S. C.
8 Feby 1850

From the Foreign Mission Board Historical Files, AR 551-8.

My daughters desire their very respectful remembrance, to you, my Brother, & My son Francis would do the
same, if he were present.
My personal regards to your lady
& family.

Yours in the Gospel, my
dear brother, with Christian regard
William B. Johnson
Edgefield C.[ourt] H.[ouse] S. C.
8. Feby 1850

Marker at the gravesite of William B. Johnson located in the church yard of the First Baptist Church, Anderson, South Carolina, which was placed there in 1909 by the South Carolina State Baptist Convention. "The tombstone is a shaft of classic simplicity with drapery denoting the scholar," wrote Miss Woodson (p.162). Photographs are courtesy of Mr. Gene Smith, Edgefield, South Carolina.

Appendix F

Gravesite of William B. Johnson and Historical Marker in his memory at the site of the Johnson Female Seminary, Anderson, South Carolina

Dr. William B. Johnson passed away quietly during the night of October 1, 1862, at the home of his son-in-law, Col. G. F. Townes in Greenville, South Carolina.

At the South Carolina State Baptist Convention, meeting at Darlington in 1863, pastor J. Scott Murray proposed that "a committee of one from each constituent of the body be appointed to raise funds to erect a monument over the remains of the honored brother" (p. 162). But being as it was that the country was in the midst of a devastating Civil War, these plans were not to be realized for another 46 years.

"It was due to untiring efforts of Mrs. R. C. Hoyt, a former student at Johnson University that the State Convention erected a monument to his memory" (p. 162).

The granite tombstone and shaft were placed over W. B. Johnson's grave at Anderson, South Carolina in 1909. Johnson had been a resident of the town during the last five years of his life and the citizens had "unanimously requested that his body be interred there" (p.158). The site has been carefully maintained in the churchyard of the First Baptist Church at Anderson.

Appendix C

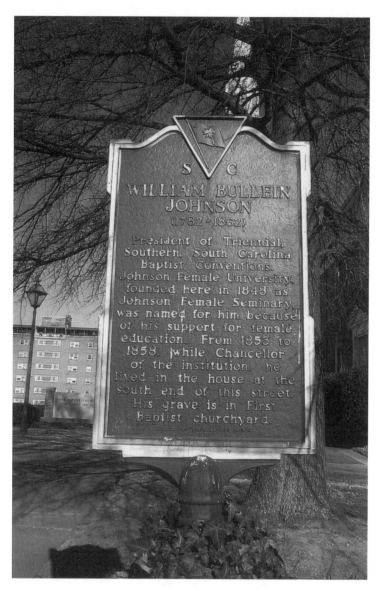

Historical marker erected by the First Baptist Church of Anderson, South Carolina in 1920 to the memory of William Bullein Johnson, "President of Triennial, Southern, [and] South Carolina Baptist Conventions." Photograph courtesy of Mr. Gene Smith, Edgefield, South Carolina.

Indexes

Publishers note: These indexes are to Hortense Woodson's *Giant in the Land; The Life of William B. Johnson*, and do not include the material in the appendixes.

Index of Persons

Indexes

Indexes

Indexes

Indexes

Indexes

Indexes

Indexes

Watkins, Zedekiah - 64, 148

Watson, Harry L. - xvi

Watts, Isaac (1674-1748), *English Independent hymnwriter* - 22

Wayland, Francis, Jr. (1796-1865) - 85, 91, 103-105, 109, 123

Welch, Bartholomew Trow (1794-1871) - 109

Welch, James Ely (1789-1876) - 37

Whately, E. L. - 83-84

White, John Ellington (1868-1931) - 48

Wilcox, Mr. - 94-95

Wilkerson (Wilkinson), J. G. O. (1785?-1859) - 69

Williams, Thomas J. - 24

Williams, William (1821-1877) - 153

Wilson, Thomas - 69

Wimbish, John S. - xv

Wimbish, John W. - 82

Woodson, Agatha Abney - 111, 165

Woodson, Elizabeth - xv

Woodson, Hortense Caroline (1896-1990), *biographical sketch of* 165

Woodson, Tucker Everett - 165

Worthington, Samuel D. - 60-61

Wright, John E. - 151

Y

Young, John (1764-1855) - 37

Youngblood, Patience - *see Patience Youngblood Butler*

Biblical Persons

Abraham - 1

Adam - 10

Barnabas - 117

Dives - 22

John the Baptist - 30

Joseph - 1, 117

Lazarus - 22

Lydia - 9

Nicodemus - 70

Noah - 1

Paul - 1, 117

Indexes

Index of Subjects

Indexes

Indexes

Indexes

Indexes

Indexes

Indexes

Indexes

Indexes

West, the - 21, 100, 108, 118, 138
Western territories - xi
White Sulphur Spring (VA) - 40
White Throne, the Great - 159
Wicked, the - 13
Wilcox, County (AL) - 92
Windsor, VT - 37
Winnsboro, SC - 65
Woman's College of Furman
University - 149
Women, higher education for - x,
84-85, 146-151
Word of God - 1, 26, 42, 69, 122,
142, 161
World War II - vii
Worldly conformity - 131
Worship, public - x, 17, 47, 50, 75

Y

Youth, education of - 58

Z

Zeal - 37, 46, 48, 61, 71, 76, 116,
124, 129-130, 135
Zion - 74, *songs of* 76

Indexes

Index of Churches

Baptist churches are shown in regular type with dates of constitution when known. All others are italicized and otherwise indicated.

Pastorates of William B. Johnson:
- Euhaw, SC January 1806 - December 1808
- Columbia, SC October 1809 - December 1811
- Savannah, GA December 1811 - 1815
- Greenville, SC November 1822 - 1829
- Edgefield, SC October 1830 - January 1845; and January 4, 1846 - November 2, 1851

The Published Works of William B. Johnson arranged Chronologically

Publisher's note: The following list of the works of W. B. Johnson is not a comprehensive one, but does include his more significant productions. And while we would note our disagreement with some of the views expressed by Johnson in these publications, they remain key documents in understanding his life and thought.

"An Admonition Against Worldly Conformity;" *The Circular Letter of the Charleston Baptist Association, presented at the Meeting of the Association at Jeffer's Creek, South Carolina, November 3, 1810.*

An Address to the Inhabitants of Georgia and Adjacent Parts of South Carolina. Savannah Baptist Society for Foreign Missions, 1813.

An Appeal in Behalf of Baptist Missions, 1813 or 1814.

Love Characteristic of Deity. A Sermon Preached before the Charleston Baptist Association, Monday, November 4, 1822. W. Riley, Charleston, South Carolina, 1823.

The Alarming Condition of the Churches, 1823.

An Oration on the First Jubilee of American Independence, Delivered at Greenville, South Carolina [July 4, 1826]. Republican Office, Greenville, South Carolina, 1826.

"On the New Birth;" *The Circular Letter of the Edgefield Baptist Association,* 1830.

The Sovereignty of God and the Free Agency of Man. A Sermon Delivered, Lord's Day, May 30, 1842. At Providence Meeting House, Abbeville District, South Carolina, and Published at the Request of the Congregation. W. F. Durisoe, printer, 1842.

A Church of Christ, with Her Officers, Laws, Duties, and Form of Government. A Sermon, Delivered, Lord's Day, September 22, 1844, at Gilead Meeting House, Union District, S. C. and Published by

[251]

Request. W. F. Durisoe, printer, 1844. Second edition printed by William J. Baner, New York, 1848.

The Gospel Developed through the Government and Order of the Churches of Jesus Christ. H. K. Ellyson, Richmond, Virginia, 1846.

Reply to the Address at the Edgefield Village Baptist Church, to the Other Churches Composing the Edgefield Baptist Association. T. Moore Knox, Abbeville, South Carolina, 1854.

For further reading on the life of William B. Johnson and the origins of the Southern Baptist Convention, the following are recommended:

Charles D. Mallary. *Memoirs of Elder Edmund Botsford.* Particular Baptist Press, Springfield, Missouri, 2004.
 Edmund Botsford was an early mentor to W. B. Johnson and this work, originally published in 1832, contains valuable correspondence between Botsford and Johnson, especially concerning Johnson's conversion and early ministry.

Mark Dever, editor. *Polity: a Collection of Historic Baptist Documents.* Center for Church Reform, Washington, D. C., 2001.
 Included in this collection is the complete text of W. B. Johnson's work on church polity, *The Gospel Developed through the Government and Order of the Churches of Jesus Christ* (Richmond: H. K. Ellyson, 1846).

Thomas J. Nettles, editor. *Southern Baptist Sermons on Sovereignty and Responsibility.* Sprinkle Publications, Harrisonburg, Virginia, 1980.
 Contains a brief but helpful biographical sketch on Johnson, along with the text of his sermon, "The Sovereignty of God and the Free Agency of Man, Delivered Lord's Day, May 30, 1842."

Robert G. Gardner. *A Decade of Debate and Division: Georgia Baptists and the Formation of the Southern Baptist Convention.* Mercer University Press, Macon, Georgia, 1995.

C. C. Goen. *Broken Churches, Broken Nation: Denominational*

Indexes

Schisms and the Coming of the American Civil War. Mercer University Press, Macon, Georgia, 1985.

Hortense C. Woodson. *History of the Edgefield Baptist Association, 1807-1957.* Edgefield Advertiser Press, Edgefield, South Carolina, [1957].

Memoirs of Elder Edmund Botsford

Compiled and edited by Charles D. Mallary

"Among the early Baptist ministers in South Carolina, one of the more influential and colorful was Edmund Botsford (1745-1819). He was nurtured in the faith by Oliver Hart, was a contemporary and fellow-laborer with Richard Furman in the Charleston Baptist Association, and a spiritual father to William Bullein Johnson, John M. Roberts and others. He was a capable minister, an involved worker in the Charleston Association, a writer and a mentor to young ministers. Yet he is practically forgotten in South Carolina Baptist history....This reprinting of the *Memoirs of Elder Edmund Botsford* by Particular Baptist Press will help introduce him to a new generation of Baptists." — *J. Glenwood Clayton, from the Introduction*

Edmund Botsford was an English-born immigrant to colonial South Carolina who rose from obscurity to become a key figure among Baptists in the South. He was eulogized for having been a "faithful minister of Christ, and highly respected for his correct, exemplary conduct" (*American Baptist Magazine*, March, 1820, p. 310). This biography has not been reprinted since the original edition was published in 1832, though it is recognized as an important sourcebook for American Baptist history. "Edmund Botsford lived at a critical time in the development of South Carolina Baptist life. He was involved in making decisions that shaped the life of Baptists in the South for generations." (*from the Introduction*). Perhaps the most rewarding part of this volume however, is the spiritual counsel given by pastor Botsford in a series of letters to his various friends.

"Mr. Botsford had a strong faith in the Savior's abiding presence, and he enjoyed much of the Spirit's power in his heart. His labors in Georgia were eminently blessed, and he is revered as one of the illustrious and heaven-honored founders of the Baptist denomination in that state and he has the same distinguished position in the Baptist history of South Carolina." (William Cathcart, editor, *The Baptist Encyclopedia*, 1881, Vol. 1, p.119).

Cloth. 251 pages. This first volume in our *Charleston Association Series* has been completely retype set and fully indexed, with 8 illustrations and a map. $25.00 plus shipping.

Particular Baptist Press
2766 W. FR 178
Springfield, MO 65810
(417) 883-0342